WRITER WAYS

A Helpful Guide to Novel Writing

by Tim Susman

writing as Kyell Gold

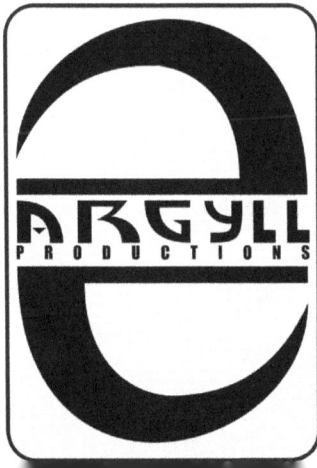

Writer Ways: A Helpful Guide to Novel Writing
Production copyright Argyll Productions © 2025
Text copyright © Tim Susman 2025
Published by Argyll Productions
Dallas, Texas
www.argyllproductions.com

Cover design by Christine Foltzer

ISBN 978-1-61450-678-2

First Edition Trade Paperback

This book is dedicated to my first and best teacher, my mother, who taught me not only the basics of writing, but curiosity and kindness as well.
I think she would've been proud of this.

Part 1: Planning

Chapter One

How This Book Works

Who is this book for?

The short answer is: if you picked up this book, it's for you. If you're looking for a book to help you get started on your novel, or unstuck on your novel, or even if you just have a vague idea that you want to write a novel one day, this will help. But even if you've written a novel or two and are looking for ways to make the next one better, there's help in this book for you. I find that revisiting writing advice is useful because there are a lot of things I know, but that aren't necessarily at the front of my mind when I'm writing. Getting a refresher every now and then brings them back there.

At the time of this writing, I've written thirty novels (counted as 50,000 words or over, plus one at 49,900 that you could count if you want). Each one has been a different journey, and each time I learn something about writing novels. I've also taught several one-hour workshops on novel writing and have taught at week-long writing workshops. Over the years, I've heard a lot about where people get stuck in writing novels, and what's helped them get through those patches, to add to my own experiences. So I figured that rather than only helping people who can come to a panel, or the even smaller number that can attend a week-long workshop, I'd try to put the things I've learned into a book so they're accessible to everyone.

What you can expect from this book

This is an overview of what I think about when writing a novel. It probably contains most of the things I consider, although I always feel like I'm leaving something out. So each subject is intended to be a foundation, to give you enough information to work with and a place to start from if you want to find out more. Many of these subjects have entire books written about them alone, and if you are interested, I encourage you to go find those other books. But I'm writing here the kind of book I want when I'm writing a novel: a little bit about each topic, enough to remind me to think about it as I'm writing. For beginning writers, I tried to present each topic the way I would teach it. For advanced writers, I hope it will serve as a refresher; I know that having written a few books, I find it easy to fall into a pattern, and reading up on the craft again helps reset that pattern, reminding me of other possibilities I might explore with new projects.

I wrote this book in a lot of small sections, so you can easily go look up a particular aspect of writing whenever you want to refer back to it. Each section is pretty short but to the point, and includes my thoughts on that subject, plus an example and optional exercise. I put the sections in about the order I think of them when I write a book.

We're going to start with the preparations, the stuff you do before you've even written the first word of the novel, because this will help immensely with problems that come up down the line. I'm sure you've heard of outlining, and we'll spend a while talking about the different ways you can do that, but we'll also cover some techniques to get you thinking about the shape of the novel and where it's going to go before you even start it. Even if you're a discovery writer, or "pantser," these techniques will be helpful, as they'll at least give you touchstones to keep in mind as you write. We'll also set down some ideas for the process of writing. As you may have heard, a novel is a pretty big project to tackle.

After that, we'll move into the actual writing part. As we go through the stages of the novel, I'll talk about techniques in plotting, dialogue, description, world building, character arcs, and a bunch of other stuff that comes up in the actual writing. We'll work through the "soggy middle," the part of the book between the exciting opening and the cool ending where you don't really know where your story is going, and we'll get through that to the ending, making sure that the ending is a satisfying one.

Whereupon you can go back to the beginning and start revising! I'll present some revision plans and talk about techniques that will make revision feel more manageable, and where to get help if you need it.

The idea behind this book is to give you more tools to help you create the best version of your story. But there's a balancing act here: all of the advice here has worked. A particular piece of advice may not work for your current project, but it might in your next one. Or it might work in a way you can't see right away, but if you give it a chance, it'll pay off down the road. Ultimately, this is your book, and if something I suggest in this book feels wrong to you, you don't have to do it. And because my favorite craft books have included plenty of examples, I'll reference some of the books I've read, and some I've written. I've tried to use fairly high-profile examples to increase the chance that you'll already have read them, but not everyone has read everything.

No writer reads only one craft book, at least not in my experience, but I hope this one will prove one of the ones you keep around.

Novels Are A Lonely Business

When I started out writing, I knew what a finished novel looked like. I'd read a lot of them. But I didn't know what happened between "I have an idea" and "here's a book." So a lot of my early books were written by vaguely aiming at that finished product, with a lot of stumbles in the process. As I wrote more books, I learned what worked for me, but what really helped my writing was finding writing workshops and listening to what worked for other people.

If you have the chance, I highly recommend finding some other writers to check in with while you're writing your novel. Perhaps all of you can follow along with this book, and keep encouraging each other as you get through the various stages of it. Checking in not only gives you some reassurance that other people are going through the same problems you are—and gives you a chance to collectively solve those problems—but it also provides some accountability. Some people struggle with spending months or years on work that nobody will see until it's done, and if this is your first novel (or one of your first novels), it's hard to have the confidence that you can even finish, let alone produce something worthwhile.

Forty or so books in, I still look at a WIP (work in progress) and have doubts about it. Now I have experience and confidence, not to mention a good set of writing colleagues to reassure me and give me honest, actionable feedback. But I started two novels before I finally finished one, both of which foundered somewhere in the middle before I abandoned them.

It would have been nice to have someone writing along with me, back in those early attempts. Even if it wouldn't have made a difference to the books being finished (both stories are flawed, based on what I remember of them), it would have given me something to compare my work to, to reassure me that I was on the right track.

Someone To Write Along With—If You Want

So what I'm going to do in the course of this book is share with you my progress at every stage as I was writing my fantasy novel *The Price of Thorns*. I have copious notes and a pretty good memory of this recent experience, and I'll share how the story developed, how I wrote various parts of it, and what it looked like at different times. You don't have to have read *The Price of Thorns* for these sections; I'll explain the story as we go along. But this will obviously contain a lot of spoilers for the book. If you haven't read it and would like to at some point in the future, you can skip these sections. They'll be set off so you can easily jump past them, and I have plenty of examples from more well-known books (and a few from my own and those of friends of mine, because, well, this is my book).

I hope that by sharing my own journey from spark of an idea to completed novel, I'll give you some confidence in your own journey. I sure wish I'd had something like this when I started out.

After the examples from *The Price of Thorns*, I'll have a short exercise to help you use what I've just talked about. These are practices I've found helpful, and I hope they will help you too (a lot of them boil down to teaching yourself to read critically).

IMPORTANT! Your Book Is YOUR Book

There's a lot of advice in this book. Sometimes I say "this works for me but might not work for you," but often I just say "this is a good thing to do." The important thing you have to remember when reading this or any other craft book is: your book is *your* book.

I'm going to tell you about a lot of things that have worked for me in the past. Have I used every one of these pieces of advice in every one of my books? Hell, no. Would I like to have? Maybe. I think of this book as a (non-exhaustive) list of possibilities for writers. Here are a lot of things you could do. They've worked a lot of times in the past. None of them are obligatory. I think—and many others think—that a lot of these suggestions will make your book better. But you have to reach a point where you understand why that is and you agree, or else you're just forcing your story into a shape someone else told you about.

What I want you to have at the end of this process is a story you are happy with. If you read my section on theme and think, "that sounds like it's a lot of work and I don't think it will work with my book," *don't change your story*. I'm trying to give you tools to build a story with, and maybe they'll click for this book, maybe on the next book, maybe the one after that. What I would suggest is at least giving them a try. Every story I write, I try to do something new or try to improve on something I did previously. That might mean "I don't think I got the romance quite right, let's try it again," or "I think I need practice with description so I'm going to build a lushly-described world." You can say, "for this next story I'm going to think about theme from the beginning," for example.

And my voice will be (hopefully) only one of many contributing to the success of your book. We'll go through what to expect in the revision section, but even before you get to the point of showing your story to other people, your writing teachers and writing books are other voices telling you what you should do. As with revision, you need to learn how much to listen to them.

There's an ideal balance of openness and confidence that every writer needs. Too open, and you'll forever be changing your story to fit what the last feedback said, or the last technique you read about, or the last thing you saw another author do. Too much confidence and you'll shut yourself off from feedback that might make your book better. You need to be able to take in feedback, imagine new paths for your book, and then also evaluate them to decide whether they make the book more like the book you want to write.

This is a hard balance and I don't know that any of us ever achieve it perfectly. But that's what community is for. Hopefully you have other writer friends and colleagues you can exchange ideas with and build up trust with. If you do that, it will be easier to accept feedback from them and imagine what your book could become. And they, in turn, will know what kind of book you want to write and will be able to help you get there.

But the important thing to remember is that at the end of the day, it doesn't matter so much what other people think of your book (unless you've signed a contract and owe a manuscript to someone); this book will be out there forever with your name on it. So make sure you're happy with it.

Writing Groups

A writing group can be an incredibly helpful resource. Having peers to pass my manuscripts around to made a huge difference in the quality of my novels. I know it's not easy to find writing groups, though. I had writing friends for years before I found a group that matched my skill level and enthusiasm. When I say "found" a group, these were groups that I helped start, from a small number of friends who were as interested in forming a writing group as I was. You can also find existing writing groups to join.

I found my first writing group just by perseverance. I kept reaching out to people in the furry writing community, and eventually found several others who wanted to share stories and writing tips. We started getting together, and though we don't meet as regularly as we used to, and the membership of the group has changed, the group is still together.

I found my second writing group by taking evening classes in creative writing. In the second class I took, I met someone I vibed with, and we took another class together and then he invited me to a screenwriting group he was starting. That one is also still going.

The last place I've found a writing group is by attending a residential workshop. In 2011 I went to Clarion, the long-running science fiction and fantasy workshop that lasts six weeks. Our class bonded, and I'm still in touch with many of my classmates. A few years later, I went to the Novel Architects workshop run by Kij Johnson and Barbara J. Webb, which had been recommended by my Clarion classmates (and Kij had been one of my Clarion instructors), and through that workshop met more people who would form the core of another writing group I'm in.

Three writing groups is a lot (even though one is screenwriting only, and another meets only monthly), but you can find your own group in any of the above ways. Local writing communities are a good place to start, as are evening or adult education classes, and workshops. There are many of these out there for any level of available time and money that you have. In addition, if you attend conventions, go to writing panels and talk to the other people attending those panels. You might find other writers this way to start a new writing group with. Even if you don't all live in the same area, you can still meet online (all my writing groups now meet primarily online).

Online is another place you can look for writing groups. There are a number that exist online, and you can find them through social media (e.g. Facebook), or in other online writing-focused communities. Look for one that matches your interest, as specifically as you want, and read their rules carefully. Some may have specific requirements for new members, and some may not be open to new members at all. You can also find friends in these online spaces with which to found your own writing group.

Starting a writing group

Here are a few hints on starting a writing group from my experience with them. None of these are hard and fast rules; you can certainly have a writing group that defies some or all of these suggestions. In my experience, though, these rules help groups last longer and be more productive.

First, and probably most obviously, it's important that you all get along. You want to be able to spend years with these people sharing your creative work, and if one of them rubs you the wrong way, that's going to be very difficult. You won't always know right away if there will be personality conflicts down the road, but if you feel tensions and stresses that will make it hard for you to trust someone with your creative work, better to not join a group with that person than try to make it work for months or years.

Under the umbrella of "getting along" is setting ground rules for the discourse within the group. Even if you're all politically aligned, maybe you don't want group discussions to turn into hour-long political discussions. Make sure everyone agrees in general about how the meetings are going to go and what is okay to bring up. Maybe you need to separate writing discussion from social time, or maybe you don't.

Second, it's best if everyone is around the same level with writing ability or careers or both. If you have one polished, published author and a few who are just starting out, or one beginner in a group of authors with agents and contracts, then the feedback is going to feel unbalanced. Additionally, the questions some people in the group are facing with their career are going to be different. A writing group can succeed with this imbalance, but it works better if everyone is generally aligned.

Third, it's important that everyone's enthusiasm levels are close. If you have someone who wants to meet every week and is producing words for the group to read regularly, they're not going to coexist well with someone for whom writing is an occasional hobby, or someone who writes very slowly and doesn't have time for weekly meetings, at least in a smaller group. If you find a larger group (some I've heard of have thirty or more members, though I've never joined one that large), these kinds of imbalances can work because there are enough members writing to keep the group active, and it will be there for the ones who contribute less frequently. This doesn't mean that people have to contribute every week. Writers go through dry spells, life happens, and so on. But everyone should be committed to the same schedule, and even if someone hasn't written, they should show up willing to read and discuss and be part of the community for the group.

Don't get discouraged if your writing group fizzles out in the first few months. It happens. People often overestimate their available time or energy in the exciting flush of starting a group. Often you'll find a person or two from a failed attempt who are good enough writing colleagues that you want to keep in touch with them, and you can be the core of a new group. Eventually one will stick, and if you find the right people, it can be an important resource for many years.

Chapter Two

Can You Write A Novel?

What is a novel?

Presumably you have read novels, so your answer to this question might be "a big thick book," or "a long story." Those are both accurate, but I want to dig down a little more into what a novel is from the perspective of someone writing one.

The first time I set out to write a novel, I started with a scene that was very strong in my head, and then I tried the exercise of "if I were reading this story, what would I want to come next?" That's not bad, and it worked better the second time, and on the third try I would finish a book mostly using this method. Relying on your memory of the books you've read is a good foundation to start novels from, and in fact, most of us became writers because we loved reading and wanted to create our own stories, so it's natural that we would model our books on the ones we loved.

But when it comes to creating your own novel, there may be elements you didn't register consciously because they weren't important to your enjoyment of the story, or elements you didn't register because you weren't reading as an author. It can be frustrating to try to re-create the feeling of a favorite story only to find that something's missing, and you don't know what. So it's worth taking a step back to think about all those books you loved and what you loved about them, where they differed, and what things you want to keep for your story. This is going to be different depending on what novels you read and what your story is, so as with all advice, take the below as a guideline to find the things you're interested in for your own story.

A novel is a journey

Where a short story is about a point in time, I think of a novel as a journey. When you read a novel, you're following either a plot or a character from a starting point through several adventures to an end point. There is usually a plot question to hook the reader early on, and a character question to keep them engaged through the story. The character "question" is some lesson about how to live in the world, which sounds didactic when reduced to that sentence, but it really just means that the author wants to show the reader something they've learned about the world, and they're using the characters in their story as a "living" example. We'll talk more about this later, don't worry.

This journey, because it's novel-length, is rarely simple. Often the endpoint isn't visible from the beginning. In Lloyd Alexander's *The Book of Three*, Taran's journey begins when the oracular pig he cares for at the farm runs away and he foolishly chases her. That event, though simple, seeds everything that follows: the pig is disturbed by a terrible future she saw coming; Taran foolishly chases her because he wants desperately to be a hero. His destiny will be to become a hero by helping to fight the terrible future she saw. So the journey winds through twists and turns, as the characters and the reader discover the full scope of the story.

Even in a fairly "straightforward" novel, the kind of plot

that will engage the reader necessarily moves through a series of events. Many contemporary novels have some kind of twist, or multiple twists, but that's not always necessary; the point is that you have the room for them. After all, a novel is a considerable undertaking for a reader—not at all the same as the time it takes you to write it, but still a requirement to sit down and ignore their phones and other distractions for many hours. So you need to give them a reason to do that. The character journey is what invests the reader in the story, and the plot is what engages them. Either of those by itself can be enough to get someone to continue reading, but they are most powerful when they work together.

Another common feature of novels is world building. In a short story, you don't have a lot of time to develop the setting for the reader, so you have to rely on quick shorthand. But in novels, especially in SFF novels, you have the space for much more development, and one of the reasons readers pick up books in this genre is to be transported to a new world. But even if you're not writing in the SFF space, where the need for world building is obvious, the novel allows us for space to discover the world of the story. *Moby Dick*, set in a very real time, devotes several chapters to explaining ships and whaling to a general audience. *The Remains of the Day*, Kazuo Ishiguro's classic novel set in an English manor house in the 1930s, spends a good deal of time explaining how a manor house works and the expectations of the servants in the house. In both cases, the details of these settings serve as a foundation to the story, both anchoring the reader in a time and place and showing how the characters are affected by the world they live in. Understanding how your characters interact with the world is an important part of the story that we'll spend some time on in Act 1.

Lots of room for characters and other elements

Novels also often (not always!) have a large cast of characters. You have a main character and an antagonist, but you have room to introduce an ally for both of them as well as a number of other side characters. In fact, a number of common plot elements of novels involve these side characters: the reversal (ally becomes enemy or vice-versa), the foil (a side character who embodies one of the paths the main character could take but shouldn't), and "recruiting the team" (collecting the group of characters to support the main character), to name a few. Subplots are often motivated by side characters as well, and often readers will end up as attached to a side character as to a main character (or more). Side characters can even go through their own character journeys, generally less elaborate than that of the main character, and those journeys can explore paths you don't want to take your main character down.

You can also have multiple main characters. I've done this on many occasions in my books, most famously the two-POV *Out of Position* series, but I've also had three POV characters in a book. Having multiple main characters means that you are writing two (or more) interwoven stories. Even if the main characters spend time apart, it's important that the stories relate to each other thematically and that they dovetail when it's time to come back together.

A novel can also include the development of several different relationships between those characters. Of course the main character will have one or more relationships, but in the space of a novel you can also conceive of a relationship between side characters that might be interesting. In The Lord of the Rings, the developing friendship between Legolas and Gimli is a wonderful part of the story.

The size of a novel also gives you space to develop a theme throughout the book. A theme links several elements of the book together and can lead the reader to look at situations in a new way. Sticking with The Lord of the Rings, in the section on theme I'll talk about why I think one of the themes of that series is places one feels safe, or just "home." Thinking about that, when you look at some of the plot points, you can see where Tolkien is commenting on what it means to have a home, and how real and immediate the threat to that safety must be to stir someone to take action.

I'll cover this in more detail throughout the course of the book, but it's important to have an idea of the elements of a scope of a novel before you go into the planning process. Think of these as the cool things you get to do when you write a novel.

Novel-sized Problems

The size of novels offers challenges as well as opportunities. Many of the problems I hear about from aspiring novelists relate to the size of the novel. So I'm going to run down some of the most common problems I hear about, and the way we'll prepare for writing the novel will have these problems in mind. You can skip this section if you're familiar with the problems you can run into while writing a novel, but I think that understanding the problems we're trying to solve or reduce will help understand why we're going to spend the next few chapters thinking about the novel but not actually writing it yet.

Even though the first part of this chapter was not an exhaustive list of all the things you can do with a novel, it was still a lot to take in. You might be passionate about your story, but it's daunting to remember all the twists and turns of the plot and what's going on with the side characters and all the different features of your world, not to mention building a consistent theme throughout. That's where a lot of people struggle with the actual writing of a novel.

Is my idea novel-worthy?

I've had many people ask if an idea of theirs feels "worthy" of a novel. That's a very valid question to ask, after all, because you're going to be spending months, maybe years, working on this story, and if you spend all that time only to find out that the book isn't going to work, or that the idea won't be sustainable across a whole book, it feels like a huge waste of time.

Unfortunately, it's an impossible question to answer, because the value of a novel is in the execution. The idea behind some great novels sounds pedestrian if you strip it down that far: "an escaped convict builds a new life for himself and must sacrifice himself for his daughter when his identity is discovered" does not sound anything like the grandeur of *Les Miserables*; "some rabbits find a new home and then have to defend it" doesn't suggest the brilliant characters and social drama of *Watership Down*; "English schoolchildren fight off the advance of the evil magic of the Dark" doesn't tell us about the fabulous world-building and drama in the five-book *The Dark Is Rising* series. Similarly, you could send me your two-page synopsis that reads like it has all of the proper plot and character elements, but that still doesn't tell me how you're going to execute that idea. Even in science fiction, a genre where a good idea can carry a story farther than in other genres, you have to be able to build a competent novel around the idea. Really, the only person who can judge whether an idea is worthy of a novel is you. We'll talk about that in the next chapter, The Novel-Sized Idea.

Has it been done?

Related, people sometimes worry that their idea for a novel is too similar to another one that already exists. In general, I don't think that's something you need to worry about too much, because, as noted above, the meat of the novel is in the execution. When I was a youngster, I read a fantasy adventure called *The Sword of Shannara* in which a young hero with elf and dwarf companions has to find a magical artifact to defeat a dark lord, while in another storyline, a prince must oust his insane brother from the throne while the dark lord attacks them. It was so obviously influenced by The Lord of the Rings that everyone saw the similarity as soon as it was released. And yet, the book did very well, and the author (Terry Brooks) has gone on to develop his own style. In the wake of the success of Game of Thrones, any number of fantasy books have come out with some political intrigue around a signature throne. If this is the story you want to tell, go ahead and tell it. Your version of it will be different from anything else that's been written. (With that said, if you write something obviously derived from a well-known story, be prepared for that to be mentioned often as people read your story.)

Where do I start?

Having settled on an idea, the next big question is where to start. There is a lot of advice to be had about this, which we'll discuss, but the problem is that a novel is so big that decision paralysis can set in. You'll think about one starting point, but that doesn't give enough background for the world; another starting point is too far from the start of the actual story; another is a scene you really want to write but it doesn't lead into anything easily. Fear of a blank page is normal for a writer, and it's even greater when you've got a project the size of a novel looming over you.

The good news is that (we will return to this theme often) you don't have to figure out the best place to start your story in order to start writing. The important thing when faced with a blank page is to start somewhere, anywhere. You will go back and edit the novel and you can change the beginning if it doesn't feel right to you. I have erased scenes and added scenes at the beginning of novels to make the beginning feel more right, and that is a natural part of the editing process. It's not something you have to worry about before you start your novel.

That said, there is value to planning out the story so that you have an approximate idea of where you want to start. A lot of the advice I'll give you around first drafts follows this theme: you *can* change anything on revision, but if you spend some time planning before you start writing, you will reduce the things you *have* to change.

Planning also helps with the most common problem I hear people encounter while writing a novel:

Getting stuck in the middle

This can happen for a lot of reasons: people lose the thread of the story, or they get bored of the story (or more excited by a newer, shinier story!), or they get interrupted while writing and can't find the momentum again.

These are all related but slightly different problems to solve, and fortunately the same solution helps with all of them, and that is outlining. Losing your place in the middle of a novel, whether through distraction or getting lost in the weeds of a scene, is something that happens a lot, because, as I've said, novels are big. Imagine trying to beat a video game by only playing it for ten minutes every day. After a few months, you might forget where you'd started, why you were trying to beat this particular level, where you intended to go next.

So what we do before we start a novel is we think about the structure, and that helps us prepare an outline. The outline will serve as kind of a walkthrough of the novel (if you'd like to continue the video game analogy—if not, I have a road trip one later), reminding you what your milestones are and providing guidance at a more granular level.

This helps you remember what the thread of the story is if you get too caught up in scene writing and lose sight of it. It reminds you what you're excited about getting to next if you get bored of writing (or gives you an option to skip forward—we'll talk about writing out of sequence, too). And it's a guide for where you were headed next if life gets in the way and pulls you away from your writing for a while.

If you're allergic to outlines, don't worry! When we get there, I'll say this again, but you only have to put as much energy into the outline as you want, and you can make it look like whatever you like. A lot of people who are discovery writers prefer not to outline ahead of time because they say it takes the joy out of finding the story as they write, and that's perfectly fair. As with everything else in this book, take the advice that's helpful to you and leave the advice that isn't. Plus, as we'll discuss, you can always go without an outline until you need one, and then stop to make one. I know because I've done that. In the early days before I outlined every book, I tried discovery writing, and often I would get lost halfway through. No problem; I started where I was in the story and then wrote an outline for the rest of the book.

So with all those problems in mind, let's go ahead and start planning the novel you're going to write.

Chapter Three

Ideas

The Novel-Sized Idea

I've already told you that the execution is the important part of turning an idea into a novel, and you have probably rightly concluded then that it's possible for any idea to become a novel. The question you should be asking is whether the idea you have is one that *you* want to turn into a novel.

This idea that you want to turn into a novel is one that you will be living with for at least the better part of a year. Some of my friends have been working on their novels for multiple years. And I think a lot of the trouble people run into in the middle of working on their novels can stem from not being sufficiently excited about the idea they started with.

You are the only one who knows whether you'll be able to sustain interest in an idea for a year. Here's how I do it: I generally don't start writing a novel unless I've been thinking about the idea for months. If it's stuck in my head and I'm still exploring it months after I thought of it, then chances are pretty good that it's going to hold my interest for enough time to get it written.

I'm a character-based writer, and a lot of this book is going to focus on character-centric novels. If that sounds scary or intimidating, it shouldn't; most Western novels are character-centric these days. There are exceptions: mysteries and heist stories are often plot-centric (the puzzle is the point), and there are branches of science fiction and horror that can be very idea-centric (the effect on society as a whole is the point), but even in those genres it's common to devote some time to the changes a character goes through. Agatha Christie's mysteries are plot-centric but have characters at the heart of them; Stephen King's horror is often centered around the extremes of human experience.

But most fantasy novels and most contemporary novels follow a character's growth, or that of multiple characters. George R.R. Martin's *Song of Ice and Fire*, adapted to the HBO show *A Game of Thrones*, follows the growth and change in a whole cast of characters, weaving that into a larger story about the changes facing the world, but never losing sight of the fact that it's individual people who shape and suffer those changes.

So great, if your idea follows a character's journey, and it's something that's stuck in your brain so you can't shake it, you just have to write it, then you're good. If you're not quite there, let's talk a little more about ideas.

Message and theme

Personally, I like for my story ideas to have a message in the way I talked about in the last section, having a character live through a journey that leads the reader to a conclusion about life. That doesn't mean that the plot has to be about some life lesson, like an After School Special. A common thread through my stories is having characters find fulfillment through acknowledging who they want to be in the face of a society or family or peers trying to tell them to be something else. Sometimes the plot is all about that identity (as in a coming-out story), but sometimes the character growth is what helps the main character navigate the plot. In *Green Fairy*, I wanted to include the dangers of online relationships, which turned into a theme about being deceived by appearances. Sol, the main character, has to mature and accept his own identity in order to understand and overcome the problems posed by (1) his online boyfriend, and (2) a mysterious ghost from 115 years ago. In *Red Devil*, I wanted to write about toxic families, and Alexei, the main character of that book, has to understand his own identity to navigate a world of high school drama and a ghost of his own. *The Price of Thorns*, which I'll be talking about throughout this book, ended up having strong themes of personal redemption and responsibility that are illustrated by Nivvy's journey, but there's also a plot involving magic and an ancient sorceress.

Themes like these are present throughout many of your favorite books, and they are strong ideas even when they're not the plot of the story. Usually, the message is conveyed through the actions and choices of the hero as they learn to change the way they see and interact with the world. Sometimes (in a tragedy) the lesson is conveyed by the hero failing to change. In either case, it's worth thinking as you develop your idea about what the success (or failure) of your hero says to the reader. Even if you come at this novel-writing project with the defiant thought that you don't want your story to have a message, readers are going to read something into it, because that's how we read. Mark Twain famously opened *The Adventures of Huckleberry Finn* with the lines: "Persons attempting to find a motive in this narrative will be prosecuted; persons attempting to find a moral in it will be banished; persons attempting to find a plot in it will be shot." That hasn't stopped thousands of critics and English teachers from finding messages in Twain's book.

Like that, but better

Now on to the more visible parts of your story. Often, especially with beginning writers, your ideas are inspired by something you love. You want to write The Lord of the Rings but with furries, or a trans-friendly Harry Potter. This is fine! A lot of artists start out inspired by work they admire. Obviously, you can't just write "the same story as Harry Potter but Ron is trans," or something like that, so what do you do with that idea?

You make it more yours. Think about what parts you really liked, and which parts you didn't, and focus your story around those. *Fifty Shades of Grey* famously began as *Twilight* fan fiction, before E.L. James renamed the characters and took the supernatural out of the setting. So if you like the idea of a magic school, you're not alone (there have been many even before the success of Harry Potter, and there are an order of magnitude more now), but what about it appeals specifically to you? In the case of *Fifty Shades of Grey*, what E.L. James was interested in exploring was the power dynamic between an older man and a younger woman, and she added her own interest in the BDSM scene (disclaimer: there are better books for exploring the BDSM scene; Cecilia Tan, longtime writer of erotic SF, wrote *Slow Surrender* specifically to provide a more accurate portrayal of BDSM).

The Final Scene

Another type of idea I see often with writers is the Final Scene idea. Inspired by some Final Scene from a favorite work, like the Death Star blowing up[1] (or an iconic scene that doesn't have to be the final scene—Aslan sacrificing himself at the Stone Table), you set about to reproduce that same feeling with your own story. What was difficult for me in that stage was that I had not consciously paid attention to the character building that led up to that moment and invested the weight of emotion into it. So when I would write my versions of those stories, I took it as understood that we all liked my Luke Skywalker character, or my Aslan character, and assumed all the weight of story that led to that point.

---

[1] I have been mostly trying to use books as examples in this text, but when looking at stories that inspire writers, movies are a much more common currency these days than books. I imagine that far more of you have some emotional reaction to "I am Iron Man" than to "From Hell's heart I stab at thee."

When we get to a novel structure, though, you have to build that weight of emotion, and that's where a lot of people get stuck. So if you have a Final Scene idea, it's worth examining it to figure out where its appeal is to you. Which character do you find most interesting? For example, in the Aslan sacrifice scene, are you more interested by the noble powerful figure who sacrifices himself to protect the foolish youngster, or the foolish youngster who is forced to confront the consequences of their actions? The second is a better character to base a novel around because they are learning a lesson, but you can also put your own spin on things. What lesson could the Aslan character learn from sacrificing himself? Do you want that to be the final act in a story, or a turning point?

Reading Critically to Improve Your Writing

A lot of this requires learning to read critically, and there's some difficulty in that. Understanding what gives a story and a scene its power means going back through a text several times, looking at how characters are introduced, what actions they take, what the consequences are, and how their behavior changes after that. How does the author make you care about the scene you love so much?

Learning to read critically is probably an entire book unto itself, and somewhat outside the scope of this one (although many of the exercises incorporate some reading and analysis). But it's a valuable skill to cultivate, whether or not you're struggling with an idea, and it doesn't mean giving up reading for pleasure. For me, it necessitates a second read to go back and understand the impressions that a first, casual read gave me. I felt this way about this character, these are the moments I felt were most engaging; then on a second read I go back and try to understand why the prose sparked those feelings. Like examining brushstrokes on a painting, it can show you some of the intention and craft behind the work, and that will give you some background when it's time to make your own.

So if you have an idea that is a big emotional scene, but is too big for a short story (imagine the Death Star blowing up as a short story, before we truly understood the menace of it or the sacrifices that Luke made to get to that point), thinking back on other works that inspired you to understand how you might build to that scene.

However you get there, you should have in mind something of an idea that will become your novel. It's important to remember that this idea is a starting point. It's an entry point to get you started writing your novel. It might be that at the end of it, you look back on this idea and think, "yep, I wrote the novel about that idea." Or you might think, "oh, the novel wandered quite a bit from that first idea." Most likely it'll be somewhere in between. And that's okay! You don't know exactly what's there yet. You just know there's something that will lead you to a place you want to explore. For now, that's all you need.

Summary Points

• The idea for your novel should be something you'll be excited about for at least a year.

• Think about why you want to write this idea. What are you aiming to say to your readers?

• If your idea is inspired by another work, be sure you understand what it is about that work that really appeals to you.

Example: Ideas

The first record I have of my idea for the book that became *The Price of Thorns* was in a series of AIM messages I sent to myself in 2011:

> [08:54] : Magic fantasy-ish setting where hero has encountered this queen who has lost her kingdom, lost everything, and hero is trying to help her. And the queen keeps insisting that they go to this fairy for help, and the hero is like "I don't know, everyone says she's evil" and the queen is all like "no, no, she's misunderstood, she'll help us."
>
> [08:54] : And they eventually go, and the fairy throws them into some horrible prison place, of course.
>
> [08:54] : And the queen is devastated and the hero is like, "I *told* you she was evil, why did you think she would help you?"
>
> [08:54] : and the queen says, "well, she always did before!"
>
> [08:55] : And lo, it is revealed that the queen was actually an EVIL queen and so the hero is now caught in the dilemma of "oh shit do I keep helping her or what?"
>
> [08:55] : Because she seems like a much nicer person now.

Now, if someone sent me this idea and asked me to look at it critically as a novel-sized idea, I would say, sure, there's maybe a novel there, but who's your main character? Are you focusing on the queen's redemption? Or are you focusing on the hero's ability to forgive past actions? It looks like the focus is on the hero (first clue: I called him "hero"), but at this point I think the queen's redemption is perhaps the stronger storyline, unless it turns out that the hero was hurt by her past actions and has to figure out how to forgive her.

More to the point, this is not even the climactic scene of this novel. This is a decision point for sure, but it's far more likely to be around the inciting incident[2] than the final battle. But this moment of revelation had something in it that grabbed me, so what was it? Here are a few of the things that I liked about it, in no particular order:

• Fairy and evil queen strongly suggest a fairy tale-adjacent world. I love fairy tales and the simple yet often bizarre world logic they employ.

• I specify magic with the "fantasy-ish setting"; magic was a concept I enjoyed a lot in my reading but hadn't managed to successfully write about all that often. When I thought about magic, it tended to be very rulebound, as if I were in a D&D rulebook. Characters have X amount of mana, and the spell costs Y, with a Z-minute recovery period. But that felt just like science fiction to me, only with less well-described energy sources. What I *wanted* from magic was more nebulous, a kind of magic that was much more about imposing one's will on the world, with some vague rules so that nobody was overpowered (you can only affect what you see, maybe, and there's a cost in energy so you can't set off a nuclear explosion-level Fireball). That kind of magic reveals character a little more intimately than "you start with 20 mana and if you study for a month you can learn the 1-mana spell Light, which you can cast once every fifteen minutes." That's just fancy guns (and to be clear, there are interesting stories to be written about societies in which magic is that accessible to everyone—I just didn't want to write that kind of magic). Fairy tale worlds abound with witches and fairies and djinni and other powerful beings who can wield magic according to some rules, but the rules are beyond our knowing. And the magic tells us about them. That's what I was chasing.

• The surprise reveal of a character's past (a "Usual

---

[2] If this term doesn't mean anything to you, don't worry; we'll talk about it later in the Structure chapter. Short version: it's the moment that propels the character into the story. This specific moment is more likely the decision that commits the character to the story, which usually comes a bit after the inciting incident.

Suspects" moment) is one that I enjoy a lot. That moment has appeal. (Amusingly, there isn't a big reveal of that in the final book—it's more an accumulation of moments.)

• Lastly, a reformed evil queen. The reformed character suggests a character change, which is always interesting. Why is she reformed? What was that journey like? And the evil queens of fairy tales feel like the least reformable people in our literature, to be honest. Think about it. "Yes, I poisoned my stepdaughter because the magic mirror told me she was prettier than I was, but I would never do something like that now." That character change was interesting to me.

So I had all those elements, and I had just been to a transformative writing workshop (Clarion, summer 2011), so I was all fired up to do something cool. As you will see over the course of this book (if you are unfamiliar with *The Price of Thorns*), the evil fairy scene stays in and is not just after the inciting incident because of the peculiar structure of the first act, but the details of the scene are radically changed. I kept the setting and the characters I liked, but the story and the focus change around quite a lot. There is another book to be written that hews more closely to this idea, but I am very proud of the one I ended up with, and this starting point had enough hooks in it to get me there.

Exercise: Ideas

If you have an idea already:

• Write down 1-3 stories (books or movies, but at least one book) that inspired or are similar to your story. (When querying, these are called "comps," and they help the agent or editor understand who else might enjoy your story.)

•   Write down in one sentence what's most exciting about this story.

• Now write down the ways in which your story is different from the comp or comps you listed.

• Look at that list of ways your story is different. Which ones are most important/attractive to you?

From this exercise, write down the part of your idea that excites you the most. This is a useful thing to hold onto as you write your story.

If you don't have an idea yet:
• Write down five of your favorite stories (books or movies, but at least one book). They don't have to be all-time favorites, just five stories you've been thinking about a lot lately.
• Write down in one sentence what's most exciting about this story.
• Make a list of the things you really like about those stories, including (but not limited to):
  - Setting
  - Characters (one specific character)
  - Character journey
  - Plot
• For each of the things you liked, think about why you like them. What makes them relevant to you?
• Are there any places where you think a change would make the story more interesting?
• Are there any of those elements that remind you of something in your own life? Ideas you want to express to other people or the world?

Chapter Four

Thinking About Your Novel

Pitches: The Cool Stuff

At some point, you will have to tell other people what your idea is for this book. There are a lot of different ways you can do this, some better than others. I have had people tell me about their book in a twenty-minute-long detailing of the plot after which I still wasn't sure what the book was about. That wasn't a big deal; he wasn't asking me to buy it or help him write it. But as you work on your novel, you'll want to talk about it to people who can help you, whether you have a writing group or just some helpful fellow writers.

To be able to do that, you need to have a handle on what your book is about. This is an important step for yourself as well, because with a big project like a novel, it helps to have something small you can focus on. People often have a photograph or some other image (in the furry fandom, we can easily commission an artist to draw a concept sketch—for years I had a drawing of the main character from the Calatians series in my office while I was writing it), but as writers, I think it's valuable to refine your novel idea down to something you can not only tell other people quickly, but remind yourself of.

You're maybe familiar with the concept of an "elevator pitch." The idea came from Hollywood, and the setup is: you get into an elevator and the only other person in it is your absolute favorite director. You have until the elevator gets to its destination to sell them on why your story is the next project they want to direct. This is shorthand for the idea that it's very useful to have a quick, elegant, one- or two-sentence summary of your novel that makes the listener think, "Yeah, I'd like to read that."

As you already maybe know, though, boiling your brilliant idea down to two sentences is far easier said than done, let alone two sentences that will hook any listener. So I have a few tips that might make that process easier.

Crafting your pitch

Whenever someone asks for advice on their novel project, I usually ask them, "Why are you excited to write this story?" Think about your answer to that question. Remember that at one point, the movie "Snakes on a Plane" was titled "Pacific Air Flight 121," until Samuel L. Jackson pointed out that "Snakes on a Plane," the working title, was better. He's right! That tells you what's cool about the movie. Your "cool thing" could be anything from "it's about snakes on a plane" to "I got really excited about this language I made up so I wrote an adventure story to explore it."

The important thing at this point is to identify what appeals to *you* about your story, not to figure out how to make it appeal to other people. If you have difficulty boiling it down to a couple sentences, the way I handle that is by iteration. Start by writing free-form all the things you find cool about your story. That gets rid of your "blank page" problem and gives you something to edit. Then look at all the stuff you've written and see if it can be compressed into a shorter description, and if not, which parts of it really stand out to you.

The pitch will change as the project matures. The "cool thing" you start with might not be the coolest thing about the finished book, and might not even survive to the final drafting. But it's important now, because remembering that pitch is going to be one of the things that guides you through the long process of writing the novel. Keep it on a post-it note on your monitor or on your laptop, somewhere you can see it and remind yourself as you're struggling through a second-act malaise, what is cool about this book.

This first thing, the "cool stuff," is for you, not anyone else. As you try to refine your pitch to show other people, your friends and writing colleagues will be able to help you figure out what parts of your "cool stuff" have broader appeal. Depending on your comfort in showing your work to other people, this is something you can do now, or you can hold off until you're writing, or until a first draft is done. I have found that sharing ideas with writing colleagues I trust can be really helpful in ironing out story wrinkles that I hadn't seen or couldn't address on my own, as well as adding new ideas that I hadn't considered, but I also know that especially early on, it can be scary to show your half-formed idea for a novel that doesn't exist yet to other people. Building the trust with other writers that allows this is important to your growth as a writer, as I mentioned in the section on writing groups.

When you've gotten your "cool stuff" pitch to the point that it can guide you through the book, there's another area that's worth spending a little time on: the themes of your book.

What is a Theme?

I had a long conversation with a colleague about what a "theme" is, and what it's not, so I'm going to define what I mean for my purposes this way: By theme, I mean a conceptual situation that is explored several times over the course of the novel, often from different points of view. I use the word situation to distinguish it from things like setting and subject matter—a theme, the way I'm talking about it, explores a situation that affects how a character relates to the world. It relates to your message in an abstract way. For example, if you're writing a book about an alien invasion in which the hero has to learn to work with others to repel the invaders, one theme you could stress throughout the book is the importance of being able to put the community's needs ahead of your individual ones. You could even get more general and explore different sacrifices you must make to join a community and what benefits you get from it.

I know, I know, when I started writing, "theme" was something I didn't give any space to in my planning. I just wanted to write stories, and "themes" felt like they belonged to Huckleberry Finn and The Scarlet Letter, something high school students had to write essays about. Besides, themes would often find their way into my work whether I planned them or not.

On the one occasion when I got to get a book signed by Anne McCaffrey, author of the Pern books and many others, she was talking to someone about a paper that had been written about "the Cinderella theme in Anne McCaffrey's books." Indignant but amused, she said, "there's no 'Cinderella theme' in my books. I should know. I wrote them!"

Even then, as I ran through her books in my head and counted the instances of a female protagonist who goes from rags to riches, I understood that themes could end up being expressed in your work even if you didn't intend for them to be there. Later, when I started writing, I figured that whatever themes showed up in the work would make their own way in, and maybe someday someone would write a paper on them and then I'd understand how other people read my books.

It took a few books, and the feeling that there was some unifying aspect to them that I could improve, before I started really paying attention to theme. I find that theme work is most effective in the editing and revision stage, when you can look at the whole story written down and see what themes suggest themselves (and what's crept into your story). Thinking about it in the planning stages, though, can also be helpful. As you're in the weeds of writing the novel, wondering what this subplot should be or what this character's deal is going to be, having at least a clue to the themes you want to explore will give you a starting point.

I know this is all a little vague, so here's an example: my coming-of-age furry novel *Waterways* is about an otter figuring out that he's gay and then figuring out how to tell his family, his friends, and the world. The message I was trying to send was that it's always better to be honest about who you are and true to your identity than to hide it because you think that's what other people want. There are a couple strong themes in the book, and the main one is balancing your identity with the expectations of the people and the world around you. So while the main character struggles with that, he meets a fox who encourages him to be fully himself, a bat who was kicked out of her house when she came out, and another otter who is repressing his identity. All of these people are navigating the difficult waters (imagery intentional) between allowing their family's and society's expectations to shape them, and being true to the person they feel they are. They are facing the same questions as the protagonist, so the choices they make illuminate and inform his.

So that's all I mean by thinking about your story's themes. What are the decisions your character is making that are important for you to explore? If you have them written down, then as your side characters come up, you can think about how they relate to your main theme, what choices they might have made that are different from your main character's, how their situations might be different, how they inform and illuminate the journey your main character is on. Sometimes your main character will learn directly from them; other times their stories are there for the reader.

It is also possible, even likely, that as you write, you will discover new themes and perhaps decide that some of the initial ones are not as interesting. Certainly when you get done with the first draft and embark upon revision, you should look back and pick out which themes were most important to you, so you can strengthen them as you revise. But you'll have less work to do if you started thinking about themes early on.

An exercise that can be helpful as you think about theme is to write down an idea board of things that might fit into your book. These can be scenes, situations, or just images that seem to fit. One of my friends, Alisa Alering, used this idea board method when planning her debut novel *Smothermoss*, just writing down images that fit with her concept of what the novel was going to be. When she had a full palette of ideas and images, then she started to see the shape of the story emerge from there.

Summary Points

• It's useful to be able to summarize your book, even just for yourself at the beginning. Start with the "cool stuff," the thing(s) that excite you about your idea. Keep that handy and visible as you write.

• Early on, it's good to think about themes and imagery as this will be helpful during the planning process.

Example: Themes

I told you already about a lot of the things I liked about the original idea for *The Price of Thorns*. One of those, specifically, made it to an idea board I made up at a writing retreat: the idea of redemption.

I spent a lot of time talking around themes, and trying to define them and such, and this is why I think examples are good: themes can be really simple. Redemption is a really broad theme, but it's a strong one. It contains a situation with a history (some bad action), the consequences for that history, and a desire for change. Redemption was also front of mind during a lot of the late teens, as people tried to come back from public or publicly revealed misbehavior, and so there was a lot of discussion about what people felt personally and what might be expected from society.

A redemption arc also has a lot of potential for character growth. There's a natural progression of growth from a character feeling they deserve redemption to attempting to earn it on their own terms to understanding that they have to earn it on the terms of the people they've wronged. So there's lots of fertile ground there for a character arc.

The other theme, related, that shows up in my early planning is the idea of reparations. I'm not sure this is a separate theme so much as an aspect of the first one that I wanted to focus on. In this case, I was curious about what an evil queen from fairy tales could do to redeem herself. Part of that involved making reparations for the wrongs she'd done. So I had to think about which fairy tale I was thinking about—or maybe more than one—and then if the queen had hurt one person or family (as in Snow White) or a whole kingdom (as in Sleeping Beauty), and what redemption and reparations would look like in either of those cases.

Settling on redemption as a theme also helped me think about the thief's character arc. He would be the central character, and so he would also be looking for redemption, with the queen's arc maybe serving as a template for his more personal story. I like to have resonances in stories like that, with larger world-scale arcs mirroring smaller, more personal ones. I had already figured that the thief had to have fallen on hard times to agree to take this job for a woman with no money, but now I knew that the hard times were at least somewhat of his own making.

The other element, which was more of a way of exploring theme rather than a theme itself ("motif" is a word we could use for that if we wanted), was that this book was going to have a lot of stories in it. This is probably not a difficult conclusion to come to in a book inspired by fairy tales, but setting it down helped me think about the role that stories would play in the book. The queen's evil deeds would have been set down in fairy tales that would have been told throughout the land, such that the thief would have heard of them. Those are stories that everyone knows and agrees on, although even in this case there are often multiple versions of the same fairy tale (as we know from our cultures; for just one of many examples, look at how the fate of Cinderella's older sisters is often left out of re-tellings of that fairy tale). But we all tell stories about ourselves as well; a thief who's been kicked out of his guild might initially tell himself the story that he's been unjustly persecuted—just as the evil queen might at first tell herself the story that she's the victim. This parallelism makes their journey toward understanding richer.

I didn't worry too much about coming up with a formal pitch for the book at this point, but in my head (and in my filenames) it was "the evil queen story." When I described it to friends, my pitch was "a thief takes a job to help a mysterious woman steal a kingdom only to find that she's the evil queen from fairy tales." This left out a lot—for example, he doesn't know right away that she's the evil queen, and in my mind, the point of the story where he learned it was going to be the point where he'd been turned into a weasel and she was his only hope to get changed back.

Still, that's not a bad pitch. I still use it when talking about the book informally. It sets up the world (a fairy tale world, a fantasy world where there are thieves and queens) and sets up the problem: if you took a job and then found out that the employer was someone terrible, what would you do? It's maybe not a super relevant message today—I believe anyone taking a job in our world that isn't at a small business assumes their employer is terrible—but it's an interesting one. The connection to fairy tales is also engaging. It's not unique by any means; even before *Wicked*, we've been interrogating the characters of villains in fairy tales (I know, *The Wizard of Oz* isn't technically a fairy tale, but it's a fairly close approximation by modern standards). But it doesn't have to be unique! It just has to have a hook for the reader—and, more importantly at this stage, for the writer.

Exercises: Pitches and Themes

1. Pitches

    A. Choose three books you remember well (either favorites or recently read) and write a one-sentence pitch for each of them. Review the pitches and refine the language to convey as much information as possible about the setting.

    For example: Your pitch for *Watership Down* might start as: "A group of rabbits search for a new home after theirs is destroyed." But a lot of the book is about the dynamics of the group and Hazel's growth into leadership, so you might revise to focus on that: "A rabbit who convinces his friends to leave their warren in search of a new home must learn to become the leader they need." If you like, you can allude to the scale of the adventures and the setting, and maybe take out that "learn to" —it's accurate but in a pitch, it's not necessary. Then it becomes: "A rabbit who convinces his friends to leave their warren must become the leader they need during their dangerous odyssey across the British countryside in search of a new home." That's decent, isn't it, for a one-sentence summary of *Watership Down*?

    B. Take your pitches to friends both familiar with the books and not familiar. Ask them if the pitches sound engaging or compelling. Workshop them to see how you could improve them.

    Some people will tell you, "oh, personally I don't like X or Y, but I like A and B, but I'm weird, so don't listen to me." If you think they'd be interested in the book you're pitching, and they're just fixating on one aspect of it, then you can tailor your pitch to make sure other potential readers like them will engage with it. If you think they would not like the book (or they know they don't like the book), then you can still ask something like, "even if you don't like YA books, is there something that might make you interested in picking one up?"

2. Theme

A. For those same three books, try to identify one or two themes that are central to the books. Then for each of the themes, list situations in the book that fall under that theme. Don't be afraid to make it a stretch. If it occurs to you that it might be linked, go ahead and write it down. If you are doing these exercises collaboratively, it helps if you all do at least one book in common so you can discuss what parts are related to the theme.

B. Settle on a simple theme that fits your story (family, identity, justice, etc.). Now list five ways you could explore that theme with your story. You don't have to use *any* of these, but if you come up with ideas, it will help you recognize patterns as you're developing the story.

Chapter Five

Structure

Making Structure Work For You

We (as humans, not me and you the reader, although honestly, us too) have been telling stories for as long as we've been able to. The first use of language was to tell stories—probably very simple ones like "Hey, there's a lion over there. Remember lions eat us? We should go a different way."

As we evolved, so did our storytelling. Now, there are really two basic elements to a good story: first, the reader should always want to know what happens next (we usually call this "engagement," even though the way it's used around social media companies makes it feel gross to me); second, the story should leave the reader with something—a message, a lesson, a feeling—that made it worth reading or listening.

In a short story, this is easier to accomplish; you have limited space, so you don't have to hold the reader's interest as long and you have to get right to the point. When you're asking people to sit down and spend hours reading a novel, it becomes a little more complicated. I've read novels (even highly acclaimed ones) that just didn't keep me engaged. I've read others that left me wondering what the point of them was.

(As an aside, it's worth noting that no book is going to be for everyone. There will be people who pick up your book and can't get into it. I've had people say about the same book, "the message was delivered with a sledgehammer" and "it took me a long time to figure out what the book was trying to say." The best you can do is make sure that the people who are your intended audience will get it.)

As we have evolved in our storytelling (novels are a relatively recent human invention, but plays have been around for millennia and myths longer than that), we've worked out some of the ways to make sure your story keeps the reader engaged and delivers a satisfying ending. That starts with what we call structure.

Structure, loosely, is how the elements of a story are put together. We talk about the elements of the story in an abstract way, for example, "the point where the protagonist commits to the story," which is a different event in every story but is present in most of them (otherwise you wouldn't have a story). Most of the stories we have read follow a similar structure—some are better at disguising it than others—and when the structure is flawed, the story is usually less effective.

So we'll look at the most common Western story structure, and then at a couple other structures, and you can start thinking about the beats of your story with that framework.

By far the most common structure in Western storytelling is the three-act structure. It's most documented in movies, but the Novel Architects workshop in Kansas teaches a modified three-act structure, and Alan Watt's book *The 90-Day Novel* also uses it. If you read screenwriting books, you'll have encountered it in Blake Snyder's *Save the Cat* as well.

Three act structure can be broken down like this:

ACT I: We are introduced to the protagonist and their world. Something happens to shake up that world. The protagonist chooses to act (commit to the story).

      ACT II: The action gets more complicated. More obstacles and enemies appear, until the protagonist loses allies and hope and has to make a difficult choice (commit to change).

      ACT III: The protagonist's choice leads to a final conflict, and the story's problem/question is resolved.

Chances are you can see these bones in most of the stories you're familiar with. It's a simple structure, after all, and not too far removed from "Hey, there's a lion over there." We meet someone, learn they have a problem to solve. But there are obstacles—otherwise it would be a very short story (like the comic about "Breaking Bad in a country with socialized medicine")—and the protagonist has to figure out how to deal with them. Finally the problem is solved, and the world finds a new stability (or not, but at least the old problem isn't there in the same form anymore).

Acts I and III are pretty straightforward: introduce the world, the character, and the problem in Act I; solve the problem and give us the wrapup in Act III. It's Act II that most people run into problems with, and for my advice with that, I'm going to talk about characters.

The Structure of Character Development

When I think about structure, I pair it with character development. Remember all that talk about theme? Theme tells the reader what kind of message motivates your story. Structure is how you package that message. But the character journey is how that message is delivered.

So as you're trying to write out the beats of your story, think of them from the perspective of your character. In a lot of cases, the motivation for your story is that your character is facing a difficult situation and has to figure out how to navigate it. Because the story is often about learning (or not learning, in the case of tragedies), the character starts out trying to solve the problem with what they already know. That proves insufficient, and they have to learn a better way to deal with the situation, which often involves having to change in a way that is uncomfortable for them.

That last part is important. If the change were easy, we wouldn't be writing a book about it. So the character is going to resist it at every turn, and the plot is the way the author (you!) steers them to a point where they have no choice but to make that hard change (this is related to the adage that the author can use a coincidence to get characters *into* trouble, but not out of it —they have to get themselves out of trouble, or the ending won't feel earned).

Writing your story beats, think about your character and what you know about them, and what they would do at each turn when confronted by the story events. Then as the author, figure out what would need to happen in order for them to reasonably make the decision you need them to. If you can do this organically, it will make the story feel natural to the reader. People are generally more sensitive to whether characters behave realistically than whether the plot is realistic (which isn't to say that in the case of wildly unrealistic plots, people are universally forgiving, just that they are more forgiving of crazy plots as long as the characters enmeshed in them are behaving realistically). It's also worth remembering, though, that what seems realistic to you might not seem realistic to other people with different experiences, but that's a problem for your beta readers to identify. Right now, you only have your own experiences to work from, so that's what you need to rely on.

This will serve you well when you get into the weeds of Act II (or the "soggy middle"). This is the part of the story where your character is on their way, but the end is still far away. There are a lot of things that can happen in this space: try-fail cycles (the characters try something, it fails, they learn and try again), reversals (an ally becomes or is revealed to be an enemy, or vice versa), side quests and/or side characters introduced, new complications or obstacles, and one of my favorites, the false victory.

A false victory often works well at the midpoint of the second act, because it involves a changing of goals (we thought we'd won, but it turns out we need to do something different or additional) and it also takes the reader on an emotional journey, as victory turns into disaster and the character has to regroup. It breaks up the long second act and re-energizes the reader as they head into the dark part of the second act, where often everything seems lost before the character turns things around.

The second act is also where you can bring in a lot of action from your antagonist. The antagonist isn't necessarily a villain—in a romance, an antagonist can be the love interest, the person the protagonist is opposed to falling in love with until romance wins out in the end. But in general, the antagonist is the person who most directly opposes your main character, who tempts them away from the path you want them to follow, often by representing the "wrong" choice.

We will talk more about the antagonist in a later section, but it's important to consider the story from the antagonist's point of view as well. We've all read stories in which the villain seems to act just to be evil, or simply to block the hero, with little motivation or clue as to what they actually get out of it. "To rule the world," sure, but why? If you spend some time thinking about why that character is your antagonist and what they want, your story will be stronger for it.

Other story structures

Besides three-act, there are a couple others worth talking about. If you took English in high school in an English-speaking country, you have probably read one of Shakespeare's plays and so at least have been exposed to five-act structure. It's not used much anymore, but here's a brief overview of how *Romeo and Juliet*'s structure goes:

Act I: Characters and world are introduced (Romeo meets Juliet)

Act II: Rising action, ending in a dramatic event (Romeo and Juliet fall in love, tensions rise, ends with Romeo killing Tybalt)

Act III: A major turning point in the story (Romeo has to flee)

Act IV: Falling action (Romeo is exiled, Juliet plans to fake her death)

Act V: Dramatic finale (deaths of Romeo and Juliet)

If you squint at this, you can see how you would fit that story into a three-act structure, maybe with Tybalt's death as the midpoint of Act II. But this does give you a different structure to fit a story into, and maybe thinking of it this way will work for you.

Another structure that's more common in non-Western work is a four-act structure called *kishōtenketsu*, which is not conflict-based. It's broken down like this:

Act I: Introduction
Act II: Journey
Act III: Twist
Act IV: Conclusion

You can find stories that follow this structure in places like urban legends as well as many non-Western stories. One famous example is the film *Parasite*, which won the Oscar for Best Picture in 2020 (I will avoid specific spoilers, but if you haven't seen it, you should). It begins with an introduction to the world, where we see rich and poor people living separately. As the journey goes on, we follow a poor family trying to improve their station by offering services to—and taking advantage of—the rich family. The twist comes when they discover that they are not the only people doing this, and the conclusion leaves us with a world in which we see the division between rich and poor but understand the inequality in a way we didn't before.

Story Templates

As you think through your structure, there are some templates that can help you think about paths your story might take. These templates take the beats of story structure and get more specific about them to direct your story in a particular direction.

One of the most famous is the "Hero's Journey," described by Joseph Campbell in 1949 and popularized by George Lucas and others after he credited it for helping him write the first *Star Wars* movie. In the Hero's Journey, the main character ventures into danger (in Campbell's original writing, often the underworld) to bring back something valuable to their community that will improve their lives. There are many common elements, such as the mentor character who helps prepare the hero on their journey and then leaves them partway through, so they have to complete the journey alone.

A modification of this template is the Heroine's Journey, described by Maureen Murdock in 1990. This template is more focused on the main character learning to integrate two sides of their nature (often masculine and feminine), as they begin in a community that emphasizes one side, but feels out of place there. They travel to another community to explore the other side of themself, and then finally return with knowledge that helps the original community integrate both sides. (Gail Carriger has written a book called *The Heroine's Journey* with a different story template.)

Another template I've used in the past is Lester Dent's pulp story template. It's intended for short stories, but you can apply it to novels; that just means you have a lot more to fill in. In brief, Dent recommended that you split your story into four parts. In the first three, you get your hero in trouble, then more trouble, then so much trouble it's hard to see a way out of it. Then he does get out of it by using his own resources and information he's gathered in the first three parts. Each part transition is marked by a surprise or reversal.

You can look up more about any of these templates online, or find others if they feel more suited to your story.

Summary Points

• Story structure is an established order of the basic beats of a story that will be familiar to your audience. You don't have to build your story around it, but it can be helpful to point out and fix potential weaknesses in your story.

• Three-act structure is the most familiar to Western audiences, but there are others.

• Story templates have more specific beats for particular kinds of stories and can be helpful in those cases.

Example: Structure

As I was working on *The Price of Thorns*, I was looking at a traditional three-act structure with a dramatic midpoint. Working on the structure was the first time I really thought about putting the story together concretely; before that it had been a collection of ideas I really liked.

I knew I wanted the thief to be turned into a weasel at some point early on. Ideally this would happen when he'd discovered that the evil queen was evil, and that put him in the awkward position of needing her help to get his human form back. I wanted this to happen early on, because there's only so long you can draw out the tension of one character not knowing something about the other before the reader gets tired of it. So that was likely going to be the end of Act I, the thing that committed the main character to the rest of the story.

After that, the structure got more murky. I planned a scene where the queen wanted to get rid of the weasel and tried to kill him, but he had to prove his worth to her. They would go on the rest of the quest and then finding the powerful thing that let her regain her kingdom would be the midpoint. That changed their goal from "find the thing" to "use the thing." He would help her regain the kingdom, and along the way would teach her what she needed to learn to become a wise ruler, no longer the evil queen of fairy tales, and she would learn what she needed to do to make up for the deeds of her past.

Before I set down a more formal structure, I put up a big sheet with post-it notes of things that I knew happened in the story. I added notes as I brainstormed with my writing group, in an approximate order of where they took place in the story. Here in the notes you can see some things that emerged in the final novel and some that did not. One of the ideas I loved was a support group for people who had been turned into animals, and there was an idea that the main character would meet a romantic interest in that group. I only knew vaguely that this happened toward the end of the story.

Armed with these ideas, I set about figuring out how the story would go. You'll notice from the post-its that around the middle of the board, below about the PLAN B note, the notes are very light on plot and are much more focused on what I want to come out of the plot at this point. The Queen and Thief bond over stories. She tells him lies that he finds out; he reveals the lies in the stories he tells about the Thieves Guild. How does all this happen? Good question. That's where the structure comes in.

At some point I knew that the Thief and Queen would have to be in opposition, just from a narrative standpoint. They couldn't be working together the whole time; that makes for a less dynamic story. If there are going to be lies and reveals, there will also have to be conflict (this is a Western story structure). But at the end, I wanted the Thief and Queen to learn the same lesson, one that reveals that I was watching *The Good Place* at this time: "What do we owe to each other?"

She realizes the error of her ways; he comes to terms with being turned into an animal and realizes that he wasn't really happy as a thief. And throughout, you can see the importance of stories that I'm putting into this.

So where did I go from a structure standpoint? Here are the earliest notes I can find where I laid out the structure more concretely:

> 1. The Spire
>
> Setup: Nivvy, a thief thrown out of the Guild (he thought he was more skilled than a fellow thief on a job and while he was right, his actions got that thief captured) and currently serving a punishment for being caught in a small town, which he considers the low point of his life, is approached by Bella, a once-noble woman who wants him to help her regain her rightful kingdom. Despite the fool's errand he thinks her job is, it offers him a way out, and any way out has to be up. He accepts.
>
> Inciting Incident: Bella takes him first to the lair of a fairy (in a volcano near a town called Spire) who is pretty clearly evil. Nivvy has a chance to back out but decides his talent as a thief is equal to the task and goes ahead with it.
>
> First turn: The theft fails spectacularly. The fairy turns Nivvy into a weasel and throws him and Bella out. Now Nivvy is sure he shouldn't

have taken Bella's job, but she's his best chance of getting changed back, so he's stuck with her. They shift to looking for a powerful magic item (the Drowned King's Regalia). Bella refuses to take responsibility for what happened to Nivvy; he persists in blaming her for it. Here she reveals that for the last thousand years she has been imprisoned in a cavern as punishment for her supposed crimes (which she does not admit to), and only escaped when the magic holding her dwindled to nothing. She views the loneliness as the worst thing in the world (but will not say that yet).

(Also: Nivvy is a trans man, which doesn't come into the story much but is noted because as a weasel he does not wear clothes at first—I think he will get little weasel britches later for that reason—anyway, the queen notices and there is a conversation about it and the queen accepts it and that's generally it.)

2. The Drowned City

Midpoint: They find the item at a place that reveals something monstrous Bella did as queen (she flooded a valley and the prosperous capital city it contained). For the first time, Nivvy connects her to the Evil Queen of stories he's heard. He tries to stop her from getting the Regalia, but this leads to her almost dying. He saves her and then can't stop her from getting the items. (Here she praises his skill as a thief.)

His focus shifts from getting turned back to talking her out of taking over the kingdom. Her perspective is that she's been punished for her crimes and that the stories were exaggerated. They come across another reminder of her evil deeds (and/or she uses the Regalia brutally to escape a situation he could've managed) and Nivvy gets a sense of how they have affected people through the years. He finally tries to steal the Regalia from her and she catches him and almost kills him but he escapes (he speaks her Unspeakable Truth to her—that she doesn't actually deserve anything she's had or wants—and she speaks his to him—that he is alone in the world because he pushes everyone away (? Maybe not, will work on)).

3. [Nivvy's hometown]

Valley of Death: With nowhere to go, he reflects on getting kicked out of the Guild and how it affected his fellow thieves. He realizes he has to make amends to them and enlist their help, which also requires him to reach out to other magically transformed animals (whom he'd previously shunned) to help him get there.

4. [The Conquered Kingdom]

They arrive—too late. Bella has taken over the kingdom. They try to steal the Regalia from her but are all caught and imprisoned. But Nivvy turning on her has wounded her because she viewed him as a kindred spirit and so she demands that he explain himself to her, and he tries to tell her about his understanding, that to be worthy of respect you have to extend it to other people as well, and that the more you try to make people like you, the more alone you'll be.

She confesses that she doesn't have anyone to talk to now that she's Queen, she feels more alone than ever, and that wearing the Drowned King's Regalia has made her think about him and what she did to him and his people, and then all the others—but it's hard to think about that, to open that door, because then she feels she's shutting herself back in the thousand-year cavern. Nivvy tells her that when she opens that door she lets other people in and that that's the only way out of the cavern. They talk about the endings of fairy tales and he says she can rewrite this story.

She agrees to give up the throne and spend her life working to repair the damage she did. Nivvy, staying a weasel, works with her along with some of his animal and thief friends.

It looks like around part 2 that I started adding plot to what was on the idea board (and here's the first mention of Nivvy being trans, an idea I liked). Here too is where some character work comes in: Bella refuses to take responsibility for what happened. This is a core of Bella's character, that misfortune is a thing that happens to her, not something she causes. Identifying it here was important. At this point the goals of the story shift (this is a good signal of a midpoint). Bella wants to use the Regalia to take back her kingdom, while Nivvy tries to talk her out of it now that he knows who she really is.

Part 3 is where I was applying traditional structure to figure out what was missing. The end of the second act is usually a "Valley of Death," where things are the worst for a character. They've lost support and have to make a change. Hence Nivvy reaching out to other magical creatures, in effect accepting his new status once he escapes Bella and has no more options.

Part 4 embodies the message I was trying to tell with the story, which is that connections and other people are important. Bella gets what she wants but it isn't really what she needed, which was someone to talk to. And you earn that by treating them with care. Nivvy has had to learn that lesson, sort of, and he now imparts it to Bella. She understands that she has to make up for her past behavior.

One last note: you'll see the phrase "Unspeakable Truths" in there. I picked this up from Kij Johnson, who in talking about the arcs of relationships (as opposed to characters), points out that characters lie to each other early on, but at some point in the story must say to each other the truth they are trying to avoid. This fits well with the character needing to learn something about themself in order to overcome their obstacles. It doesn't always happen, but it's often an important point in a character's arc and in the development of a relationship. I'll talk more about it in a later section on characters.

Hopefully as you compare the idea board to that first attempt at a synopsis, you can see the progression from ideas about what I want the stories to be to a structure to make that happen. It's not a firm plot—there are a lot of things like "she catches him but he escapes," which are vague signposts for things I will figure out the specifics of later—but it's still got more shape than the idea board which is just "what story about himself does he arrive at?" and things like that. This feels like a story I can write.

Exercise: Structure

1. Pick three books and list out the main plot points. Identify:
  • The inciting incident
  • The point where the main character is committed to the story
  • Any point where the goal changes (this includes a plot point that starts or concludes a subplot)
  • The point where the main character needs to commit to a change in strategy or in philosophy in order to "win" the final battle
Answer the following:
  • Are there any plot points that don't really affect anything (where the characters' goal and situation is the same after as it was before)? Why do you think they're there?
  • Can you map this onto any of the structures listed? Don't try too hard to force it; it's as instructive to see where something doesn't fit as to see where it does.
  • Are there places in the story that feel forced, or flat? How would you change those?

2. Thinking about the story you want to write:

List out any of the main structural points you already know from the list above. It's okay if you don't have them all yet.

>> A. For each of the points that is still blank (if any), come up with three to five possible events that would fit into that spot in the story. How can you make each of these work with the story you want to tell?

>> B. Come up with five possible subplots that would work with your main story. Think about how each one interacts with the main story. What counterpoint or different message does it provide to your reader or main character? What aspect of your world does it reveal?

Chapter Six

Outlining

Oh, no! Outlining?

A lot of writers have strong reactions to outlining. When I used to object to it, I guess I thought it was getting in the way of starting the story I was excited about getting to. Or it felt too academic—I used to have to make outlines in college, I'm sure, although I can't remember for what anymore.

But the more I wrote, the more I realized that an outline was a valuable part of preparing for writing a novel. The parts of novels that tripped me up inevitably came after I'd exhausted the initial burst of excitement from starting it but hadn't yet gotten to the conclusion. Most of the time, I found myself stopping in the middle of the novel to make an outline of how I thought the rest of the book was going to go. When I realized that, I thought it would probably be good to have that outline at the start of the book.

The other objection I hear is that people don't want to plan the story out because it takes the excitement of discovery away. And hey, I still love the thrill of discovery as I write a story, and I can tell you from experience that an outline doesn't have to take that away.

An outline represents the shape of the story as you see it at the beginning. But you will almost certainly diverge from the outline as you write the story. This is fine and even expected! As you dive into the story, the characters will become more real to you than they are at the beginning, and you will see more possibilities for them and for the story. Writers talk a lot about throwing away their outline as they get into the writing of the book itself.

So…why bother? If you're just going to throw the outline out, why go to the trouble of writing it?

This goes back to what I said at the beginning, about keeping the story of the novel in your head in some form. For me, at least, writing out an outline tells me what I want the story to look like and where I want it to go. This is like having a map when you set out on a road trip. Even if you end up taking a different path to your destination, you know that a path exists. That gives you the confidence to diverge from it if you need to.

The other thing you might be asking is: didn't we just make an outline in the last section? The one on structure where we had to figure out the plot beats?

Well, sort of. The idea of the structure section is to look at the broad strokes of your story, the milestone events that are turning points. The idea of the outline is to find out how those are connected. We want to drill down to the scene level, so that ideally when you're done, you can read through your outline and have a pretty clear sense of what your novel is going to look like when it's done. (Except, of course, it will probably not look like that when it's done.)

How do you make an outline?

When I first started writing outlines, I didn't know what an outline is supposed to look like. There weren't at the time a lot of examples of people sharing their outlines. It took me a little while to realize that it didn't matter what the outline looks like, because it's *only for the writer*. If you feel like you want a formally structured outline like:

I. Part I
    A. Chapter 1
        1. Scene 1
        2. Scene 2
        3. Scene 3

… and so on, then great, build your outline that way. If you'd rather it be less structured, just a list of scenes, you can do that too. You don't even have to make it a list. You can just write it as a synopsis, if that works for you.

If you use Scrivener, as I do and many writers do (http://www.literatureandlatte.com, I don't get anything for this but it's a good writing tool), you'll find it useful to break up your scenes because that works well with Scrivener's corkboard interface. You can make each scene its own entry and put your one or two sentences in the Summary section, and then as you go through, you'll have reminders of what you were intending to write in each scene.

As you're building your outline, there are two main precepts to keep in mind:

1. Remember what each character *wants* at that point in the story.

With that in mind, what's the next logical step for them to take? At the same time, what does the antagonist want? What are they doing at the same time?

Remembering what your main character wants, let alone the antagonist and all the side characters, is difficult when you're trying to build out the plot of a great big novel where you've already decided on the milestone points. You may (probably will) reach points where it feels difficult to wrangle your characters toward the plot points you've set up (this happens more while you're actually writing, but it can happen at this outlining stage as well).

This is why I asked you to think about theme before story beats. If you haven't thought about what you're trying to say with your story, then you will find it harder to restructure the plot based on what your character now wants. And you should be constructing the story in this direction. Following a character's wants is what makes a story feel organic and real.

It's often more difficult to think about your side characters' or antagonist's wants as you go through a story. "Antagonist antagonizes" is a common note I make in my early outlines, but it's important to understand *why* your antagonist is antagonizing. If you don't think about that, your villain is going to run the risk of becoming just a personified obstacle, someone who always does the most inconvenient thing for the protagonist because it's the most inconvenient thing and for no other reason.

Every character in your book should have something they want at some point—most points—in the book, and act accordingly. Your job is to channel all those wants into the story you want to tell. Part of that is making sure you have the correct characters in the correct circumstances, and the other part is listening to those characters as you craft your story.

2. Make sure your scenes affect the story.

This is a principle put forward by the creators of South Park in a famous video from around 2017 (search YouTube for "Writing Advice from Matt Stone & Trey Parker @ NYU"). Their philosophy is that the words that connect your scenes— the words you would write in between the scene summaries if you were writing out a synopsis—should be either "therefore" or "but," never "and then."

In other words: what happens in one scene should directly influence what happens next, or the next thing that happens should interfere with the flow of the story. In novels, you can have several storylines going on at once sometimes, so if you're jumping around from one point of view to another, apply this rule within those storylines.

It's a good one to keep in mind when you're thinking about plot, because it keeps the reader engaged in your story. When the events of a scene have consequences that are felt in the next one, that creates momentum, a sense of motion. When you end a scene and the next one doesn't seem to draw anything from that last scene, the story feels more static. There's less energy in the plot.

In addition to making sure that each scene follows from the last one, you also have to make sure that the scenes move you along on your plot and character arcs. When each scene is finished, at least one character's situation should have changed. They should have satisfied a small want, or be a step closer to— or farther from—realizing a larger one. They may realize that someone they thought was an ally is an enemy, or vice versa. This change should then inform the next scene.

The end result of both of these is to remind you to think of the story as a connected, dependent series of scenes, driven by the characters and resulting from their actions and decisions. It's also framed and shaped by the setting, which gives context and consequence to those actions. We'll talk about each of those things in detail farther along, but for now just remember that the purpose of writing the outline is to get a feel for how all these elements work together to build your story.

Summary Points

- Planning your story with an outline will likely save you time in the revision stage.
- An outline can look like whatever is most useful to you.
- When planning scenes:
    - Remember what the main character(s) want in each scene.
    - Make sure the scenes affect each other.

Example: Outlining

Here is the next stage in the outline I wrote for *The Price of Thorns*. Since I'd written down some scenes already, some of this had been written before I started the outline, but this covers what was written and my ideas for what had yet to come:

- - -

Nivvy, a thief from the mid-latitude coastal town of Copper Port who has been expelled from the Thieves Guild, is on a large wooden wheel of punishment in a backwoods desert town to the north when Bella, a mysterious woman with an air of decayed elegance, approaches him with an offer. She claims to be a deposed queen who seeks help regaining her kingdom. With few other options, and the great potential of reward, Nivvy agrees to work for her even though he knows very little about her.

They travel to the town of Spire, near which Bella says a friend of hers lives that they need to steal a magic item from. Because Nivvy is unfamiliar with Spire, they hire a guide: Zein, a hawk who used to be human but was transformed into an animal by magic (Zein, of indeterminate gender, calls themself a "former-human"). Nivvy stops Bella from killing Zein as they are about to leave Spire, which Bella deems necessary because she doesn't want anyone to know where she's heading.

They ride three days to a volcano where the only settlement is a temple to the fire god Bouli. Bella reveals that her "friend" is a fairy who lives in the volcano, and she and Nivvy ascend to find the friend's residence. When Nivvy first meets this fairy, who calls herself Scarlet, he sees her as a fearsome djinn, but a moment later she takes the form of a genteel lady in a dress. She guides them through several caverns filled with battle trophies and magic artifacts, and Nivvy spots the chest full of rings that contains the ring Bella has asked him to steal.

He makes an excuse to leave the two friends talking together, but as he leaves the cavern he can still hear what they're saying. Bella doesn't appear to know this, as she tells Scarlet more than she has told Nivvy about her past. Scarlet asks her about a place called Glaederigdal, and Bella confesses that she drowned an entire city a thousand years ago to protect her daughter's honor. This revelation comes with bad timing just as Nivvy has found the ring he was meant to steal and leads him to drop the lid of the chest he's holding, shocked by the revelation that his employer is a many-times-over murderer and more than a thousand years old.

In a moment, Scarlet has discovered him, and in revenge turns him into a weasel.

Bella defends him, threatening the fairy with what may be a bluff, and she and Nivvy are allowed to escape with the ring. But the ring, which allows the wearer to assume any form, is useless to Bella. Magic works differently now than it did in her day: now you must know an item's story to use its magic, and she does not know the ring's story. But Nivvy hears her muse that there might be an alternative.

In the night, unused to his new body, he wakes hungry and decides to go look for food. After a tussle with some rats, he drinks a little wine and passes out. He wakes in the morning to find himself in a cage and Bella gone, along with most of their supplies and, most unforgivably, Nivvy's dear companion, his horse Rahila.

The priests hang his cage in the library as they try to get him to speak to them, which gives him the chance to trick a visiting court official into freeing him and bringing him back to Spire. There, he searches out Zein again and proposes to hire them to take him to Glaederigdal, which is the only place he can think of that Bella might have gone.

To find out where that is, they visit one of Zein's friends, a storyteller who says that it is a very old name. While there, Zein misgenders Nivvy without realizing it, because his naked weasel body shows his biological sex (female). The storyteller directs them to Glaederigdal, now a lake in the mountains as a result of Bella drowning the kingdom.

Zein flies there while holding Nivvy in their talons, which is frightening but very efficient. When they get close, Nivvy insists they fly over a town as a more direct route, which leads to Zein being shot by a hunter. Nivvy scares the hunter away and then drags Zein to the nearby forest and hunts for food, afraid they're going to die.

He stumbles upon an ancient hippie living in the forest amid a clearing of peaceful animals and brings him to Zein. The hippie, Frankh, takes them both in and tells them about his goddess Aska, a gardener who loves all her subjects.

After a night with Frankh, Nivvy wakes with his determination to reach the lake feeling muted. He realizes that Frankh has drugged him and all the animals, and runs away, leaving Zein behind but promising himself that he'll return to rescue them.

He reaches the lake and after a day, Bella and a man from the nearby town arrive. He gives her a small magic item that allows her to stay underwater indefinitely, and she descends to look for something, but comes up angry. Nivvy reveals himself to her, and she asks him to go into the lake to retrieve a crown for her, promising to make him human again if he does. He doesn't fully believe her but doesn't have many other options, so he takes the magic charm and dives.

After a long swim and exploration of the palace, he finds the crown along with a ghost guarding it.

The ghost accompanies him back to the surface, although because its language is a thousand years old, he can't understand a word it's saying. At the surface, Bella asks Nivvy to give her the crown, and the townsman tells him not to. Bella cuts his finger off, which Nivvy notices is wearing the ring he stole from the fairy, and then throws dust in his face. She tells Nivvy that Scarlet has taken possession of the man's body and that the dust will temporarily remove her powers.

Scarlet confirms that it is her, and tells Nivvy not to give Bella the crown, but Bella tells him that with the crown she can turn him human again and so he gives her the crown. She orders Scarlet to transfer all the fairy's power to her and Scarlet obeys. When she has all the fairy's power, she restores Nivvy's human form and then turns the townsman's horse into a dragon and flies away on it, leaving Nivvy with his horse and the ghost of the prince.

The ghost leads him to the severed finger, which still has the ring on it, and when he picks up the ring, the fairy/djinn speaks to him. Scarlet managed to transfer herself into the ring and now tells him that he must stop Bella; because he took the crown, it will not work for him or on him (the crown must be given willingly, so it will work for Bella because he gave it to her). She translates the ghost's words as he tells Nivvy the story of his ancestry and the crown and how Bella murdered his whole kingdom (not to protect her daughter), and Scarlet tells Nivvy that he has to promise to get the crown back and/or defeat Bella before the ghost will let him be.

He promises, knowing he doesn't have to keep his promise, and the ghost leaves them. Nivvy wants to rescue Zein, and Scarlet says she will help if he brings her back to her volcano so she can live out her remaining years in peace (she thinks without her power she will survive maybe a decade). He agrees, and she reveals the story that will make the ring work so that he can disguise himself as Frankh's goddess and take Zein back.

This plan works, but drugged Zein doesn't want to be rescued. As soon as the drugs wear off, they fly back to Frankh, but return that night saying that when they saw the lake, they remembered that Nivvy knew they wanted to see it and took them there, and then realized that he'd rescued them, and nobody else had ever gone out of their way for them.

Scarlet tries to convince him to go after Bella, telling him that the fate of the world hangs in the balance, but he thinks she's just mad and wants revenge.

I think the first act ends with Nivvy getting turned into a weasel because that's where the goals change and he gets committed to the story. The first half of the second act ends with him being turned human again as Bella gets the djinn's power.

So I'm working through the second half of the second act. Here I have to get into something that will drive Nivvy to take on the most powerful magic being in the world.

What he actually wants more than anything is a community; what he fears is being alone. (His hope in working for Bella is that he will be allowed back into the Thieves Guild somewhere, maybe back at Copper Port or in her kingdom.)

Scarlet's idea for defeating Bella is a magic mirror that shows your true nature (because Bella has founded her identity on a lie, a story she's built over the years of how she was wronged). He takes Scarlet back to her lair and refuses to go after Bella because it's not worth it. Instead he tries to get into the Thieves Guild in Spire (the city near Scarlet's home), disappointing Zein, who does believe he should go after Bella. But they send back to Copper Port and we find out the real story of why he got expelled: he was working a job with another thief and left that thief to be caught, and eventually executed (he may not know that the other thief was executed). They want to take him prisoner but he gives up his faithful horse (who is not as faithful as he imagines but allows the Guild members to lead her away), and because these Guild members aren't invested in the guy he betrayed, they figure having a horse is better than having a prisoner and they let him go. He's left with nothing and decides to go back to Scarlet's cave and steal the ring so he can pretend to be someone else and join the guild again. Zein spots him leaving the city and goes along with him and finally convinces him to go after Bella by asking "what kind of story do you want to be told about you?" He realizes that in all the stories he grew up admiring, the hero remained true to himself, and he doesn't want to hide and become someone else. So he goes and gets the mirror (hand mirror) and the ring and goes off to confront Bella.

A strong theme in the novel is stories, and in the second half of the second act, as Scarlet is telling Nivvy the truth of how things happened with Bella/Rose back a thousand years ago, they discuss the nature and purpose of stories (Scarlet has no need of stories that teach a lesson and is frustrated that people change the events of stories from what happened to fit emotional beats), which is why I want stories to be involved in the climactic moment.

- - -

You can already see how the story's changed since my first attempt at putting structure to it. Where Bella and Nivvy originally traveled together to the lake, as I was working through the plot scene by scene, it felt to me more dynamic if they were separated at this point. A journey together would need to have a lot of external obstacles created; if they're separated, and Bella is Nivvy's best chance at returning to his human form, then Nivvy has a strong need to find her again, and a lot of natural obstacles in his way (he's caged by the priests, he's a weasel without a horse, etc.). This section between Nivvy turning into a weasel and the Drowned Kingdom did not have a whole lot in it in the last version, but when I made this change, it became a much more exciting and engaging adventure to write.

In addition, it added conflict between Nivvy and Bella. One of the things I realized later on was that all the inflection points of this story involve characters making decisions about their relationship to other characters. After Nivvy turns into a weasel, he really needs Bella's help—and she rejects him. This is a strong character moment for her, proving that she can't let people get close to her, and it sends her down a path away from the redemption arc I'd planned for her. Fortunately, neither the redemption arc nor the "journey together telling stories" got lost; they just got repurposed.

Bella taking Scarlet's power was a new twist, one that also added conflict to the story and unexpectedly opened up a new arc for me. Scarlet was now the companion on the journey, someone with far more stories than Bella but also with a character trait that brought a lot of tension to her relationship with Nivvy (and to a lesser extent Zein): she sees everything amorally. She lives in a world where power was the only right. If you had the power to impose your will, you had the right to use it. Now that she's powerless, she believes her life is over, but Nivvy and Zein try to convince her that there is more to life than power. So she gets a redemption arc that is less straightforward than Bella's, but also (strangely) less difficult to deal with. And this took me a while to articulate, though I felt it in this outline: because Bella was human and understood what she was doing, her evil actions make it much more difficult to redeem her. Scarlet has done arguably way worse things, but because her actions stemmed from a different moral system, her redemption can simply be thought of as teaching her about human morality.

As for the "journey together" arc, that works better after the Drowned Kingdom, because here is where Nivvy has what he wanted: he's been part of an amazing story, he's got his human form back, and he has some perspective on the world. He has a friend (Zein) with whom he might form a partnership (joining the Thieves' Guild in Spire). So this is a reflective period where we get to hear some stories of the world as Scarlet tries to convince him to go after Bella, and at the end of that there's a dramatic event that drives him to do the right thing. I don't have the dramatic event in this outline, but I knew something needed to go there.

The takeaway from this is that as I started getting more specific with the detail about what had to go into the story, I started finding details that strengthened and changed the story I wanted to tell. Bella is more of a villain in this version; Scarlet and Zein have greatly expanded roles. But at the same time, the second half of the book is still a little fuzzy. And that's okay! As we move forward with the writing, we'll discover where the story wants to go.

Exercise: Outlining

By now you have an idea of what the exercises are going to be, I'm sure. The best way to practice outlining is by doing it, breaking down scenes and seeing how they relate to each other. So take a book you like, and from about 3 chapters (2 if they're long chapters, 4 if they're short), write out a 1-3 sentence description of what goes on in each scene.

That in itself is a good exercise, working backwards from something that already exists so that when you have to create your own outline, you have a feel for the relationship between a scene and the scene summary. But keep going from there:

  • Write them down in a way that feels natural for you to organize and read. Try a couple different ways—on lined paper, in a spreadsheet on a computer, on post-it notes—and find one that works for you.

• Now go through the scenes and look first at how they connect. What words can you write to connect those scenes?

• For each scene, write down the main character and what they want to get out of that scene specifically. If you can, write the same for the other characters in the scene.

• Write down how the character has changed in the scene, if at all (what have they learned?). Write down how the plot has advanced (has the ultimate goal changed? The immediate goal?).

What you're hoping to get out of this is a feel for the structure beneath the scenes. It's easy to get caught up in the writing—that's what we hope happens when we read—but when you're planning and writing, you have to make sure that there's a strong underlying structure to the scenes you're writing. As we get into the actual drafting, we'll talk about how to dress up the scenes and all the tools you have to do that, but it's important to understand the purpose before you start the writing.

Chapter Seven

Four Levels of Story

Four Levels of Story

I learned the idea of four levels of story from Kij Johnson and Barbara Webb at the Novel Architects workshop. They posit that any story can (and a good story should) have four different stories going on at different levels of the narrative.

We have already talked about two of the four levels. The Personal story is the character's arc, how they grow and change over the course of the story. The Plot is the sequence of external events that moves the story forward. Both of these were covered in the Structure section (and we will return to both in more depth a little later).

The other two levels are Interpersonal and World. The interpersonal story is the story of the relationship between the main character and others (sometimes one particular other), kind of an external reflection of the internal character journey. And the world story is the larger period of change happening around the character.

World

Let's start with the world story and work our way down. The world story is often the least well defined of all of them, but even if it's in the background it's there. In *Watership Down*, for example, the world story is simply that the rabbits' world is being encroached upon by man. There is no real arc to this story, no endpoint or fighting back against it; it is the period of change that defines the world they live in. This era of change sets the story in motion, and after that is felt mostly in setting; the men aren't pursuing the rabbits throughout the book (although man's presence touches their lives everywhere and eventually the rabbits use this to their advantage). In The Lord of the Rings, by contrast, the world story defines nearly every part of the adventure. The book is described as a chronicle of the "end of the Third Age," in which magic diminishes greatly in the world, and the plot—to destroy the One Ring, also for Aragorn to become King, and yes, I am greatly simplifying a three-book epic—relies on that world story in a way that *Watership Down*'s does not.

The world story is important as an aspect of world building because it introduces the space into which the plot can take place. A question often asked of writers in critiques is "why this protagonist, why now?" Part of the answer to that must lie in the world story. At a time of transition in the world, customary behaviors and practices will stop working, or will be less effective, and people need to find new ones. Problems will arise that nobody has had to solve before, and this is where your protagonist comes in. In Lord of the Rings, the hobbits' behavior of isolation is made impossible by the threat of Sauron. Literally, Nazgul invade the Shire, which has previously been safe from encroachment.

Usually—not always—the world story will not be personally directed at the character. It's larger than them, a sea change that they happen to be caught up in. A country is transitioning from peace to war, or the other way around; an isolated community faces interaction with an outside world; a growing population puts strain on a community's rules. Often the main character will either represent this change or be affected personally by it, but the change is not directed *at* them. Sauron didn't rise back to power specifically to destroy Frodo, but Frodo is nonetheless personally affected by his growing power and hunt for the One Ring.

In "special hero" narratives, the main character can precipitate a world story. In *The Dark Is Rising,* the second book in the eponymous series, Will Stanton reaching his eleventh birthday brings him into the Circle of Old Ones as the last, which sets in motion the final conflict between the Dark and the Light. In The Lion, the Witch, and the Wardrobe, it's the arrival of the Pevensies in Narnia that begins the events that bring about the fall of the White Witch. So in these cases, the world story is, to some extent, about the protagonists, but even in these cases, there are larger forces at play.

Plot

The plot is the engine that drives your character through the story, the series of events that push your character to make choices they previously wouldn't have. The plot is often intertwined with the personal story (or character arc), because the character's choices directly affect what's happening in the world around them and the progression of the story, and in turn, the events that result from those choices force new decisions onto the character.

The plot and the interpersonal story are the two stories with direct stakes for the protagonist. The world story may have consequences; in the case of Lord of the Rings, for example, if the hobbits fail to destroy the One Ring, the world will be plunged into darkness. But the end of the Third Age is still at hand; even if Sauron had been successful, magic was continuing to diminish. It just would've been a lot less comfortable transition for most of the inhabitants of Middle-Earth. But the stakes to Frodo specifically are the survival of the Shire and of the hobbits' way of life. The larger stakes provide more tension in the narrative, but for Frodo, the Shire is what is important. The Shire's survival is the stakes of the plot.

Stakes are important to the plot because they motivate the protagonist, and represent the consequences of their decisions. When I say the plot must pressure the protagonist to make choices they otherwise wouldn't, that's because there is something at stake they desperately need to save, or to achieve. Their choice is between personal growth to achieve that goal, and refusing (or being unable) to grow and change, and losing this goal. In a tragedy, the protagonist does not meet the moment, and the goal is lost (more on stakes later).

So the plot has to be believable (within the continuity and context of the world, and the tone of your story—what works as the plot of a farcical P.G. Wodehouse novel would not work as the plot of a serious Kim Stanley Robinson science fiction novel) and the goal has to be something that matters to your protagonist so much that they will endure previously unimaginable changes or situations in order to accomplish them.

In Western storytelling, the plot is usually centered around a conflict: the protagonist wants something but is being blocked or challenged; or someone else is trying to do something that will have (to the protagonist) terrible consequences and they must stop them. "Conflict" can be broadly interpreted here. In a romance, the "antagonist" is the love interest and the conflict is over whether the two (or more) will get together by the end. In a mystery, the conflict is between the criminal, who has set out a puzzle, and the detective, who has to solve it.

Romance and mystery are interesting genres in terms of plot, because in both these cases, the *outcome* of the plot is rarely in doubt. There are very, very few mysteries in which the case is not solved (though sometimes the criminal may get away), and similarly few romances in which the main characters don't get together at the end. The genres determine a lot of the conventions of the plot, and in this case the outcome is much less important than the journey. What clue will tip off the detective and how was the puzzle set? What grand gesture will convince the love interest to get together?

I'll talk more about what makes for an effective plot as you get farther into writing the book.

Interpersonal

This is the storyline that shows your protagonist's relationship with the other main (or near-main) characters in the story. Kazuo Ishiguro, in his Nobel Lecture,[3] touched on the importance of relationships in fiction—not just the growth of characters in a character arc, but the growth of their relationships within the story.

In a romance, the interpersonal relationship is sometimes the entire stakes, but there are often side relationships—with family, with best friends—that are also affected by the plot and can be nearly as important.

Even in books that aren't romances, the relationships can be as important or more important than the plot. In Patricia McKillip's wonderful Riddle-Master series, the trilogy hinges on the relationships between Morgon and Deth, and Morgon and Raederle; the book ends on the closure of those relationships rather than on the effects of the plot or the world, even though the plot and world story were quite important.

So as you're going through your book, think about the main relationships in the story and how they evolve over time. What's interesting about them, what goals do each of the people have for the relationship (whether conscious or not)? How do the events of the plot affect the relationship? This doesn't mean that each of the characters has opposing goals, though they might, but they might want to accomplish the same goal in different ways. Ultimately, their perception of the relationship will change over the course of the story. I'll go more in depth into relationships later on in the book.

Personal (Character)

This is the traditional character arc we talked about in the

---

[3] The lecture is about the small moments that influenced his writing, much more than just about relationships in fiction, but that's a large part of it. Video and transcript available at the Nobel Prize's website: https://www.nobelprize.org/prizes/literature/2017/ishiguro/lecture/

structure section, how the events of the book will teach a character a lesson, providing them an opportunity to grow. The lesson they have to learn is often not one they're conscious of, but something necessary to improve their world. As the story starts, the protagonist is in some equilibrium with their world, but it's not an ideal place. Their life seems to be missing something, and maybe they realize this, as Taran does at the beginning of the Prydain Chronicles (though he is mistaken about what it is missing), or maybe they don't, as Mr. Stevens doesn't at the beginning of *The Remains of the Day*.

The events of the plot will intrude on the main character's world, jarring them out of their familiar habits and settings and sending them on an adventure. The stakes of the adventure, as we discussed above, should be something so important to the protagonist that they are worth the risk and danger of the adventure, worth trying multiple ways to succeed, and finally, worth changing the protagonist's beliefs and supplying them with the lesson they have to learn.

The reason we do all this over the course of a novel is to build the tension, build the stakes, and build the struggle. A short story in which a character overcomes an obstacle can be effective, but the journey of a novel shows us how much a character has to go through to change their world. A longer journey and harder struggle invests the reader in the story; following the character through the hardest times and watching them succeed in the end is uplifting (or, in the case of a tragedy, watching them fail anyway).

But the journey has to make sense. It isn't fulfilling if a character beats their head against a wall for 300 pages (metaphorically) and then on page 301 suddenly realizes they have to value the lessons of their ancestors, especially if they were told that back on page 10 and ignored it for most of the story. We want to see them take the advice in the wrong way, encounter people who took a different path (one that's open to them), and be tempted to abandon the adventure. When they finally make the correct choice, learn the lesson, solve the puzzle, we cheer along with them and feel their satisfaction.

We respond to fiction in many ways as though it were real. Certainly the personal and interpersonal arcs of your novel are ones that people will most relate to in their real lives. I will talk throughout this book about character arcs and how to make them believable, because I think this is the heart of any book. Even a plot-driven story like a heist or a mystery can have a character arc for its protagonist, and it's often the character arcs that stick with people from a book—or at least, that stick with me. I remember few of the details of the narrator's raft trip in *Life of Pi*, but I remember vividly his conversation with the insurance investigators and his revelation at the end.

Summary Points

• A novel can have multiple stories going on at once. There is a story about the world, the main story (plot), a story about relationship(s) between characters, and a personal story about the main character. The more these stories feel related and depend on each other, the stronger the overall story will feel.

Chapter Eight

The Writing Process

Your Writing Process

After all this planning, you still have to figure out how you're going to write seventy or eighty or a hundred and fifty thousand words. If this is your first novel project, that's a daunting task. Even if it isn't, it's worth reviewing your writing habits to see how you can put yourself in the best position to get through writing a novel. I've met a lot of people who've gotten stuck in the middle of writing their novel. The planning we've done so far is one good measure to prevent against that; the other is building good writing habits so that you can weather the inevitable obstacles that will come at you in the months you're going to spend working on this novel.

<u>Expectations</u>

You will find various pieces of advice telling you to write every day, to write 250, 500, 1000 words a day. You know yourself best and know how quickly the words come for you. Some people write a very fast first draft and can write 1000 words a day easily; some people spend more time crafting their sentences and go more slowly. What's more, some people respond well to missing a goal, taking it as a challenge; others don't respond well, taking it as a failure. Some people need to give themselves permission to take a day off here and there; some people know if they miss one or two days, they'll find it harder to get back to the routine. You know how best you work, so find a goal that is reasonable and that suits your temperament.

When you've set your goal, do your best to meet it every day. Recognize, too, that your best may not always meet your target. You're the best judge of how much to push yourself and how much to give yourself slack. And you'll need to do both to finish a novel.

There will be days when you're frustrated with the story, or when you're not in the mood to write. There will be days when it feels inconvenient to write. You can give yourself a break once in a while, but ask yourself: do I need to take a break or do I just want to? If you get into the habit of taking breaks, soon enough it'll be easier and easier to do so. You'll find yourself not having written for days on end because it wasn't convenient or exciting, and once you fall out of the habit, you've got to build it back up from scratch.

On the flip side, there will be times when you can't get words down that day. There will be sick days, travel days, emergencies (hopefully not too many), company, and other life events that cut into your writing time. If you miss a day, that's okay! But you should try extra hard to get back into the groove the next day. Trust me—it makes it so much easier if you build up your routine.

Setting a daily goal is useful because it can help you set your expectations for how much time this project is going to take. This is something that you'll get a better feel for the more often you do it, but you can still make a guess. Your outline will tell you about how many scenes are in your book, and depending on how descriptive you like to make them, you can figure out how many words go into a scene. For me, it's an average of 1500, ranging from 1000-1800 in practice, and I average three scenes per chapter. This isn't a formula for you to follow—your chapters might be shorter or longer, your scenes might be more economical or more expansive. Only you know what fits your style. But if you go through your outline and you figure you have ~70 scenes, and you write 1500-word scenes, that's 105,000 words as your target. If you write 1000 words a day, it'll take you just over three months to finish a draft. If you write 500 words a day, six months.

I think it's important to have that expectation in your mind as you start the writing process. Knowing it's going to be three months, or six, or nine, or a year, helps you moderate your expectations. A common source of frustration with writing a novel is "I've been writing this for weeks and I feel like I should be farther." Knowing that it's going to take a while helps you push off that feeling. If you wanted, you could print out a calendar and X out every day as you go along, like in a cartoon, so you can see your progress visually.

And you can change the schedule as you write. If it turns out your scenes are closer to 1200 words, or 1800, you can change the timeline. If you find yourself adding in scenes as you write (I do this all the time), you can change the timeline. A writer friend of mine keeps track of how many words he's written for each section of his outline and uses that to project how long the rest of his outline will take to write. Be as detailed or as loose as you feel comfortable with; the important thing is understanding the scope of the project so you don't get discouraged.

(There are other reasons people get discouraged in the middle of their book, but we will get to that later.)

Accountability

I talked about writing groups and writing communities at the beginning of the book. Having writing colleagues during the writing of a novel can be really valuable. Sometimes you can set up writing sprints, times when you all log into a video call to check in and then spend 45 minutes or so working on your book before checking in again to see how you've all done. For some people, it's immensely helpful to feel that you're in a group where writing is expected to happen during a certain time, and to have other people you feel you owe that writing to.

You can also be accountable to your writing group or colleagues without having that real-time interaction. Schedule a regular check-in, probably no less frequent than every couple weeks, and report on your progress to each other.

If you don't have a writing group, then if you'd like to be accountable to someone, ask a friend or partner to check in with you regularly on how the writing is going. Even if they don't really understand what's involved in writing a novel, having someone to talk to about your process as it goes along can be very helpful.

Space and Time

People have different ways of setting aside time to write every day. Again, you know yourself best and will have to figure out what works for you. But here are some techniques that have worked for me and others:

• Set aside a particular time of day. Get up a half hour earlier; go to bed a half hour later. Schedule an hour before dinner or after dinner. Use part of your lunch hour. Make that your writing time every day until you get used to it.

• Set aside a particular place to be your writing place. Don't write in the living room with the TV and the game console; write in the backyard or write on your porch or write in your car. Write in the coffee shop down the street.

• Find friends (or just other writers, they don't have to be friends) who want to write at the same times. Some groups will do sprints, periods of up to half an hour usually where everyone checks in and then writes together, heads down. You can do this online if you are not fortunate enough to have writers local to you, but there may be writing groups near you that organize sprints in libraries or coffee shops.

- One writer friend and I hold regular writing streams (separately), where we share our screen for an audience. She also reads aloud to an audience while editing. I don't do this for all my projects—I'm protective of some of my first drafts—and you might not be comfortable with it either, but if you are, it works well to have a group expecting you to show up and write at a certain time.

• If you can't find people to write at the same time, find a group to be accountable to on a daily or weekly basis. It helps with my motivation if I'm writing not only for myself, but to have a number to tell a group at the end of the day.

• Give yourself a small reward—a cookie, a YouTube video, something—when you've reached a goal for the day.

AFK (Away From Keyboard) Time

The time you spend at the keyboard is important, of course —that's where the words get put into the draft—but almost as important is the time you spend away from the keyboard. The story needs time to develop in your head before the words will come down onto the keys, and that development time can happen anywhere. If you ride public transportation or even have an easy drive in to work, that's a great time to be thinking through your story.

When you don't spend that time away from the keyboard, the development time has to happen while you're sitting at the keyboard, and that cuts into your writing time. I definitely noticed that my productivity suffered when my mind was preoccupied, whether with family health situations or world politics or a global pandemic. When things were really bad, even my time at the keyboard wasn't very productive. Those times are going to happen, and you have to give yourself some grace to deal with the things on your mind. It's bad enough worrying about family or the world without then adding the stress of beating yourself up because you didn't make your writing goal.

But when you have the space, it's important to think through your story. Again, figure out what works best for you, but what I find helpful is going back through the last scene I've written, reviewing what happened, and thinking about what's going to happen next. What am I most excited to write when I get back to the keyboard? Often if there's a complicated action scene, I'll spend three or four days working through it in my head, thinking through all the moving parts until I find the arrangement that works. But whatever stage of the manuscript I'm in, the time at the keyboard always goes better if I've spent time working out in my head what I'm going to type when I do finally sit down.

Follow your outline…or don't

I told you when I talked about outlines that you would be straying from yours. What this means is that you will be learning more about the story as you write it. The early chapters, clearest in your head, will remain the closest to your outline, but as you fill them out, you will add details that will change the course of the story, maybe only a little, maybe more. My experience is always that my story gains its own momentum, and I refer to my outline less and less. I'll still look at it for the major beats I need to hit, but sometimes even those change if the story shifts enough.

The other way you can diverge from the outline is in the order of writing. One would imagine that you would start at the beginning of the story and go on until you reach the end, and that is usually how I write. It allows the story to grow as you write more of it. If there are scenes I'm excited to get to, I'll put them in the outline, but the story might change before I get there, so I don't usually write them ahead of time.

However, I know people who say that you should write the scenes you're excited about, and if those scenes aren't the next ones, skip the next ones and write the exciting ones. You can stitch them together later—or maybe you'll find that you didn't really need those intervening scenes. That'll give you more work in revision, but it also keeps your momentum going through the writing of the first draft, where it's easy to stall if you're not engaged in the scene you're working on. If this appeals to you, then try this out and see if it works for you.

Summary Points

- Writing a novel is a big task. It will likely take you many months or possibly years.
- Plan your time as best you can. Set expectations for each day of work, but give yourself some grace.
- Figure out what tricks work to motivate you. Accountability to others, rewards for work, setting aside a particular time or place to write are all things that have worked for others.
- Use your outline as a guide but don't feel obliged to follow it if the story takes you away from it.

Part 2: First Draft!

All right. We've put off confronting the blank page as long as we can. We've got an idea board, pitches of various lengths, and an outline. It's time to put down actual words, first draft words. You can use this book in two ways: The chapters in this section will cover a lot of things you'll need to know as you move through Act 1 of your novel draft, and the next section will be helpful for when you've been writing a while and are in Act 2. Last, we'll cover the endings (Act 3) and revision. So you can read through as you write—and I'll be sharing examples from those parts of *The Price of Thorns*—but the chapters are also designed to be referred back to at any point in your writing process. Feel free to skip ahead to the chapter that's most relevant to what you want to do right now, and jump around as needed.

A few things about first drafts as we get started here. These are themes I'll come back to often, but let's just get them down here so you can come back and look at this section if you need to. Then I'll talk about the exercises and examples in this section so you know what to expect.

The most important thing about first drafts is that they are allowed—even encouraged—to suck. At this stage of your novel, the important thing is getting all those ideas out of your head and onto the page so you can see what you've got, and at the same time allow yourself the freedom to play with your ideas as you explore them and try new things. One of the biggest problems that faces writers at any level is pressure and expectations. It's hard enough to write without having a voice in the back of your head constantly saying, "That's not good enough," as you try to get your first draft done. Reminding yourself that this first draft is not going to be what you publish, and may not even be shown to anyone, gives you more freedom to get your words down.

Editing, as much as many people hate it, depends on having something to work with (obviously). The process of getting a manuscript ready to send to an agent or editor or to self-publish it involves several steps; you don't have to get it perfect on the first step. When I write, I have a first draft and then a revision pass, then I show it to my critique groups and have probably two more revision passes, and then a proofreading/final edits pass. So when I'm first-drafting, I'm mostly concerned with getting down some words that will be useful in the next step—and my own first revision pass, before I show it to anyone else, is there precisely because I don't want my critique group to waste time correcting all the little typos and mistakes and continuity errors that I can easily find going through it myself. I want them to work on the things that aren't as obvious to me.

There are people who put a lot of care and effort into their first drafts and produce near-publication-ready manuscripts. I have a friend who wrote short stories in a single draft. If this is a path you feel might suit you, go for it! The reason that I (and many other people) recommend a "let your first draft suck" approach is that, especially for writers starting out, the effort and time needed to make a publication-ready first draft is so much more intensive as to be daunting. If you're someone who's just trying to get their first or second novel draft done, psychologically it tends to be much easier to break up the process into shorter steps, so that you can feel a sense of accomplishment after the first draft, after the revision, after showing it to your beta readers, etc., rather than spending months or years perfecting a first draft without anyone to appreciate or encourage you. For all that writing is a solitary profession, the contributions of other people to your mental health are important and considerable.

So. You're ready to write your sucky first draft. The second thing to remember is that all the planning you did was just to give you a framework to write the story. As you write it, you'll come up with new ideas and new characters and new subplots, and you may change how some key events happen, maybe even the ending. This is all fine. The structure you give a story at the high level helps you understand the possibilities when you're in the weeds of actually detailing the adventures, so that when you come to a place that feels uncertain to you (what should happen next?), you have a roadmap to refer back to. But that structure shouldn't be too restrictive, because the first draft is where your creativity really shines. The story will end up different, and that's okay.

With that in mind, the last thing I'd like to say about first drafts is what I think of as the "third cab" rule, based on a Sherlock Holmes story ("The Final Problem") in which Holmes tells Watson not to take the first cab outside the train station, because it was sent by his enemies, nor the second, because they will anticipate that he might be suspicious of the first cab, but to take the third. I think of this when faced with a "what's going to happen next" question. Often the first thing I think of is going to be the first thing lots of people will think of, something popular culture has made very common. This will be fine, but is less likely to reflect my unique experience. I try to think of another thing that could happen, and then a third, and often I'll stumble on something that's unusual enough to be exciting (it's not always the third thing).

This doesn't always happen during first drafting, but if you're pausing to think about what's going to happen, or thinking about what you've just written—something that inevitably you will do and should do in between writing sessions —use that time to dream up different and interesting possibilities. As one of my screenwriting teachers said, "You have to give people what they're expecting, but also surprise them."

Chapter Nine

Chapter and Scene Breaks

The Rhythms of Story

I occasionally get questions about how long a chapter should be, or where to break a chapter. These happen often enough that I think it's worth writing a short piece on my philosophy of chapters and scenes.

Chapters: Breaks and Length

In one of my earlier books (*Out of Position*), the story was made up of five stories in almost a Fibonacci sequence of length: a short story, one twice as long, the third one the length of the first two, and so on. The book was broken up by those stories, but—you may already have anticipated—the last story was over 50,000 words by itself, basically a short novel. It had scene breaks, but I wrote it all in one go and so there were no chapter breaks. Technically I suppose that is the longest "chapter" I've written. Only one person ever complained to me about that last section having no breaks (when it came time to record the audiobook, I worked with the narrator and made chapter breaks that I added to the e-book). Their problem with it was that there were no pauses for them to know when they could take a break from reading the book. I thought, "I don't want you to stop reading!" But people are used to a certain rhythm when reading, and a story broken up into chapters is part of that rhythm, so a 50,000-word stretch without a chapter break is a bit much.

In general, I try to write chapters to be 2500-5000 words in length. A scene usually runs me 1000-2000 words, and a chapter is anywhere from two to four scenes. If you want numerical guidelines, there you go. Your scenes may run longer and therefore your chapters will run longer; you may write more economically and have shorter chapters.

In a structural sense, I break chapters by feel. Some authors like to end their chapters on a cliffhanger, to encourage the reader to read on (an exemplar is in *The Hound of the Baskervilles*, whose second chapter ends with the line, "Mr. Holmes, they were the footprints of a gigantic hound!" and about which one writer—sadly, the quote has stuck in my mind, but not the source—said, "The title of the next chapter may be the least-read chapter title in literature."). Others like the chapter to take place at a break in the story, a pause where the reader can reset and, as that reader of mine wanted to do, put the book down. Choose whichever you like; and remember, nothing stops you from mixing these techniques in the same book, if you like.

A cliffhanger, if you use that structure, generally follows an action or a revelation that puts the characters in a new, dangerous, and/or unexpected position. For this to work at the end of the chapter, it should occur at the end of a scene, and since we're talking about chapter breaks anyway, let's talk about scene breaks too.

Scenes

A scene is a story in miniature. If you think of a story as a character pursuing a goal and overcoming obstacles, a scene contains all those elements. It ends when the goal has been achieved or the obstacle has proved so formidable that the character has to find another way of achieving the goal. It doesn't always mean that the literal location of the story changes. Sometimes a new character is introduced, sometimes a character leaves; anything that changes the goal ends the scene. A scene can also be used for exposition or setup, usually at the beginning of a chapter, but if there's no goal in the scene then it can quickly become static. At the end of the scene, some progress has been made in one of the four levels of story, some change that informs where the next scene should go. Remember the "therefore/but" rule from the section on outlining, and we'll talk more about that when we get to talking about plot.

A chapter, then, is a collection of scenes that go together. What "go together" means is up to you; you don't always have chapter-paced intermediate goals for your characters to pursue. I have definitely moved scenes between chapters before when revising, deciding that a scene worked better grouped with the previous scenes than the following ones. Anytime I wrote a book with multiple main characters, I always changed chapters whenever the POV character changed. In the Dangerous Spirits series, this led to the shortest chapter I've ever written, when I wanted to show one character's reaction to another character's story (the short explanation is that one of the stories is a comic being drawn by the primary protagonist, but she's not entirely in control of the story so she's experiencing it as it happens). That chapter was, in its entirety: "Seriously? *Seriously?*" I don't recommend that as a general practice, but it was an effective structure for breaking the story at a cliffhanger and showing another character's reaction to it, keeping the reader aware that she was watching it with them.

Keep in mind as you write this idea, that a scene is a story in miniature, a chapter is a collection of scenes, and a book is a collection of chapters. This kind of fractal view of stories will be helpful when we talk about the tools you have to reinforce a message or show variations on a theme in your story. Rather than simply a series of points along a single line of story, scenes can meander. Characters can make wrong decisions in one scene that resonate down the line in another. Scenes can focus on any of the four levels of story (though when possible should include movement in more than one).

As you write and explore the way you can use scenes, you'll gain a feel for how to group them together into chapters. There's no wrong way to do it (except maybe, as I did, by not doing it at all, but even then there are ways to make that work).

Summary Points

• A chapter is as long as it needs to be, but somewhere between 3,000 and 7,000 words feels about average. As you write, you will get a feel for how long you like chapters to be.

• A scene is a story in miniature: characters enter wanting something and have some sort of interaction toward their goal.

• A chapter is a collection of scenes that go together. What "go together" means is up to you.

Example: Chapter and Scene Breaks

The first chapter of *The Price of Thorns* consists of three scenes, as I read it. The overall goal of the chapter is for Nivvy to escape the wheel he's tied to somehow.

In the first scene, we are shown his problem, given the goal and the obstacle, and we see him attempting to escape via prayer as two boys throw tomatoes and rocks at him.

In the second scene, Bella appears and engages him in conversation. She seems as down on her luck as he is, and she says she needs to hire a thief. Nivvy is dismissive, but eventually realizes that this might be his chance to escape.

In the third scene, Bella tells him she needs help stealing a kingdom. They negotiate over this and Nivvy agrees to take the job. Bella agrees to free him from the wheel.

You could argue, perhaps, that scenes two and three are actually just one scene. I think the second scene ends after another farmboy comes to throw a rock at Nivvy and Bella is powerless to make him leave. This makes her a little more sympathetic to Nivvy and he agrees to listen to her job. The conversation leading up to that is different in tone than the one that follows, so I think of them as separate scenes. In the second scene, I would say that Bella also enters with a goal (all characters in a scene should have a goal of some sort): to see if this thief, to whom she's been led, is the right one for her. Nivvy's goal is to see if this woman can get him off the wheel somehow. In the third scene, Bella's goal is different: she's told Nivvy the job and her goal is to convince him to take it. Nivvy's goal is to figure out whether she's in her right mind enough for him to agree to the job, and ultimately, his chapter-long goal of getting off the wheel takes precedence.

Exercise: Chapter and Scene Breaks

Pick two or three books you know well and read through the first chapters. Try to identify where the scenes end. Do you agree with where the author put the chapter break?

If you feel ambitious, take a book you've recently read and look back at all the chapter breaks. How many were cliffhangers and how many were pauses in the narrative? Were there any places where you might've broken up the chapter differently? Was there a place where you were annoyed by the cliffhanger?

Chapter Ten

Sentences and Paragraphs

Building Blocks

By the time you get to the point of writing a novel, you might not be worrying much about sentences and paragraphs. You use them without really thinking about them: a sentence has a subject and action, often an object and maybe a dependent clause or two. A paragraph is a group of sentences that goes together...somehow. And it works, in general. But it's worth going back through how we construct sentences and paragraphs as you embark on this novel.

As a caveat, this section will be useful again—maybe more useful—when it comes to revision. The most effective way to hear how your sentences and paragraphs sound and flow into each other is to read them aloud, and that's my final stage before handing any book off to a publisher, not something I do as I'm writing. Still, every now and then as you're writing, you'll trip over a sentence that sounds off for some reason, or a paragraph that doesn't work quite the way you want it to. It's good to have some ideas about what might be going on when that happens.

Sentences

First, sentences. We are taught very early on that a sentence has a subject and a verb, and that sentences without both of those things are fragments, and that sentences with too many of those things are run-on sentences. We know that some verbs are transitive (there can be an object associated with them that the verb's action applies to, for example, to eat—"Lee ate the donut") and that some are intransitive (they do not take an object; for example, to sleep—we can describe how Lee slept, but Lee doesn't "sleep the bed" or "sleep the meeting."). We know about prepositional phrases ("Lee slept on the bed" or "Lee ate the apple from the commissary") and adverbs and adjectives. We know how to put together a sentence.

What we—or at least I—did not get taught early on was about the rhythm of sentences. Some of these things are intuitive: short, active sentences feel punchier; longer descriptive sentences stretch out and slow down the action (but longer sentences that cram several action phrases next to each other can have the opposite effect). What this means, if you think about it, is that each sentence is an action. The "action" can be establishing a background, or can be a character's thought, or could be a punch in the middle of a fight, but each sentence expresses a discrete idea.

Think about how the following examples sound:

> The car screeched to a halt. Lee jumped out and slammed the door behind him. He raced up the stairs into the museum.

> As soon as the car screeched to a halt, Lee jumped out and slammed the door behind him. He raced up the stairs into the museum.

> As soon as the car screeched to a halt, Lee jumped out and slammed the door behind

him, then raced up the stairs into the museum.

The car screeched to a halt, double-parked on a busy street, but Lee didn't care. He opened the door, jumped out, and slammed the door behind him. Barely stopping to lock the car with the remote, he raced for the stairs, took them two at a time, and then burst through the doors into the museum.

They all use the same verbs and language. The first example gives us three actions in short succession, each one part of its own sentence. The second combines them into two, pulling the readers's attention away from the car and giving more weight to Lee's hasty actions. The third combines them into one, still giving weight to Lee's actions, but putting the two actions into the same space. The fourth gives a lot more setting detail with the actions, which slows down the reading just a little.

Of these, I like the second and fourth best, but that doesn't mean the others are wrong. I like separating the two actions so the reader has time to focus on both of them. But there might be cases where you want the sharp punctuation of the first case, or you want the quick flow of the third.

And this is an action scene. In an emotionally charged scene, or a detailed description, the flow of the sentences will be different. As you vary your sentences, you'll get a feel for which ones give the narrative the pace that works best with the subject matter.

It's important, too, to vary your sentence length and structure, unless you're deliberately using repetition for effect. It's easy to spot repetition when you're using short sentences, a little harder when you're using the same structure in longer sentences over and over. For example, I have a habit of starting sentences with a gerund in a dependent clause, like: "Scrolling through her contacts for the right number, she weaved through the crowd outside the gallery." I like the economy here; rather than having to say, "She scrolled through her contacts, and while she did that, she weaved through the crowd," the above form gives you someone doing two things at once. Unfortunately, I like the form so much that I sometimes use it when it's not appropriate, as in: "Walking up to the door, Lee knocked firmly." (This sounds okay, and most people would read it as "Lee walked up to the door and then knocked firmly," but using the gerund in the opening clause should indicate that the action is taking place throughout the rest of the sentence. Lee is not still walking up to the door as they're knocking. That's a short example of how actions are contained within sentences.) This can result in paragraphs where every sentence starts that way. You might not notice it while you're writing, but you'll certainly pick up on it later, and some of your readers might too.

Using repetition intentionally can produce an effect of monotony that can be useful sometimes, or can play the sentences off each other in an interesting way. Experiment with those effects and see how they sound to you, and if you like the effect, use it in your prose.

If you like thinking about sentences and how they're put together, I recommend the book *Artful Sentences: Syntax as Style* by Virginia Tufte, which goes into amazing levels of detail about sentence structure.

Paragraphs

Paragraphs are a collection of sentences that go together to describe a series of connected actions. The easiest way to know when to start a new paragraph is when a new character is speaking; every time the speaker changes in dialogue, you should start a new paragraph. Beyond that, use your judgment. The end of a paragraph is a small pause, a break in your prose before the reader moves on to the next one. So you'll want to think about what groups of sentences fit best together. Sometimes it will be easy and sometimes there will be cases where there's no clear right answer. I often find myself moving sentences between the end of one paragraph and the beginning of another as I try to figure out whether an action belongs with one group or another.

I find it difficult to talk about in the abstract, so here's an example from my book *The Revolution and the Fox* (Calatians book 4):

The Salon held not only tables, but the string quartet producing the music that filled the building. Alice and Emily found an empty table and sat there, while Kip and Malcolm chose the nearer side door and climbed the stairs behind it. Their ravens flew ahead of them up the stairs while Kip helped Malcolm through the crowd to the first floor and up the empty stair to the second.

The first room they entered was empty enough for the ravens to rejoin them without worrying about being jostled by crowds. Kip lifted his nose to the scents in the hall and caught many new ones, while Malcolm murmured, "So many colors."

Red paper lanterns hung all along one side of the room, below which hung the Chinese flag and another flag with three concentric circles on a black background: red the outermost, then green, and a bright gold at the center. Men—Chinese sorcerers, Kip presumed—stood near the flags in black robes with red trim, and each one bore a gold pendant around his neck. One was in the process of casting a spell that created a beautiful pattern of frost in the air.

On the other side of the room, the green, red, and white of the Egyptian flag hung behind a trio of men in green robes. Unlike the Chinese sorcerers, they had two tables in front of them draped with green cloth and bearing a pair of elaborate white birdcages at either end that held green parakeets with red bills. Between the cages lay some books, a bottle, and a few small glasses.

The first paragraph introduces us to the Salon, and what happens here is that the four characters split up; two stay behind while two others go up the stairs. If I'd wanted to, I could have perhaps described the Salon in more detail, then put Kip and Malcolm walking up the stairs into a second paragraph. Similarly, I could have combined the second and third paragraphs, so that the vivid room description was associated with their first steps into the room. But I wanted to give the impression of space first, and then show the Chinese sorcerers on one side of the room, followed by the Egyptian on the other.

Separating out the second paragraph lets you see their reaction to the space first. I liked that because it creates a small amount of tension and sets an expectation for what we're going to see. The last two paragraphs could also be combined to give a description of the room all in one paragraph rather than separating out the two sides. But splitting them up makes me feel like we take in one side, then there's a pause before we turn and take in the other.

But there are many ways to rearrange this passage to achieve a particular effect. The takeaway from this example is to look at the places where I chose to break the paragraphs and think about how a different break would affect the prose. Ultimately, the choices you make about where to break paragraphs will dictate the pacing with which your reader moves through your prose.

Writing is made up of a series of these decisions. What word works best? What groups of words make up the right sentence? What group of sentences makes up the right paragraph, and what paragraphs make up the scene, and what scenes make up the chapter? Some of these decisions will be made unconsciously as you write, but your prose will be the most effective if you think about as many as you can.

Summary Points

• Sentence structures can affect the rhythm of reading. You should also think about varying your sentence structure so it doesn't become noticeable to the reader.

• Paragraphs are collections of sentences that describe a particular action or series of connected actions. You can move sentences around between paragraphs to change how the action is described.

Example: Sentences and Paragraphs

Here's a section from *The Price of Thorns* that I'll use to talk a little about sentences and paragraphs:

> The priests of Bouli did not have a wide range of food that day, but they did have fresh roots and greens from the nearby forest, along with a small amount of meat and copious amounts of weak wine. There was grass for Rahila, which she ate with some indifference.
>
> Nivvy enjoyed the meat and veg, most of it roasted with aggressively hot spices the like of which he hadn't had since Copper Port. He expected Bella to comment on the spice, but she ate the food as calmly as anything. He wasn't even sure she tasted the spices. The priests ate with them, and over conversation they discovered that there was a holy place two thirds of the way up the volcano but that it was very dangerous, and the priests did not recommend that travelers go near it. Why dangerous, Bella asked, and the oldest of the priests said vaguely that sometimes priests and acolytes didn't come back from travels to it. He remembered one such and waxed eloquent about the devotion of his friend, that Bouli must have thought highly of him to take him so early.
>
> Bella managed to wrangle vague directions to this holy place in between several more warnings and attempts to point them to the more casual path to the top of the volcano, which was a splendid sight. Because Bella couldn't be bothered to respond with the appropriate pleasantries, Nivvy took over the conversation to assure the priest that they would indeed take this safer path and would

pay their respects to Bouli at the top of the volcano.

They were shown to separate rooms, Bella's near the female priests and Nivvy's near the male ones, and Nivvy was secretly relieved, because for the last two nights he'd been worrying about whether Bella slept or not, and having her in a separate room would allow him to sleep without worrying that she was staring at him all night long.

There are a few decisions in this bit to talk about. The first paragraph's focus is "what was there to eat?" There are only two sentences here. The first details the human food, and the second the food for the horse. It made sense to me to split them into just those two sentences, knowing that later I was going to spend a little more time on the experience of eating the food. I could've split the first sentence into two or maybe even three, but this wasn't something important that I wanted to spend time on.

The next paragraph is one where I think there's the most flexibility to change. I could, looking at it, have put the first three sentences in the previous paragraph with the rest of the food commentary (with some massaging) and then combined the next two paragraphs to be the "conversation over dinner" paragraph. That wouldn't have been bad. What I've opted for instead is the first paragraph that describes Nivvy and Bella eating and their first conversation with the priest. I bundled these together because this gives you the impression of them sitting down to dinner. The second paragraph goes on to Bella following up the conversation and getting directions for their hike the next day, and Nivvy concluding the dinner.

There are a lot of long sentences in this example, too. The last paragraph's single sentence could have been split into two (the second would start with "Nivvy was secretly relieved"), but that would put more emphasis on them being shown to their own rooms by making it its own sentence, and I didn't want that; I wanted that to be linked to Nivvy being relieved to be sleeping in a different room. There's a subtle difference between "Because X happened, Y resulted" and "X happened. Y resulted." The first tells you both events but makes Y more important; the second makes them more or less equal.

In the second paragraph, there's some good variety in how the long sentences are structured. Just in the first three, the first one is a simple "Nivvy enjoyed the meat and veg," followed by a long adjectival clause (basically a long dependent clause modifying a noun or group of nouns) describing how spicy they were. The second sentence starts similarly, with "He expected," but the subject of "expected" is not a simple noun, but a verb phrase, and the following is not an adjectival clause, but an independent clause describing how she ate. The two sentences appear similar in length and structure, but they're different enough to make them feel different when read. And then the third sentence is very simple.

This example is by no means perfect, but that's why I chose it. It illustrates how there's not always an absolutely right answer grammatically, only the answer that comes closest to conveying what you mean.

Exercise: Sentences and Paragraphs

Simple exercise here. Take three or four paragraphs of prose (not dialogue) from your draft. Paste them into a separate document and play with the sentence structure. Make the sentences shorter or longer, vary the structure or force them into the same structure. Then look at how the paragraphs are broken up and move sentences between paragraphs—put the last sentence of one paragraph at the beginning of the next (where it makes sense), or vice versa. Break up a long paragraph into two.

The idea here is to break out of the trap of first drafts. Often when we write our first draft, if we're not open to change, the words begin to look like they are in their final form. The longer we leave them, the harder it is to imagine them moved around. By practicing here—and I recommend doing this exercise periodically—you will open yourself up to see new possibilities for your writing that will perhaps reflect your vision more accurately or more elegantly.

Chapter Eleven

Character Introductions

Character Introduction: Who Are You?

All right, let's start writing!

What? Oh, right, the blank page. Picking where to start your book is a difficult choice to make, but the good news is: you don't have to make it right now. Seriously! When you get to editing and revision, that's when you'll decide where the best starting point is. For now, let's focus on introducing the reader to your character.

This is a good place to remind you that one goal of your writing is to keep your reader engaged. You get a certain amount of leeway at the beginning of a book, but with so many things vying for someone's attention these days, you need to give people not just a reason to keep reading, but a desire to keep reading. Two main ways to get someone engaged enough to want to read more is to (1) give them a puzzle they care about, or (2) give them a character they care about and something that character wants.

We'll talk about the puzzle later, with plot. In introducing them to your character, you need to make them care about the character quickly. The best way to do that is to make your character interesting (and sympathetic or relatable), and one of the best ways to make your character interesting is to show them doing something.

Eventually, you'll want to show them that this character wants something that will precipitate the story, and then there's a natural desire to read on to see if the character gets it. But to start, a character-driven book will introduce its main character either trying to get something or trying to get away from something (in peril). So let's focus on that and see what we can reveal about your character.

Introducing Your Character

In the first chapter, and ideally the first couple scenes, you need to give the reader a sense of what your character is doing (and maybe why, though you can leave that to be discovered later), a sense of your character's physical presence (so they can build a picture in their head),[4] and a sense of their place in the world. The good news is that you can often accomplish this all in a single scene.

Let's be fair; you could accomplish it in a single sentence: "Ven, a six-foot tall accountant in the Royal Department of Magical Resources, was going to have to find out who'd misreported a spell used last month in Ficklesburg, or else they'd

---

[4] The amount of description you want to give your main character early on is up to you. There is a thought that if you leave the description sparse, it's easier for the reader to identify with them; on the other hand, many readers like to build up images in their mind and so they appreciate a good description of the main character to start with. I have done both in my books, and so I'd say the most important part of the physical description is one or two traits that stand out about the character, so at least the reader can build a partial mental image.

never get to sleep again." There's something to be said for jumping into the action like this, and in a short story you absolutely have to. But in a novel you can take your time. Sometimes—especially in SF and fantasy—people like to have a few paragraphs or even a few scenes to get to know the world and how it works when things are going well before we delve into what's messed up that the main character has to fix.

So whatever it is that the main character is doing doesn't have to be the main problem of the story. In fact, in a novel, it's usually better if it's not. Because this is going to be a long journey, one technique is to start the character off with a small, personal problem, which will then escalate into a larger one as the story goes along. *The Hitchhiker's Guide to the Galaxy* begins with Arthur Dent noticing that a bulldozer has come to knock his house down, which seems like a fairly large problem until he is made aware that a construction fleet has also come to destroy the whole Earth.

There's a saying that I got from a workshop that is one of the most helpful things I learned about character: character is best revealed through interaction. This saying holds over a lot of areas, but its applicability here is that it is much more entertaining for your reader to learn about your character as they are moving through your world trying to accomplish a goal than if they are sitting in their room looking into a mirror (please do not describe your character sitting in a room looking into a mirror).

This is an offshoot of a maxim most writers are familiar with: show, don't tell. A lot of people have learned this by rote without really understanding why it's true, and some people have a contrarian impulse to say "but sometimes you have to tell" (which is true), so it's worth taking a little diversion to explain why writers are taught this.

Show, Don't Tell

It comes back to engaging the reader. When you say, "Ven stood six feet tall, with blue eyes that matched the uniform of the Royal Department of Magical Resources. She had black hair that came down to her shoulders and a rather doughy physique from sitting in front of a desk most days," for example, you allow the reader to construct an image of Ven in your head, but it's a static image. She's not doing anything.

Putting Ven into a situation where her physical characteristics interact with the world also allows the reader to construct that image, but in a way that adds information about the world and some kind of sympathy or empathy for the character. For example: "The seats on the train to Ficklesburg reminded Ven of torture techniques she'd read about where prisoners were given cells just too small to lie down comfortably in. Her physique, about which her girlfriend had said, 'You look like you've been working at a desk for the past fifteen years,' did not appreciate how close together the armrests were, and the legs that made up more than half of her six-foot height had to fold at an awkward angle just for the privilege of having her knees pressed against the seat in front of her." Now we have not just a tall woman, but a tall woman who is above average in her world and uncomfortable in the world around her. We know her world has trains and magic and prisoners and torture—we know a lot more about the world than we do from the static description of her, and we know how the world serves as context for her. Maybe the discomfort in this seat will be a metaphor for her journey through the world (one thing you can do is if you start with an image, return to that image throughout the story as a visual marker of the character's progression).

The point of "show, don't tell," is that when you *show* the reader something, they have to engage with the story to understand the meaning of what's being shown, and that activity brings them further into the story. When you *tell* a reader something, they accept it and there's no further engagement needed.

Description Through Interaction

When I wanted to introduce Kip at the beginning of the Calatians series, I used a fairly on-the-nose metaphor: he is trying to walk into the grounds of the College of Sorcery, but is prevented because the demon guarding the gates has been told to only let in humans, and Kip is a Calatian, an animal-person.

So we get the description of a Calatian (Kip has a fox's nose, but fingers that can grasp the bars of a gate, and stands on two legs, and also has a tail), as well as the way he interacts with his world (being kept from things because of his race) and something he wants (to get into the Sorcerer's College).

Here's the passage, the very beginning of the first book:

> Kip grasped the wrought-iron bars of the school's gates with his black-furred fingers and pushed his fox's nose through the gap, staring at the large limestone tower that rose from the center of the well-trimmed lawn a hundred yards away. In bright daylight the White Tower earned its name, but today's cloud cover darkened the ancient stones and showed the moss and the cracks. It might well be a Roman ruin if not for the still-complete walls and crenellation around the roof. To the left stood a large canvas pavilion, with another barely visible behind it. A stone path cut through the grassy lawn, and beyond those was a small orchard, all of it safe behind the barred gate.
>
> The fox's eyes dropped to the figure standing two feet behind the gate, an olive-skinned young man with short hair as coal-black as his eyes. "You have to let us in!" he cried.
>
> The young man folded his arms over his tan cotton tunic and looked back at Kip with a half-smile that might have held regret or amusement, or both. "I was told to admit any young men who wished to apply for admission to Prince George's College of Sorcery," he said. "And while I am sure it would cause the sorcerers great consternation were I to open the gates to admit a fox-Calatian," he gestured to Kip, and then dipped his slender hand toward Kip's companion, "and an otter-Calatian,

neither of you is technically a 'man.' I am sadly bound by the direct order I was given."

"We are men," Kip protested.

"Aye," Coppy, the otter, said from behind Kip. Where Kip talked with a Massachusetts brogue, Coppy's accent betrayed his London birthplace. "Should you like, we can pull our trousers down and prove it."

The young man's smile did not falter. "There's no need to expose what's under the clothes when the proof of your in-humanity swings freely outside of them."

I'd return to the imagery of the gates several times in the books. Along Kip's journey he is eventually able to open the gates himself, allow other people to come through them, and finally dispense with the gates altogether.

You can also tell the reader something when you have to, but in such a way that it leaves some questions open. Arilin Thorferra opens her furry magic-school romance *Saida and Autumn* with this lovely paragraph:

Two months past her twenty-ninth birthday, Saida Talirend could still usually pass for a college student, but she'd begun to feel self-conscious about it, as if her monthly stays at Mensura College perpetuated a kind of fraud. As a relative of a tenured professor here, though, she had the right to rent a little studio in the housing area—and there weren't any places *off* the campus a cat woman whose ears broke the eighty-foot mark could fit.

The first sentence alone gives us Saida's age, the fact that she visits a college campus monthly (and the story is likely to take place in a college setting), and an uneasiness in the character's situation (note the use of "fraud") that this romance will complicate in her life. The rest of the paragraph tells us that she rents a small place on campus (for monthly visits, so she's well off, but it's a studio, so she's probably not super rich) and that she's an eighty-foot tall cat woman. This also tells us that giant people are known and accommodated at the college, but nowhere else in this world. You may not have consciously thought it, but this introduces even more tension to the story: if there's nowhere else for a giant cat woman to go, and she's aging out of the college…where *can* she go?

Even though all this is told, Arilin keeps the principle of describing character through interaction with the world. Saida isn't just 29 years old and 80 feet tall; she's too old to be still hanging out on a college campus, in a world where the college is an enclave for giant people. Presumably they are other animal people, though that isn't definite here; her being a cat doesn't seem to contribute to her being out of place. But it could. (Subsequent paragraphs will reveal that it does not.)

One of the tricks I picked up from a screenwriting class is that if you want people to sympathize with your character quickly, show them either in trouble or having a sense of humor. You can see that above, where Kip is somewhat in trouble and Coppy has a sense of humor about the whole situation. I go back to that trick often, but then, my characters often have humorous takes on their situations.

You don't have to figure out a powerful starting image right now. That kind of thing will suggest itself and you can work it into the story later. But what you can do now is introduce the reader to your world and your main character in an active, engaging way.

Summary Points

- The best way to introduce your character is to show them interacting with another character or with the world.
- Show your character's physical characteristics rather than simply telling them to the reader.
- Try putting your character in trouble or showing their sense of humor.

Example: Character Introduction

Here's how I introduce Nivvy, the main character from *The Price of Thorns*:

> The tomato smacked Nivvy on the temple, bleeding juice and seeds down his cheek. "Ow!" he yelled as the teenagers laughed and strolled on by. "That one wasn't even rotten!"
>
> He rattled the chains that held him in the stocks, and spit out a tomato seed. "Wasting perfectly good food like that. Y'oughta be ashamed!"
>
> One of the two boys stopped the other one, and they looked back. Uh-oh. "Reckon he's right," the slightly lighter-haired boy said to the slightly darker-haired boy, and stooped to the ground, rummaging in the dirt.
>
> "No, no I'm not." Nivvy spoke quickly. "One of my faults, you see, I—hey! You! Uh—farmer boy! Sign says you're not to throw rocks!"
>
> The lighter-haired boy had straightened up with an egg-sized rock, or, if the gods were smiling, a clump of earth, in his hand. "Don't see nobody here minding the sign," he said.
>
> "I'll report you. When Kingsley comes to set me loose, I'll tell him." Nivvy knew that there were times in his life when it would be better for him to stop talking, but so far he had not managed to recognize a single one of them before it happened.

There's not much here in the way of physical description, but we get the setting: a pre-industrial world, or at least an agricultural part of it, and probably a secondary fantasy world, given that Nivvy is praying to a god we haven't heard of. Nivvy's in stocks, so we know both that he's being punished for something (already a hint that he's a thief) and a little more about how punishments work in this world.

What's more, being in a precarious position at the mercy of boys throwing food is putting him in peril, a good sympathetic position from which his wry humor can emerge (when he tries to backpedal on telling the boys not to throw fruit).

There's not a lot of room given the situation for physical description, but the lack of detail implies a very average physique. If he were tall, he might be bent over painfully to fit into the stocks; if he were short, he might have to be on tiptoe or something. But none of that is noted, so one can safely assume "average."

In this original version, toward the end of the scene, I do include some physical description when Bella looks at him:

> She didn't speak a word, but turned and walked away. Nivvy tried to follow her progress, but all he could do was listen to her footsteps walk around behind him and pause. He swallowed a comment about her looking at his body without his leave—it was a pretty good body, he thought, though not shown off at its best in the thin flax tunic and trousers, bent over at the waist to fit his five-foot frame into the stocks. If she wanted to say something, she would.

Now here's how Bella is introduced, not much farther on in the same chapter:

> "So this is what I've been reduced to," a harsh female voice said above him.

> He turned his head until it hurt, enough to see the red velvet dress patched with brown cotton and strips of what looked like someone's dirty white tunic. The neck and chin above it were white as china, but not china that was sitting in someone's cabinet waiting to be

liberated from its pristine prison. They were more like china one would find in the back of some peddler's cart, a mismatched set dusty and cracked, not worth the trouble it would take to shout "King's Men!" to distract the peddler as you swept the pieces under your cloak. To one side of the neck, Nivvy could see strands of black hair, but his field of view did not permit much more than that.

"Aye, well, we've both been reduced, then," he said. She wasn't throwing anything at him, and that was a good thing. "How can I be of service to you? Mind, it'll have to be on the spot here, and if it's something the two hands need to be set together to work on, well, I'll be free of these at sundown." He stuck his tongue out. "If it's this you need, well, it's a little dry, but step right up and I'll do the best I can."

We see her through Nivvy's eyes, and here is more confirmation of his vocation; he compares Bella to porcelain that isn't worth stealing. But "a mismatched set dusty and cracked" implies that at one time it *was* valuable. So we get the impression of someone who's fallen from greater status, like Nivvy. He even comments on this: "we've both been reduced, then." This creates some kind of bond between the two of them right away.

Not bad for the first couple pages. We have an idea of the setting and of our main character's role in that setting, and we know our secondary character and what they have in common already. What's more, by introducing both characters quickly, I've set up the main character dynamic of the book.

Several things changed in edits, two things most notably: First, I changed out the stocks for a wheel. As I wrote the book, the imagery of a wheel kept coming back to me as a symbol for fortune. Having him tied to a wheel in this first scene leaves him at the mercy of its movements, struggling to escape it; by the end of the book, he will have accepted that he is at the mercy of fate. Bella gives us a hint of this metaphor at the end of the chapter, when they have reached an agreement to work together:

> When finally she did speak, she regained her dry, confident tone. "I will trust in the spell that brought me here. I fully believe that within one month, our wheels will have turned, and we shall be in far better circumstances." She walked around to the front of the wheel, gave him a not-altogether-reassuring smile, and reached for the nearest binding.

(This is the revised ending; in the original ending she walks away from him and finds him again after he's been released, which is much less desirable from a story standpoint than having her be the architect of his release.)

The second thing I changed was the sexual talk. There's no hint of romance between them and Nivvy is rather ace throughout the book, so I took the crack about his tongue out.

That's how I chose to introduce Nivvy at the beginning of **The Price of Thorns**. There are a lot of choices I had to make to emphasize the things I thought were important, and I think at the end of it the reader is left with a good impression of the two characters, and hopefully anticipating a fun match between Bella's haughtiness and Nivvy's wry humor as they set off to try to steal a kingdom.

Exercise: Character Introduction

The Exercises in the writing sections are going to be a little different from the ones in the planning section. By now I hope you have your favorite stories picked out and are used to going through them looking for techniques. By all means, keep doing that. In this section, for instance, it's instructive to go back through your books and look at how main characters are introduced. But I'm going to suggest brainstorming exercises that will hopefully help you generate ideas to write the bits we're talking about.

So, for character introduction. This is often difficult because it starts the book and there's a lot of weight on it, but as we've said before: this is a first draft. Tell yourself you're going to change it in edits, tell yourself it's okay for it to suck, tell yourself you are feeling your way through the story, whatever you need to do to take the pressure of the blank page off yourself.

Then think about your main character's daily life in their world. What is their routine? The story you're telling is about a character whose life is interrupted, so what does their life look like before the interruption? Specifically, what activities could they be engaged in that reveal their character? Often, early on, you want to focus on good qualities, but maybe you want to highlight their flaws, too.

In a story sense, it doesn't matter what your character is doing when the story interrupts them, but in a character and world-building sense, it does. *The Hitchhiker's Guide To The Galaxy*, as I mentioned, famously begins with Arthur Dent, hung over, facing bulldozers about to knock his house down. This is not a usual part of his life—the bulldozers, at least, though we guess the hangover might be—but it is a perfect introduction to both Arthur and the giddy, off-kilter world created by Douglas Adams. Arthur, though an ordinary fellow with no particular powers, nonetheless feels obliged to stand up for his rights by lying down in the bulldozers' path, which both tells you something admirable about him and shows him at the mercy of larger forces. The bulldozers foreshadow the next section of the book (where Earth is scheduled to be demolished), but after that, they aren't important to the story at all.

All right, the exercise: Think about your main character and the world they live in. In your head or written down, list off some of your main character's qualities, good and bad. List off some of the interesting details about your world, things the reader needs to know about or just things you think are cool about it. Now go through the two lists. Is there a way to have your character interact with one of those unique world details that reveals one of those qualities of theirs? Brainstorm a couple until one hooks you.

If one doesn't hook you right away, build out the lists a little more, or do some more brainstorming, maybe consult with a friend ("I want to show that my character is very punctual in a fantasy world where people use elemental spirits for power," for example, would be a fun exercise for a number of my friends to play with). At worst, even if none of your ideas hook you, pick the best one and start writing it. After all, say it with me: you'll change it in edits.

An optional exercise, if you want to get more depth on your character, is to conduct an interview with them. Think of ten questions you would ask someone you wanted to get to know better and then answer them as your character. Some suggestions: "Who was your best friend as a child and what's your favorite memory together?" "What's been the best or worst day of your life so far?" "What's your mother/father like?" "What's your favorite food?" "When did you know what you wanted to be as an adult?" "What was it like to leave your family home?" "What do you dream about (daydreams and night dreams)? What are your nightmares?" If you have trouble coming up with questions, think about the significant points in your life and your friends' life and ask your character what the equivalents were for them. Don't limit yourself to things associated with your story; these are details that will help you understand how the character reacts to things, but they may never be explicitly revealed in the story.

Chapter Twelve

Inciting Incident and First Choice

Early on in your story, there will be a point where the main character faces a choice about whether to undertake the adventure. This is often, but not always, paired with the inciting incident, the event that launches the real story, and it's worth taking a little time to think about these two things, especially as "inciting incident" is often used to describe both. I use "inciting incident" to describe the event that disrupts the character's world, and "first choice" to describe the character's reaction to that event and their decision to embark on the adventure.

Inciting Incident

When we introduce the character, they are in a sort of equilibrium in their world. They have a life and a routine, although something is probably missing from it. If they want something (as we discussed previously), they have an idea of how they're going to get it.

The inciting incident is the event that disrupts the routine, that takes them out of their familiar world. In *Watership Down*, Fiver's vision is the inciting incident; in Lord of the Rings, you could pick Gandalf's return, but I think the Nazgul appearing in the Shire is a stronger one. Both of those moments signal to the main characters that their world is changing.

An inciting incident is usually something out of the character's control, an event that impinges on their lives without being invited. It strongly suggests action, but it doesn't force or compel it. That said, it has to be meaningful enough that the character is motivated to take action. In Stephen King's *Rose Madder*, the inciting incident is the discovery of a drop of blood on a pillow; in *The Remains of the Day*, the inciting incident is Stevens' employer suggesting he take a holiday (to be fair, this is a bigger deal than it sounds for a lifelong butler).

Sometimes, as in these latter two books, the inciting incident comes very close to the beginning of the story. We do not take time to observe the character in their world, or we get a scene or two that are indicative enough, and we will learn more as the story goes along by seeing how that world is disrupted (in *The Remains of the Day*, much of the story is told in flashback, so we end up seeing quite a bit of Stevens' earlier world).

At other times, especially in longer works, we get to linger in the character's world before it's disrupted. The amount of time you spend in it is up to you, really. Is the world an important part of what the character wants to save or return to? Then it's worth introducing it properly to the reader so they feel what's at stake later on. In a SFF world, authors often choose to show off what makes their world unique and interesting in the first few chapters, and readers expect and even welcome this. Mysteries also often start with a few chapters to let you get to know the players in the drama before one of them is murdered. Lloyd Alexander's *The Book of Three*, by contrast, gives us barely a chapter to get to know Taran before Hen Wen runs off, but gives us enough in that time to understand a young man dissatisfied with his farmer's work, dreaming of being a hero.

And we do get a little world building in there, enough to situate us in the world.

First Choice

The character's response to the inciting incident is to choose to take action—otherwise there would be no story. Sometimes this happens right away: Hen Wen runs off and Taran runs after her (rather than taking the safer course of returning to the wizard who runs the farm to ask him what to do). After Fiver's vision, Hazel gathers a few other rabbits and they decide quickly to leave the warren. Sometimes the decision takes a little longer, but it's important that the character make this choice.

I've heard this first choice compared to a one-way door (and the same with the choice at the end of the book, but we'll get there): once the character decides to embark on the adventure, there's no going back. Taran quickly gets lost; the rabbits can't go back to the warren once they've left (which is considered betrayal). Rose can't go back, having left her abusive husband. The story has started, and the only way out is forward.

There are times when the inciting incident and first choice are separated by more than a small space, but it's not common. You don't usually want the character floating around in indecision after their world has been disrupted. This works in The Lord of the Rings because the beginning of the first book is almost a novella of its own about Frodo and the hobbits getting to Rivendell. It isn't until the council at Rivendell that Frodo finally makes the choice to take the ring. There's enough action between the appearance of the Nazgul and that decision to satisfy us, as well as a fleshing out of the story and maybe some extra incentive for Frodo to undertake the quest.

The thing I'm highlighting and saying over and over is that this has to be a choice made by the character. If it's not, they're not committed to the story, they've just been swept up in it, and you can write that, but the reader will feel the lack of commitment. If you are finding this happening, maybe you are focusing on the wrong aspect of the story, or maybe even the wrong character (this happened to a friend of mine). And the choice therefore has to be something related to what the character wants or needs, related to the journey they're going to take through the book. Taran wants to be a hero and so running off to the rescue is perfectly in character for him (and is motivated also by his concern for Hen Wen, who is under his care). Hazel lives in a world where not every rabbit is listened to (the rabbits in charge ignore Fiver's vision) but he believes all rabbits are of value, and that decision—to listen to Fiver—motivates his departure and informs his journey throughout the book to build a more egalitarian warren.

The other thing about the first choice is that it's the first place where the main character's goal changes. They started out the story wanting something; now their world has been disrupted and they have a new goal to work toward. We will talk about how it's very helpful to reader engagement to change the goals as the story goes along, even if a goal is not replaced completely but sidelined for the moment to make way for a more pressing one. In Lord of the Rings, for example, the goal of destroying the Ring is never shelved, but more immediate goals come up ahead of it.

Portal Fantasies

There is a type of story where the character gets swept up into the action through no choice of their own, and this would seem to be an exception to the rule about their choice dictating their commitment to the story. The most common version of this in the spec fic world is the portal fantasy, in which the main character travels to a new world. So let's talk about those for a minute.

In many portal fantasies, there's a choice involved in going to the new world. In *The Lion, the Witch, and the Wardrobe*, the children can go back at any time; they choose to stay in Narnia and fight for their friends there. In Cat Valente's *The Girl Who Circumnavigated Fairyland In A Ship Of Her Own Making*, September is invited to come to Fairyland and makes a choice to take the journey.

There is a kind of portal fantasy, though, where the protagonist is dropped into the world very much without a choice. Gordon Dickson's *The Dragon and the George*, Steven Boyett's *The Architect of Sleep*, and my own book *Camouflage* are examples of this type of story. The problem here is how to show the character making a choice to engage with the story when the story has been thrust upon them. Dickson's Jim Eckert does make a choice to look for his vanished fiancée, but does not expect to wake up as a dragon; this isn't what he chose. Boyett's main character—also a Jim—walks into a cave in our world and out of it into another one; my main character Danilo similarly falls into a river and emerges in another time.

So what to do with these characters who are now deep in the story without having chosen to engage with it? There is a choice they can make, and that choice is how they decide to move forward. Even if an exit from the world doesn't seem possible, they have to adapt to their new situations, assess the world they're in, and make a choice about how to deal with these new surroundings. In *Camouflage*, Danilo, after emerging in the year 1508, is presented with a choice between joining the Church and helping the gay friends he's made, and that's the point where he dives into the story more literally than when he dives into the river.

In these cases, the inciting incident is the movement through the portal into the new world,[5] and the first choice is how they respond to their new surroundings. In these cases, the first choice doesn't happen right after the inciting incident because the character has to take some time to orient themself in the new world (as the author shows it off to the readers). But even though it feels like the story kicks off as soon as the character gets to the new world, the character still needs to make a choice about how the story is going to go.

I bring up these examples to show how the inciting incident and first choice can appear differently in different stories: they can both appear in the first chapter, or they can be separated farther along. The point is what effect each of them has on the

---

[5] In *The Dragon and the George*, the inciting incident is actually Jim's fiancée disappearing and him choosing to put on a weird headset to go after her, which plops him into a dragon's body in the fantasy world. So he technically makes a choice to go after her, though he doesn't know what the headset will do, and then his world is upended and he has to make *another* choice about how to proceed now.

story, and how they are in a sense the first step on the character's journey (we will talk a lot more about character journeys, don't worry).

Summary Points

- The "inciting incident" is an event compelling enough to pull the main character out of their normal life.
- The "first choice" is the main character's choice to undertake the journey suggested by the inciting incident.
- In a portal fantasy, entering the portal world can be but is not necessarily the first choice or inciting incident, even though it seems like a natural choice for them. Look for the place where the main character makes a decision.

Example: Inciting Incident

In *The Price of Thorns*, the inciting incident happens when Bella appears and makes an offer to Nivvy. This happens in the middle of the first chapter. The first choice, by contrast, I think happens when he decides to follow her into Scarlet's cave and steal from the fairy, in chapter seven (there are forty chapters total, to give you an idea of the placement).

Why separate them this much? Well, Bella's appearance does upend Nivvy's world, but not in a way he can't escape from. As he learns about her, we learn more about his world. His choice has to be made when he's gotten to know her better.

Up until he steps into the volcano, he can still back out of the journey. He's got a lot invested in it and still believes Bella will provide him a way back to a Thieves Guild, so it would take a lot to get him to turn his back, but he could. When he sees the entrance to Scarlet's cave, with a dead bat stretched out across it, he almost does. But he feels he's bonded with Bella, and the lure of an accomplishment he could tell a story about pushes him to move forward. And when he leaves the cave, he'll be turned into a weasel, and now Bella is the only one who can change him back and he's bound even more closely to her until the book is over.

You could also argue that Nivvy's first choice is to accept Bella's job, when he's there on the wheel, and I could see that. But I think taking a job as a thief isn't really out of character for him. Bella is a change in his world, but he doesn't understand how much until he's talked to her for a while. The important decision is when he ignores his instincts to follow Bella into the cave. This shows his search for companionship and community, and that's the underpinning of his journey. He will soon find that Bella doesn't share that desire, but Zein does, and finding them leads to him finding more community.

Characters make choices all through your story, but the reason to pay attention to this one, the one that sets them irrevocably on their path, is so you can give it the proper weight in the story, and understand how it forms part of their journey.

Exercise: Inciting Incident

For your own work: think about what incident disrupts the character's world. Now what's their response to that? Is that the moment they're no longer able to back out, or does that come later?

Try to identify these moments in other books you enjoy. How do other writers handle these moments? Does the first choice often get lost in other moments, or can you easily pick it out?

Chapter Thirteen

World Building

World Building: Where Are You?

I talked about world building in the planning stages, in the sense of figuring out what details are unique to your world. This section will be more about how you conceive of your world, and how to introduce that world to your readers.

By this point, you should know the broad strokes of your setting. Fantasy world, science fiction, contemporary, or historical? What's unusual about your world? Why is it the perfect location for your story?

In an SFF book, the setting and story are often intertwined. Science fiction, especially, is often about how an idea changes society, and so the world has to be the place the idea is perfectly part of. Ursula LeGuin's famous novel *The Left Hand of Darkness*, which explores gender and sexuality, takes place on a planet where the native people's biological sex can change.

Fantasy novels often take place in a world where the unusual and/or magical aspects of the world are an important aspect of the story. N.K. Jemisin's Broken Earth series (considered science fantasy) is set in a world where some people have the ability to control the movement of the earth, and deals with their treatment in a society that both needs and fears them.

Even other genres can rely on their setting in ways that may not immediately be apparent. Many of Agatha Christie's mysteries take place in a time of transition after World War I, when increased mobility was changing England from a country of isolated small villages to a more connected society. You can see this reflected in the number of her stories that involve a stranger coming to town or a long-lost relative returning, the whole idea that people will always have only a small circle of family and friends in their life disappearing as the country changes.

The idea of your world being at a transition point is a common one, too. We talked in the "Four Levels" section about a world story, and that's why times of transition in a world are excellent settings for a story. The world story is an easy one to tell at those times.

Ordinary World

Before we think about how the world is changing, though, it's helpful to think about the world as your character knows it. What does the day to day life of someone with your character's standing look like? Are they high on the social scale or low? What is life like for people above and below them?

It's worth spending some time on this because in the process of figuring out how your world works, you will discover other interesting aspects to it that may contribute to your story. When I was working on the Calatians books, I had to think about the effects magic would have on everything from newspapers to westward expansion.

And thinking about your character's daily life (before they are interrupted by the events of the story) gives you lots of chances to see how they interact with the special features of your world. I talked in the previous section about character being best revealed through interaction; setting works the same way. Neal Stephenson could have introduced the dystopian world of *Snow Crash* with a lot of description of how the world has changed (and in fact, a couple pages in, he does give us some colorful history in a couple paragraphs), but he starts us off with his character on a mission: "The Deliverator belongs to an elite order, a hallowed subcategory. He's got esprit up to here. Right now, he is preparing to carry out his third mission of the night." In the rest of the paragraph, his outfit is described, with components of "arachnofiber weave" and "sintered armorgel." As the book goes on, we discover that the mission is a high-stakes pizza delivery, which takes place through the setting, giving us a chance to hear about communities and businesses and roads in this world, all things that specifically affect our main character. This gives us a feel for the setting more completely than paragraphs explaining to us how we got to this place (even with Stephenson's highly effective prose).

There are some cases where you may not want to introduce the special feature of your world right away in the first chapter. If you are writing a horror novel or a mystery, for example, a story type where the central conceit is generally introduced later, then your first task with world building is to set up the ordinariness of the world, so the reader feels the disruption more strongly. At the same time, you still want to signal that something is going to happen to this ordinary world. I know, when someone picks up a mystery or horror novel, they tend to assume that something will go terribly wrong, but what you are showing the reader first is how the disruption will strike this world. A murder will, for example, be received differently on a crowded subway car than it will at a family reunion.

One way to do this is to start with an "ordinary" type of disruption that foreshadows the horror or mystery to come. For example, many Agatha Christie mysteries begin with a hypothetical murder or a rhetorical one (as in, "someone's going to kill him one day" or "I swear I'll kill her if she tries that again") that people engage with semi-seriously, but in the context of the world as it exists prior to the murder. In Stephen King's classic *The Shining*, where the horror is that Jack Torrance is manipulated and possibly possessed by ghosts, the first chapter introduces us not only to the Overlook Hotel itself and Jack's impatience with the "officious little prick" explaining the job to him, but also the tragedy of the former caretaker and Jack's history with alcoholism and losing his temper (his eventual possession is a metaphor for alcoholism).

Your job in these first few scenes is to settle your reader into the world, so they empathize more with your character's situation. In some cases—SFF stories, historical dramas—there is also an element of delighting (or impressing, maybe not in an "I'd like to live there" way) the reader with the depiction of a world they can't experience in person. John Scalzi's *Old Man's War* starts with this short paragraph: "I did two things on my seventy-fifth birthday. I visited my wife's grave. Then I joined the army." Rejuvenation and longer lifespans aren't the only different things in this science fiction world, but they are different enough to be engaging, especially as artfully presented here.

Take Your Time

Note that you don't have to, and shouldn't, present everything about your world in this first chapter. You want to give the reader enough to understand the world and sympathize with your character's situation, but as the novel goes along, one of the tricks you can use to keep the reader interested is revealing new things about the setting. Think about many portal fantasies, where the character is guided through a world new to them, revealing new parts of it as the story goes along. When the Pevensies first arrive in Narnia, what they most notice about it is that there are talking animals and it is always winter. We learn more about the winter, at least, as the book goes along, as well as other parts of Narnia.

Similarly, in N.K. Jemisin's Broken Earth series, the history of the world and of the main character is parceled out over the course of the first book, and even the limits of powers that exist in the world keep being pushed farther back as the story goes along. The little thrills of discovery keep coming throughout the series, one of the (many) things that makes it so engaging.

So it's a good idea to think about what the reader needs to

know at the beginning and what will have more impact later in the story. In a world with a lot of different rules (for magic, for politics, for anything like that), it is often easier on the reader if you introduce a little at a time and then add on every so often, when the situation calls for an expanded explanation.

Often this is the case when the world is in transition. I talked about that being a good time to set your story in; this is because times of transition are unstable, periods when people's values come into question and as their lives are disrupted, they are looking for new answers. It's a time when people in power are more desperate to hold onto it, where people without power see opportunities to gain it, where a whole lot of chaos can happen that your main character can try to control, or join in with, or take advantage of. Sometimes the story precipitates the transition, as in Lord of the Rings where the threatened destruction of the Ring is an existential threat to Sauron that he will do anything to stop; sometimes, as in the Agatha Christie mysteries mentioned above, the world is changing for reasons beyond the control of the characters and they are coping with it as best they can. The former is more usually true of SFF; the latter of contemporary fiction, Westerns, mysteries, and so on.

Horror can be either, and interestingly, horror often concretizes the changes people are afraid of. In *Rosemary's Baby* and *The Stepford Wives* (both by Ira Levin), the stories are set against the upheaval of women's liberation in the 1960's, and the horror in both books comes from men trying to control the women in their lives. In *I Am Legend* (Richard Matheson), helplessness and disconnection from society are concretized as an apocalyptic plague that has left the protagonist alone in a city of vampires; here the horror event has precipitated the transition the protagonist is struggling with.

These are a lot of things to think about as you introduce the reader to your world. But don't sweat it! Once again, you don't have to get this perfect the first time, and if these ideas don't click with you now, let them settle in your head as you write, and maybe something will click halfway through the book as you learn more about your world. Then you can go back and change these first chapters.

For right now, you do want to have an idea of how your

character's story fits into the world, both as it is and how it's changing. Keep that in mind as you guide your reader's first glimpse of the world they'll be sharing with you for the next many hours.

Summary Points

• Especially in SF and fantasy, but also in other genres, the world you place the story in is tied to the story.
• Think about what ordinary life is like for your character.
• You don't have to tell the reader everything about your world in the first chapter. Leaving little mysteries gives them something they'll be excited to find out or figure out.

Secondary World Building

On the subject of world building in general, there's a lot to consider. As with most of the subjects here, there's probably enough to fill a whole book. But I'm just going to go through a few of the points I've picked up when creating a new world.

A "secondary world," if you're not familiar with the term, just means a world you've made up that isn't Earth as we know it. The advantage to a secondary world is that you get to make up everything about it: You can tailor it to your story and put in all the interesting ideas you have. The disadvantage to a secondary world is mainly that you have to make up everything about it.

Some people get really into developing their world, and this is great but can also be a trap of its own. I've known people to get so wrapped up in the world as they were creating it that they lost sight of the story they were going to tell (or perhaps they were diving into the world building because they were nervous about how to start the story). One person got sidetracked writing out an entire dictionary for their world's language, for example. For that reason, and also because I'm much more interested in the story itself, I try to keep my world building to whatever is necessary to support the story.

That still leaves a lot to think about! I've talked about a world that supports your story, and a world at a transition point. Behind those points, there's a lot of foundation you can build, and a lot of details that will bring realism to the world you're building.

History

The foundations are things like the history of the world, the religions, the political divisions, and the culture. If your world is at a transition point, what forces are bringing it to that point? What history has shaped the world your character lives in?

It's inevitable that we look to our own world's history for examples of things that might happen, because that's the only history we have available. However! Here in the USA, we don't even get a good picture of our own country's history unless we specifically seek it out. My public school history class was a lot of memorization of names and dates from about the French and Indian War through World War II, and we skipped the Reconstruction era completely. At the time my teacher just said, "we're not going to cover this," and didn't really explain why; with the benefit of hindsight and more education, I have some ideas.

And that was just American history! We barely covered Europe and did not cover Asia, Africa, or Australia at all. When I spent a few years in a European school and learned just the basics of European history, it was—no joke—like I was reading an epic fantasy novel. I've since become fascinated with history because it contains so many interesting human stories.

The point is that if you read widely about history, even just on Wikipedia, you will encounter a lot of interesting stories that might inspire the past of your own world. If you can imagine a conflict, it has probably happened multiple times already. The fun part, the writing part, is when you take that historical conflict and shape it to your world.

At their core, most conflicts are about resources of one kind or another. Money represents the ability to get more resources; land represents the possibility of food and shelter (and sometimes other resources, precious metals or gems, for example). What are the scarce resources on your world, and who controls them? What means do they use? When I was writing the alternate history of the Calatians series, I changed some things (the date of the American Revolution) but left many others intact. Magic being a rare resource meant (to me) that it would get concentrated in the hands of governments, much like any other military might would. Magic was a tool that a few people could use to exert power over others, and governments exist to exert power, so they would naturally accumulate sorcerers. Then sorcerers became another aspect of military might. They were able to overcome the first American Rebellion, having superior communication and movement to the actual British troops of our era (who still nearly won that war), but in the long run, magic did not change very much about the way history proceeded.

Art and Culture

As you're figuring out how the power struggles in your world have gone, you'll also want to think about how they're viewed by the people who live under them. This is often represented in the kinds of art that are created by the culture. Art can be sponsored by people in power or can be created as a counterculture, and the origin is important. In medieval times, rulers commissioned elaborate portraits of themselves and their families, while the poor people told stories to each other, as of Reynard the Trickster, for example, who triumphs over the wolf and lion who represent nobility in those stories.

The challenge with art in secondary worlds is that it's unfamiliar to the reader, and so it can become clunky to bring into a story. Every time you have your character remember a favorite story or song or painting, you have to describe the art to your reader. This can end up feeling like it's putting too much emphasis on the art, when in a contemporary world you could refer to Star Wars or Lady Gaga and have most people understand what you mean (there are other pitfalls there, of course; what if the perfect art for your reference is one not many people know, or what if you're thinking of "Bad Romance" Lady Gaga but your readers think about "Born This Way" Lady Gaga?). But there are ways to do it artfully. In Patricia McKillip's Riddle-Master series, riddles (short stories with a lesson) and harp ballads are critical to the story, and walking us through them becomes part of the story; we are being told these stories within the narrative, where they are clearly important, and so they don't feel superfluous. I tried to mimic that in *The Price of Thorns*, which also relies heavily on in-world stories that have a great deal of meaning for the people of that world.

However much work you do on the culture, don't forget that no culture is universal. Within any community there will be people with differing views. Even when something is viewed as a universal evil, there will be differing opinions on how to deal with it. In Anne McCaffrey's Pern books, the planet is ravaged by Thread, silvery tinsel-like clumps of spores that fall from the sky and inflict acidic burns on whatever they touch. They're fought by dragon-riders, who burn it out of the sky before it can touch the ground. But not everyone on Pern agrees that the dragon-riders, and the feudal system that supports them, are the best way to fight what everyone agrees is an existential threat to their lives. People differ on the system of government, the leader, the religion, the way the religion is observed, which fork to use with salad, and hundreds of other things, large and small. Remember when writing about a community, especially one the main character doesn't belong to, that communities are rarely uniform, even small ones like families.

Again, as I said in the previous section, this is not information you need to process and create all at once before you start the story. You can if you want to, for sure, as long as you don't put off writing the actual story forever. If you're going to do what I do, though, build the fundamentals you need to understand for the story, and then do more as needed as you progress through the story. As I'm writing, I'll become aware of holes in my world building, either from immediate need (wait, my character's trapped in a temple, what kind of people would visit a temple who might help him out?) or from a sense that something's missing (we've talked about the people who oppose the Queen, but there must be a group that supports her, mustn't there?). Follow your instincts, remember to look to art and history, and above all remember: you'll get an editing pass to clean this all up.

Summary Points

• If you're making up an entirely new world, think about that world's history and how it brought the world to the point where your story takes place. Many of the key events in history come down to power struggles over scarce resources.

• Art and culture are how people tell their stories, and the stories of the world. What they choose to make art about and how they make that art is an important thing to know in your world.

Example: World Building

A lot of the world building I'm going to show here from the first draft of *The Price of Thorns* is also (or could also have been) used as examples for the character introduction; as I said, the best way to show character and world is by having them interact. So with that in mind…

In the first chapter, I want to build up the world a little bit at a time. We start with Nivvy in the stocks getting tomatoes and rocks thrown at him, which places it in a sort-of maybe medieval-ish time, and then there's this:

> He occupied himself for a few moments with venomous thoughts of revenge against both the merchant's wife who had felt the compulsion to check on her jewelry at sunrise, and against Kingsley, the innkeeper and de facto lawman of the town. For a theft in which all the stolen goods had been recovered, two days in the stocks was usual in every town Nivvy had stopped in. But here, Kingsley claimed four were needed, and Nivvy's attempts to persuade him with logical, sensible arguments had been met with silence as obdurate as the wood clamped around his wrists and neck.

A town where the innkeeper is the de facto lawman tells you more about this being a medieval fantasy setting, and that Nivvy had gone from town to town (knowing the punishment for thievery in each) tells you a little about the world he finds himself in. But the world here is all filtered through the character's experience.

Later on in the chapter, we get indications of the magic in the world:

> "The other thing about big things like kingdoms." Nivvy watched her feet. They

remained still under the slowly rippling hem of the tattered dress. He shifted his body to try to ease the strain on his back. "They tend to be watched and guarded by wizards. Steal a brooch from the Emperor's daughter, you might get a flight of crows after you. No great shakes to deal with if you're an accomplished dodger and scarpermancer, like yours truly. Even know a spot of magic myself. But the important things in a kingdom—say, the royal family—those tend to have heavy-duty magic around them. You know, the kind that involve the earth splitting and dragons coming down from the skies and people getting turned into animals and plants if they're not just turned inside out on the spot."

"The realities of magic are much less dramatic—" Her feet shifted, kicked at a clod of dirt.

"Tell that to my best friend Martin. Tried to steal from a wizard once, got turned into a toad."

Her voice remained flat. "That must have been terrible. However—"

"It was! You've no idea! I had to carry him 'round in a box, make sure he didn't get eaten, or stepped on. Least he could talk, though after a while he mostly tried to tell me about how different flies and bugs tasted." It helped to talk. For one thing, it took his mind off the aches and stresses; for another, people weren't throwing things at him while Bella was standing next to him.

Again, the revelation of magic in Nivvy's world is all through his own experience. But here, what I wanted to convey was that magic exists in the world…but not extensively used. A person can get turned into an animal here or there, but earthquakes and dragons and mass transformations, those are reserved for really important situations. Even Nivvy's friend was only turned into a toad because he tried to steal from a wizard. Magic on that scale isn't something a normal person will usually encounter. As we will see later, Nivvy has a few cantrips he can call on, but those are very minor spells: being able to read any language, counting coins, semi-invisibility.

It's harder to show a negative example, but the other thing I want to highlight about this first chapter is that that is basically all the world building I did. In future revisions, I went back and added a few things to make it clear that Bella has a wider experience of magic than Nivvy does and greater expectations about what magic exists in the world as a subtle hint that the world is changing, that there is less magic now than there used to be. But for the most part, what I wanted the reader to come away from the first chapter with was: this is a largely agrarian fantasy world where magic exists and people get turned into animals sometimes. But magic isn't super common in most people's day-to-day lives. More is going to be added as the story moves along, of course, but for now, that's enough.

Exercise: World Building

In a lot of ways, this exercise will be similar to the one for Character introduction. You're trying to find the details that are most important for your reader to know so that they understand your world right away.

So the exercise that I find helpful here is to list out all the interesting things about the world. Big ones, little ones, any ones you can think of. Then, looking at your outline, pick a couple new details to introduce in each chapter. Early on, you'll want to introduce the most basic things your reader has to know about the world: where and when are we, and what are the main dynamics that will be affecting your character.

As with the character introduction, you'll be looking to show how those aspects of the world affect the characters and their goals. But you'll also be looking to keep the list short. You don't need to dump everything about your world in the first chapter; you need to put in enough to spark your reader's interest.

As a bonus exercise, if it feels like something you want to do now, think about what kind of transition your world can be going through. Times of transition happen when a new resource or technology is introduced or removed from the world. Learning to build ships that could cross oceans changed the world for colonial powers and the countries they could now reach easily; railroads had the same effect on the American West in the 1800s.

In science fiction, a very common agent of transition is for a new technology to be introduced, as in H.G. Wells' classic *The Time Machine*, or for a person to arrive who sees the world in a different way, as in Frank Herbert's *Dune*. War is another popular way to embody transition in a world, as it brings with it a lot of disruption and unusual circumstances, and usually at the end of a war, the world will be changed. The Lord of the Rings is about the rediscovery of a powerful artifact that will either fall into the hands of an evil wizard (and thereby bring about a dark age on the world) or be destroyed (and thereby diminish the magic in the world), and the war that is fought to determine which fate will be realized. The ending makes it clear that it is impossible for the heroes to go back to their normal lives after the war; this is a common ending for a world in transition, but is also important because your hero should be changed by their journey.

It's important to note too that by "changing the world," I don't mean that every single person's life will be fundamentally altered (although that may be). The events of *Dune* and The Lord of the Rings will alter the lives of everyone on those worlds, but the events of *The Time Machine* only really affect the perceptions of humanity in the people who hear the story. This change arrives in a more subtle way.

It's up to you to decide what transition your world is going through and what role your hero plays in it.

Chapter Fourteen

Furry World Building

Furry Fiction: A Case Study in World Building

I write primarily furry fiction, which is stories featuring anthropomorphic animal characters. There is a rich cultural and historical tradition of this kind of fiction, and it provides an illustrative example for any writer.

Why a Furry World?

When we talk about furry stories, the world building is an important part of it. The parts of the world that differ from non-furry stories, the bits we focus on when we talk about the "furriness" of a story, are the parts of the world that are different because the characters are anthro animals (of course), and those differences tend to be centered around the ways in which we in non-furry worlds interact with animals and with our environment.

These include (but are not limited to): How are living quarters designed? What do people keep as pets (if they do)? What do people eat? Who do they have sex with, and how, and what do the cubs look like? Also, how does their language reflect their furriness?

There's a lot to think about here, and to start with, it helps to think about what furry is and what it means, at least in terms of the furry community. Furry is a community different from a fandom in that there is no central text, and one of the crucial differences between furry and, say, a fandom like the Star Wars fandom (or Star Trek, or Harry Potter, or whatever other books or movies have gathered people around them) is that furry does not have a "canon." In Star Wars, for example, there are movies that are indisputably canonical, meaning that things that happened in the movies are immutable parts of the Star Wars universe.[6] You can't have a Star Wars OC (original character) that doesn't fit into that universe somehow.

Furry, by contrast, is whatever furries define it to be. You want a Robin Hood-style fox who walks on two legs and doesn't wear pants? Want an <u>anatomically improbable taur species</u>? Want a blue unicorn with lion paws and a purple skunk stripe down its back leading to a fox tail? Snakes, birds, orcas? You do you. All of these fit into the fandom. In fact, the only thing that there seems to be a mutually agreed proscription on is that... you can't have a human OC in Furry.[7]

But you are creating your own world with your own rules. There will be, perhaps, *only* blue unicorn skunk-griffins in your world. So the first question you have to answer in your furry world building is: *Why is your world furry?*

There are a few broad categories that furry worlds fall into,

---

[6] There were books, too, a lot of them (including comics), and the world in the books was described as the Extended Universe, or EU. When Disney took over Star Wars, there was an official declaration that the EU was no longer considered canonical.

[7] Primate OCs, though rare, can be found. They seem to be rarer the closer they are to human, in my experience, so there are some lemurs, a few monkeys, very few great apes.

and these are not mutually exclusive, but thinking about them in this way can help you figure out the rules for your world. In my experience, furry worlds tend to be driven by aesthetic, metaphor, or exploration.

Aesthetic is the easy one. Honestly, I think it's a factor in most furry novels, but I'm breaking it out here because it is also perfectly reasonable to make your story furry just because you like the way animal-people look. If you're in the furry community, a lot of your interpersonal experiences have been shaped by this aesthetic, and likely at least part of your identity, too, so it makes sense to build your world along these same lines. What good is being a fox if you can't write a story about foxes?

Metaphor digs more into the point of your story, and can cover a lot of possibilities. Generally, this means that you're using a furry world to represent a real-world problem. *Zootopia* is the classic example of this, a really well-done metaphor because it uses the predator-prey dynamic to explore prejudice. Because predator-prey doesn't have any direct correlation in the real world, the film can discuss prejudice without having to drill down into racism, sexism, homophobia, etc. Furry species can also be a stand-in for class, or furries can be used to model different social structures, as in *Watership Down*. Figuring out your world building here will require you to think about what you're trying to accomplish with your story.

And just a note: it is almost always a bad idea to use furry species to represent real-world demographics (a race or culture). If you're Art Spiegelman and you want to use mice, cats, and pigs to tell your father's memoir of surviving the Holocaust in *MAUS*, then as a pretty much purely visual device used by a Pulitzer-winning writer, sure, it works. Otherwise, it's probably best for you not to envision a one-to-one relationship between a species and a real-world demographic. Animal species have a lot of cultural attachments, and if you make the one-to-one representation clear, you open yourself up to other interpretations than the one you intended.

Exploration is often an outgrowth of the aesthetic, but with more concrete details. I'm thinking about taking animal behaviors and physiology, like a wolf pack or a hive of bees, and wondering what our society would be like if we'd grown out of those origins. What if we were anthro rabbits who still wanted to live underground, or anthro starlings who couldn't stop talking to each other all the time, or anthro possums who still played dead when we sensed danger (and could emotional danger also trigger this?)? Or what if all three (and more) of those existed in the same society? How would society have to adapt? Here, also, you'll have to think about what your story is trying to say in order to make sure your world building supports it properly.

Summary Points

• Furry fiction is often born out of a desire to use an animal-centered aesthetic, use animal metaphors to tell a story, or explore society through the lens of animal behavior and/or physiology. Thinking about your goal in creating this world will help you think about what stories it's suited to hold.

Furry Worlds: Tone and Language

The tone of your story is something else to keep in mind with your world building. When planning a furry world, you want the details to match the tone. *Watership Down* is a story about society, and so there is a lot of focus on the mythology and the religion, the underpinnings of their society. *Zootopia* is a story about human problems but made accessible to all ages, so in addition to the structure of society set up to accommodate the people there (the districts, the special designs for the cars and homes), there are animal puns everywhere. They work with the tone of the story, but when the story gets serious, the animal puns fall away.

Another area where tone is important to consider is in what your characters eat. Because many animals (including us) eat other animals, that simple basic need becomes fraught if lots of other animals are sentient. In a world like the one in *Zootopia*, with that lighter tone, none of the animals eat other animals (unless they go feral, but even then there's really no discussion of them *eating* fellow animals, just wounding or killing them)—they eat bug protein. This is never really brought up in the movie, but there are background ads for "Bug Burgers," and it's discussed in some of the supporting materials. The division between predator and prey was critical to the movie but it was never actually acted out.

In *Watership Down*, by contrast, the rabbits are prey, and this is important to the central plot of the book: finding a place where they can feel safe. Rabbits are killed or captured by people, by foxes, and by other rabbits—General Woundwort trying to become a predator himself is perhaps his defining character trait.

My own solution for my contemporary furry world (Forester Universe, named after a fictional college from the earliest short stories) is to draw a distinction between sentient people and domestic animals. Basically, the domestication of animals happened much as it did in our world, because I figured if wolves and bears and foxes followed the same path to civilization, it would make sense for them to domesticate some prey species for the same reasons our ancestors did. That didn't mean *all* prey species; some of them also became sentient, but not the domesticated ones. So my carnivore and omnivore characters eat pork chops, and there are boar people, though not domestic pig people (and there are wild horses, but not domesticated horse breeds; wolves, but not dog breeds).

Food in a World of Animal People

This brings up another aspect of furry world building: the difference in how we as the reader view things versus how the characters in the story view them. How would a wild boar sitting at dinner with his wolf friend react if the wolf ordered pork chops?

It's shocking to us because this is the first time we've been introduced to this world. But you can decide what the customs are. Maybe the boars have grown up knowing there's a distinction between them and the domestic pigs, the way we wouldn't really be offended by people eating monkeys (or at least, we wouldn't take it personally, though we might be offended on an environmental level). Boars are omnivores, so they might eat pork themselves. There might be religious proscriptions against it, depending on how your religions are set up. It might be considered rude to eat pork in front of a boar, or it might be considered aggressive, or it might be fine, and you don't have to decide on just one attitude for the whole world. Different cultures and different individuals within those cultures will have different views, just as there are differences in eating and drinking customs between cultures in our world, and people who adhere more or less to those cultures.

And whatever the attitude, these people will have lived with it all their lives. Shock comes from when someone deliberately violates those norms. In our world, comparing humans to apes or monkeys is an aggressive slur; the equivalent in a furry world might be calling a boar "pork chop." But if boars have grown up around people who ate pork and have internalized the differences, they're not going to be shocked if someone orders a pork tenderloin meal near them.

The way people talk in a furry world is also worth considering. Do you want to, as *Zootopia* does, have furry puns that are more for the viewers than the characters? ("Zoogle" is funnier if you know what "Google" is, as we do but the people of Zootopia do not.) Do you want to invent a language for your people, as *Watership Down* does? These matters of style are up to you, but at the very least, you need to consider language in the context of the society you've created.

Language and Idioms

A couple decades ago, there was some debate in the furry writing community about whether the upper extremities were called "hands" or "paws" (some picked the compromise "handpaws"). Either of them works, but they produce different effects. I choose to use "paws" most of the time, to remind the reader of the furriness of the characters, but I ran into problems with deer and horses (among others), who don't have paws. For them I use "hands," and that's a distinction in my world. When I started reading Rukis's books, it felt a little jarring to me that she referred to her people as "men" and "women," something I stayed away from, but she makes it work in her stories.

When you do replace common words like "hands" or "men," you have to be careful of idioms. "Give me a hand" is a common expression, but how would it sound in a world where hands are "paws"? "Give me a paw" works, but can you similarly change "hand me that thing"? What other idioms would furries come up with? I'd advise against overwhelming your reader with furry world-specific jargon, but a few well-placed phrases here and there can really give your world a distinctive feel.

When considering diet or language, you have to consider how this society (if not necessarily its people) have evolved. What customs are in place to allow everyone to live together relatively peacefully? Ideally, your story will have something to do with these differences, though it doesn't have to. If you are exploring these customs, and maybe where they break down or can be exploited, you are telling a story that's interesting because it's a furry world.

Summary Points

• Furry worlds are made with a range of different tones depending on their audience, from whimsical to "nature is red in tooth and claw."

• Because we humans eat animals, a world full of animal-people will raise the question "what do they eat?" Are there non-sentient animals? Do some animal-people eat other animal-people? Is everyone a vegetarian or insect-arian?

• Think about the language in your world. There are expressions borne out of human culture, experience, and anatomy that may not make sense in your world of animal-people.

Furry Characters

Now you've got your furry world, let's populate it with characters: what sliders you can use to make them more or less furry, how often you should remind the reader of their species, and how to engage with the cultural assumptions about certain species.

As I talked about previously, we're privileged to be part of a community that thrives on art and includes hundreds (if not thousands) of talented artists. It's very helpful to figure out what your characters look like and then get an artist to render them (don't use generative AI, support furry artists![8]), so you have a visual reference while you're writing. A lot of writing is about details, and knowing what details to tell your reader about will help your character feel more real.

Everyone's conception of what their furry characters look like is different and unique. There's no "world bible" that we all draw from. Some like digitigrade, some plantigrade; some like generally similar humanoid forms for all species, while some prefer the species be reflected in the body proportions and relative sizes.

Describing Your Character

However you imagine your characters, you'll have to describe them for the reader, and here the age-old author's problem of "how to tell the reader what the character looks like" is magnified. In a non-furry book, the reader can safely assume that a character is human (unless otherwise specified), and, most crucially, the point of view character is almost always human, even in fantasy and science fiction. There are a few solid details you can give someone to get a picture of a human character: skin color, hair color, height, build. In a furry book, however, the point of view character is most often not human, so aside from fur color and height and build, you need to tell the reader

---

[8] I wrote extensively about this here:
http://open.substack.com/pub/kyellgold/p/essay-we-live-in-a-society

more about the character's body type. This can get awkward, and leads to a lot of furry stories starting with the character looking into a mirror (do not do this; it stalls the story and feels like the author telling the reader what the character looks like).

Your character will likely reflect the amount of "furriness" in your world. If you're imagining your wolves living in communal packs, your otters in aquatic homes, your squirrels in rickety treehouses, then your characters might skew more toward the animalistic shape. If you're writing a modern world that happens to be populated with furries, they'll look more human.

And just as it is with any character, or any setting, description is most effective when it's revealed through action or interaction. Figure out a way to show the reader what they look like as they move through their world. The first book in the Calatians series, *The Tower and the Fox*, begins with Kip demanding to be let in to the sorcerers' college. He's denied because he's a fox-person, which tells you as much about him as it does about the world he lives in.

But once you've told your reader that your main character is a fox standing on two legs, with a muzzle and bushy tail and clothes, how often do you need to remind them of that? I've read stories in which I was told the character's species once and then it was never mentioned again, and at some point in the story I realized I'd forgotten it. You can of course refer to your character by their species, a common practice in furry writing, but you can also remind your reader of their furriness in other ways. Fortunately, the standout differences between furries and humans are also important to the ways furries (or at least the animals they're based on) express emotions. Your character's ears can perk or flatten or cup toward someone; their tail can curl, wag, lash, or arch. This accomplishes the dual goal of showing the reader what your character is feeling and reminding the reader that they're a furry.

A side note: if you want your stories to be accessible outside the furry fandom, you might have to explain some of these reactions the first few times. We all know what it means when a character flattens their ears or curls their tail between their legs, and people familiar with dogs and cats might also pick up on it, but some people might not.

Describe Your Character's Experience in the World

You should also remind the reader occasionally what it means to be this character's species in the story world, another two-for-one opportunity. In the Calatians series, the Calatians (animal-people) are a minority, and so anytime Kip is in contact with humans, his species is important. He has to navigate the prejudices and expectations of the other; in fact, that is largely the obstacle of each of the books. In a fully furry world, you will have to think about how each of the species thinks about other species. We have those divisions in our world, and they are malleable: two people might consider themselves part of the same community because they belong to the same church, then find out that they live in different towns or hold different political beliefs or root for different sports teams, and that creates a division between them. In-group/out-group behaviors are believed to be some of the oldest in our history, and so you can only imagine how those would play out in a world where there is such a visible delineation between certain people.

Here you will have to take into account the cultural associations with different species in the story world, if only because your readers are going to have them in their heads. If you are aiming at the furry community, you can play off stereotypes of species in the community, but a wider audience has perceptions formed more by Disney and Aesop than by furry artists and writers. Foxes are clever and sneaky; rabbits are tricksters with large families; bears are generally good-natured and hungry, and so on. If you want to play into those types, you can. Often a fun way to play with characters is to accept those cultural associations, but have your character not fit into them: the clumsy, naive fox, or the loner bunny, or the grumpy fitness-obsessed bear. That sets up tension between their nature and the expectations put on them and can make for some good story movement.

The great thing about writing in furry worlds is that you can define everything about the world. Make it yours, and then remember that you have to bring the reader into this world you've made. Show them your characters and help them relate to the way they move through the world. We write furry characters and worlds because we love them, so let that love show on the page, and your readers will fall in love with them too.

Summary Points

- It helps to get art of your characters to use as a visual reference.
- When writing non-human characters, find the way that feels right to you to remind the reader of their non-humanness. Using interactions with the world is always a good way to do this.
- Think about how your character experiences the world, both physically and socially.

Chapter Fifteen

Dialogue

Dialogue: Say What?

Having introduced your characters, you most likely will want to have them say something. Dialogue is not only a character's primary method of communication, it's one of the most natural ways for a reader to get to know them. We talked about character being revealed through interaction; dialogue is one of the primary ways your character interacts with other characters. There are so many possible nuances to dialogue that it's your strongest tool when building your character.

Dialogue, of course, is also how a character makes their intentions known to other characters, how they manipulate and seduce and confront. So whenever your character speaks, you're keeping several things in mind, namely: what does your character intend by this dialogue, what does the listener understand, and what does it tell the reader?

That might seem like a lot, but we do it all the time in our normal conversation. In fact, I think if you write the dialogue as though it were a conversation in your head, it would at least be passable dialogue. With room for improvement, yes, but it would at least sound natural. A lot of awkward dialogue I see in stories seems to stem from one of two problems: either the author is trying to advance the plot through dialogue and hasn't sounded it out, or the author is trying too hard to make a character sound distinctive and so they've twisted their speech into a way nobody actually talks (or, related, they are trying to imitate movie dialogue but haven't established the proper context for it).

So let's talk first about how to write natural-sounding dialogue, then talk about how to suit it to each character, and lastly we'll talk about dialects and idioms and other peculiarities of dialogue.

Natural-Sounding Dialogue

The reason I say "natural-sounding" dialogue is because natural dialogue as we speak it today is full of umms and uhhs, sentences we start and don't finish, and abrupt changes of subject. We can generally follow those conversations because our brains follow them in real time and are very good at filtering out the tics and pauses so that we don't go "what did he mean by 'uhh'?" (although sometimes you notice a tic and then your brain fixates on it). But when you're reading dialogue, you're conditioned to pay attention to each word. If you use an "um" in dialogue, it's because you want the reader to know that the character is hesitating there. Most writers know this, but occasionally people want to try to write "the way people talk," and that's not how we're trained to read.

We'll talk a little in the exercises about how to learn to write natural-sounding dialogue, but the old standby of "study works where you think the characters sound good" is a good one. Movie scripts, in particular, are easily found on the Internet and mostly consist of dialogue. But the easiest test is for you to read your dialogue aloud as a conversation and see if it sounds like something people would actually say. Have a friend read back and forth if you want to simulate a conversation.

This is harder if you're writing in a different world or time than our own. We have a pretty good ear for what dialogue sounds like to us—think of the people you've met who talk oddly, how easy it is for a little quirk of speech to stand out to you, whether it's using the wrong word for something or pronouncing a word differently. But when it comes to your world, what does dialogue sound like there? In fantasy, a lot of people default to "old-sounding British English," especially in high fantasy with courts and such, but if it's not actually set in Olde England, it doesn't have to follow those patterns. Those are just the ones we're familiar with. And that can be good in some ways: it will read that way to readers who share the same background of fantasy stories you do, and if that's the impression you want to create and the audience you want to reach, then great. But most of us haven't lived in medieval England, so we're creating these voices based on someone else's impression, maybe an impression of an impression of an impression, not firsthand experience.

Think about the voices you're familiar with and see if you can't use them. If you're a professional in some field, how do your colleagues in that field talk? How did the people at your first job talk? If you haven't spent time in a particular group or community, it's not a great idea to try to adapt their voice to the page, but if it's really critical to the story, you can always research YouTube videos. As with any kind of representation, do your research, be respectful, and hire a sensitivity reader if it's an underrepresented community you're trying to represent. Even if you're not intending to code a voice to a particular group, the patterns you use might read that way, so it's best to get a lot of eyes on it.

The more difficult component of natural-sounding dialogue is to write what a character would say *the way they would say it*. This is one of those things that you'll develop more of a feel for as the book goes along. It's not uncommon for me to start a revision by noticing that the character doesn't talk in the first chapter the way they talk at the end of the book. The more you get to know the character, the more individual and natural their dialogue will sound. You'll discover little patterns of speech and certain word choices that come to define them.

Character Voice

But early on, here, you're still getting to know them. So it's often helpful to do those "get to know your character" exercises, if those work for you, like the optional exercise in the Character Introduction section. That can build up your background knowledge of your character. They probably picked up most of their vocabulary and speech patterns from their parents, but school friends and other community influences also affect that.

Even with all of that, there's going to be a process of feeling out the character's voice, and that's completely natural. You won't know until you write them in certain situations how they'll react, and that will evolve their voice. This is fine! Start with as much knowledge as you can and then remain consistent with everything you learn about the character.

When creating a character's voice, word choices mean a lot. We default to the words we know, but our characters won't necessarily know all the same words. A few choices here and there can stick out in your readers' minds and help shape their perceptions of that character. What community has your character spent a lot of time around, and what are some particular words that group might use that aren't as common outside of it? Religious groups, military groups, hobby groups, professional groups, all have their own lingo, and picking up just a few things from them can remind your audience of your character's background.

Again, as with so many things in writing, balance is key here. Pick a few word choices to highlight your character's background, but don't flood your dialogue with them. This is true of anything you are trying to do to make your character more distinctive. Dialects in particular are easy to overuse, which can make the dialogue difficult to parse as a reader.

Consider an attempt at a Cockney dialect: "Oi guv, wot yew fink yew doin' 'ere?" It's a bit of an effort to parse, isn't it? Imagine line after line of that dialogue. It would get pretty tedious quickly. You could write it instead as "Oi guv, what you fink you doin' 'ere?" That gets across a lot of the Cockney feel without making the reader parse every single word.

The trick to balance is finding those key words. In the previous sentence, "Oi" and "fink" really get the accent across, and "'ere" and "guv" cement the feel without being too difficult to parse. With a Cockney accent, the dropped "h" is what most readers think of, so you have to include that one, but for the others you could adjust words here and there to make it easier to read. And once you've established the accent, you can dial it back even more as the book goes along.

Colm Tóibín, a celebrated Irish author, is expert at conveying the lilt of Irish speech without pushing too thick a dialect in his characters' speech. In his novel *Brooklyn*, here are samples of dialogue from the first few pages:

> "I'm starving," Rose said, "but I've no time to eat."

> "You're just to call up there tonight."

> "And we are worked off our feet every Sunday here. Sure, there's nothing else open."

Note the syntax that is a little off from our American speech ("I don't have time to eat," we would say, for example) and the "sure" which is a common marker of Irish speech. These are a few lines scattered throughout the dialogue in the first three or four pages, but they give you enough of a flavor of the speech that you can hear it.

All of these tools will help your characters sound distinct from each other. One of the worries I hear a lot from beginning writers is that "all their characters sound alike," at least to them. If you hear each character differently in your head, that'll help them sound different, but this is also something you can work on in revision, once you have a better handle on the characters. Also, it's not necessarily bad for all the characters to sound similar; this is something that I think feels more obvious to the writer than to most readers. If this does worry you about your own work, though, come back to this section. Revisit your main characters and think about what makes them different in their backgrounds. What words and syntax would they use that would set them apart from the others? What would they notice more than the other characters would? What would be on their mind? All of this, expressed in their dialogue, will help set them apart and make them distinct to you and your readers.

Dialogue Tags

The most common dialogue tag is "said," which is the easiest way of explaining what a dialogue tag is: it's the verb that accompanies a line of dialogue. "Said" is the neutral one, the plain no-frills one, and there are plusses and minuses to that. The plus is that "said" often fades into invisibility for the reader, so its use doesn't trip them up as they go through the story. The minus is that it doesn't tell the reader anything more about how the line of dialogue was spoken.

I say that "said" fades into invisibility, but that's only up to a point. I read a short story once—published, by an award-winning author—that included eleven lines of dialogue in a row that all used the word "said." By the time I got to the end of that stretch, the repetition was painfully obvious; clearly this author had understood the "'said' becomes invisible" maxim but did not realize that it had an upper limit. I find that for my own tastes, three lines in a row is about as far as I want to go with it.

However, some writers go too far in the other direction, avoiding "said" completely to tell me that their main characters shouted, cried, wondered, remonstrated, reflected, mused, urged, and so on. This is extremely distracting; non-"said" dialogue tags get maybe one or two lines before I start noticing them, and if it's a big awkward one like "remonstrated," even that can be too much.

The answer is not, as you might be on your way to concluding, to alternate "said" with one of those "said-onyms" throughout your dialogue. Remember back when we talked about varying your sentence structure? That goes double for dialogue. One of the keys is that *you don't always need a dialogue tag*. You can set off dialogue with action, or leave it alone by itself (and that goes back to making your dialogue so individual that the reader can tell who's speaking without being told).

Here's a snippet from my novel *Dead Right*, in which our protagonist, private investigator Jae Kim, is talking to a mother about her daughter who's died (the daughter has become a ghost, but Jae can't tell the mother that right now):

> She was quiet for a moment, and when she spoke again her voice was cracking. "I don't

understand what happened. I haven't gotten any information about Penny and now you're talking about a ring…"

"Okay," I said. "Okay. I'm sorry. This is a really difficult time. But you saw the government agent. I'm only trying to do what your daughter would have wanted."

"How do you know what she would have wanted?" Her voice cracked again, sharper this time. "How would I even know?"

The front door stayed closed. I gauged how much time I might have. "When was the last time you talked to her?" I said gently.

She sniffed. "Months ago. Toward the end of last year."

"What did you talk about?"

"Oh, we fought. She told me she was going to make a difference, I told her that teenagers can't make a difference, that she should come home and get her education and then we could make a difference together. She didn't agree, as you can guess. Do you have any children, Mr. Kim?"

"I don't."

"Then you can't understand what it's like to have your child turn against you."

There are nine lines of dialogue there and only two "said"s. One of those I modified with "gently" because I couldn't get that tone across with just the words. The rest of the dialogue is either set off with action or left alone. I could have used dialogue tags here—"she complained" in the first line, "she cried" in the third, "I urged" in the sixth—but how much would they have added? You get the feeling from the actions and the dialogue flows naturally. Jae says "I'm sorry" and speaks gently, so you understand what his tone is here; the mother's voice cracks and gets sharper, and then she sniffs and her sentences become short. If you read this aloud, you will probably get the tone pretty close to what I intended. More dialogue tags would have cluttered up the flow.

And speaking of flow...

Dialogue Pacing

One of the quirks of beginning writers that I see often is the tendency to stop after every line of dialogue and explain how the character felt about it, what they're thinking, and what's going to lead them to say the next thing they're going to say. I'm not going to pull any specific examples, but here's one I'm making up for illustration:

> "How dare you talk to me like that?" Flip yelled.
>
> Barkley couldn't understand why Flip was so mad. He'd only talked the way he'd just seen Rose talk to him, and he held the same position as Rose. "What do you mean? Like what?"
>
> Flip's arms waved, and the short fellow paced back and forth, getting more and more agitated. Clearly Barkley's words weren't having the calming effect the manager had hoped they would; in fact they seemed to be having the opposite effect. "Like—like I'm just a worker drone! Like I don't have any opinions of my own!"
>
> Opinions of his own? Barkley struggled to figure out what "opinions" could matter when a mechanic was being told to service the spacecraft's engine. He wished Rose were here; she seemed far more able to take control of a situation, and Flip respected her. Torn between his desire to assert the authority of his position and genuinely wanting to make Flip feel better,

Barkley tried to steer down the middle. "Well, the engine needs to be serviced now, but afterwards, why don't you come find me and we can discuss whatever opinions you might have."

This is another example of telling rather than showing. Dialogue is the ultimate "show"—it's an action the person is taking to communicate with another person, and it has to address the immediate issue while also being shaped according to the mindset of the person speaking. For some people, the showing doesn't feel like enough, so they decide they have to accompany it with some telling to bring the reader up to speed. But when you do that—as we've discussed before—you remove an element of mystery from the story. A small one, but it's one less thing the reader has to engage to figure out. Smoothing the path for the reader like this over and over will make the whole work less engaging.

We are all conditioned to parse speech for clues about the other person's state of mind, and allowing the reader to use those reflexes with the dialogue in your story keeps them interested. If you tell them, "don't worry about figuring this out, I'm just going to tell you why they said this thing," then they are less engaged and more passive, and that's not what you want. You don't need to obscure things, but you also don't need to spell everything out.

There's a lot of information in the example above, but much of it is just telling the reader things that should be obvious from the dialogue. More importantly, this is supposed to be an animated, lively conversation. Pausing after each line to reassess and catch the reader up drains all the energy out of the lines.

A better way to handle this would be to have the conversation with as little interjection as possible, and after the conversation, let Barkley retreat and process what's happened. Communicate anger and confusion and all the other emotions with the dialogue itself.

Go back to the example in the previous section: most of the emotion is in the dialogue. At one point Jae pauses to gauge how much time he might have left; that's an immediate calculation that affects the conversation. The rest of it he can process when it's done, as much as is needed. If every line had been crowded with thoughts and processing, the dialogue itself would've held a lot less power.

Summary Points

• Dialogue should sound real while not actually being word-for-word real. Good movie scripts are a great resource for this. Read your dialogue aloud to see how it sounds.

• Your character's dialogue reflects their attitude and upbringing. Dialects are tempting to use but don't make them difficult for the reader to parse; a little goes a long way.

• Vary your dialogue tags, but not so much it stands out. "Said" is fine to use in moderation.

• Dialogue has a flow in the text; don't interrupt it too much with lengthy narration or internal monologue.

<u>Example: Dialogue</u>

The first chapter of *The Price of Thorns* introduces two of the main characters, and apart from some interactions with farmboys throwing things, most of what happens in this chapter is dialogue.

We first meet Nivvy—in this early draft he's in stocks—getting tomatoes thrown at him by bored farmboys:

> He rattled the chains that held him in the stocks, and spit out a tomato seed. "Wasting perfectly good food like that. Y'oughta be ashamed!"
>
> One of the two boys stopped the other one, and they looked back. Uh-oh. "Reckon he's right," the slightly lighter-haired boy said to the slightly darker-haired boy, and stooped to the ground, rummaging in the dirt.
>
> "No, no I'm not." Nivvy spoke quickly. "One of my faults, you see, I—hey! You! Uh—farmer boy! Sign says you're not to throw rocks!"
>
> The lighter-haired boy had straightened up with an egg-sized rock, or, if the gods were smiling, a clump of earth, in his hand. "Don't see nobody here minding the sign," he said.
>
> "I'll report you. When Kingsley comes to set me loose, I'll tell him." Nivvy knew that there were times in his life when it would be better for him to stop talking, but so far he had not managed to recognize a single one of them before it happened.

I wanted to start with Nivvy in a predicament because under stress, there's a lot more opportunities to reveal character. Here, his dialogue goes from an appeal to common sense (about wasting food, something that calls back to his childhood) to a reminder about the rules to, finally, a threat to bring authority into it. Nivvy has a peculiar relationship with authority, as befits a thief, and thinks of it as a last resort, and then only if it can benefit him.

His dialogue here, with the "y'oughta" and dropping some of his articles ("sign says"), is intended to mark him as casual with his language use, which is sometimes a marker of a poorer class of people (or at least less well educated than others), and here serves to place him in contrast with Bella when she shows up:

> She took a breath. "My name is Bella, and I have need of a good thief. Failing that, I have searched for a merely competent thief, and when I was unable to find one of those…"
>
> "I'll have you know," Nivvy said, completely forgetting his promise at the slight on his ability, "that I am an uncommonly talented thief."
>
> "What about your talents is so uncommon?"
>
> "No, it's an expression." He sighed. "Look, it wouldn't do to brag overmuch about things I've stolen while I'm being restrained here and who knows who might be listening to take word back to any of the various kingdoms involved, but you know the Tarisch Empire, across the western ocean?"
>
> "Yes," she said slowly.
>
> "Well, I stole the jeweled brooch of the Emperor's daughter from the topmost tower of the castle. Now, the castle itself is atop a hill surrounded by armed guards, and a wall, what's more. The tower stands two hundred feet off the ground, so I says to myself—"
>
> "I'm not interested in the details of your exploits," she said, and her feet shuffled irritably.

"Well." Nivvy cleared his throat as best he could. "Climbed right up the outside and in the window, off her bureau, picked the lock, sold it in Rivermouth for thirteen gold crowns. Say, you wouldn't have a wet cloth on you?"

"You wouldn't rather have a drink?"

"Bit tricky to manage that in this position. I can suck on a wet cloth quite passably, though." He turned and tried a winning smile, though as he turned, he felt the trails of blood sticky on his skin.

"Perhaps," she said, "if you can be of use to me."

"Right." He was no stranger to leverage in discussions, and not unaware that he held nearly none of it at the moment. "What d'you want, then?"

"I want you to steal something for me."

Here, Nivvy's casual speech contrasts with Bella's more stiff and formal speech. Eliminating a few contractions here and there does wonders to make a person sound more formal; just as Nivvy's "y'oughta" earlier gave him a more casual feel, here Bella's "what about your talents is so uncommon," rather than a more casual, "what's so uncommon about your talents," gives her a slightly stiff and formal feel. Eliminating all contractions can make her sound even stuffier (imagine her saying "would you not rather have a drink"), but I didn't want to go quite that far.

Her dialogue is very focused, too. She needs the services of a thief, and she's not interested in hearing Nivvy's stories (we will learn that not listening to someone else's stories is unusual in this world, or at least the sign of a self-centered person); she makes her assistance to him conditional on whether he has anything to offer her. These first few lines tell us a good deal about Bella as a person.

Exercise: Dialogue

One of the key aspects of dialogue is making sure that your word choice is intentional and not simply the default of however you'd talk. If you want to improve your dialogue, you have to (1) broaden your experience of how other people talk, and (2) practice intentionality in your writing.

1. How People Talk

For the first, there are a number of ways you can go about broadening your experience. One comes from a screenwriting class I took with Carl Yorke, and is very simple: go sit in a public place where people are having conversations for half an hour or so and write down verbatim the things you hear. You have to write them down quickly, because if you rely on memory, your mind will smooth them into words that fit the way you would say them. Not all of these will be useful, but over half an hour you'll hear someone use a turn of phrase you haven't heard before, or use a word or syntax that seems odd to you. These are tools for you to tweak your dialogue.

Another way, as I mentioned in the main essay, is to study movie screenplays. Pick movies with distinctive characters and look at their dialogue to see what makes them stand out. Are there lines that you could read without the attribution and still know which character says them? What in the word choice and construction makes those lines of dialogue distinct?

You can, of course, and should also look at novels with distinct-sounding characters. But novels are often harder to tease the dialogue out of, because there's so much surrounding the dialogue. A character might feel distinct to you because of all the other things that the author is doing around the dialogue. That's not bad to learn either; you have a number of tools available to you. To focus on dialogue, though, is easier with a screenplay.

2. Intentionality

To practice intentionality in your dialogue is harder. My

suggestion here is to pick a few key lines from your first scene or chapter, ideally a few lines for each important character. For each of those lines, focus on what the character is trying to convey, and then think of several alternative ways they could be said. How does each of the different ones sound? What different feel do they have? Does one of the alternates fit better than the original? Make sure to look at word choice and syntax both, and any other ways you can think of to vary the dialogue.

After doing this a few times, you will get a feel for how your character talks, and the dialogue should flow better. Return to this exercise anytime a line feels a little off, but establishing your comfort with your characters and how they talk is critical to writing good dialogue.

Chapter Sixteen

Description

Setting The Scene

You know, more or less, what your world and characters look like, but how to present that to the reader? How much detail should you include in a scene? I've talked a little about this already in the World Building and Character Introduction sections, but it's worth talking about description in its own section here.

There are as many philosophies of description as there are writers. Some people hate extensive description and want to jump to the characters and the action; others want to linger lovingly over each detail of a character's wardrobe or the shades of color in a twilight cityscape. Some readers devour every detail of a description; others skim them to get to the dialogue and plot. All this is not to say that there aren't any guidelines for writing description, only that you can be extremely flexible within those guidelines. What I'm going to talk about are best practices I've encountered as a writer and reader.

My own preference is to keep description on the lighter side. When going back through my first drafts for revision, I often find my characters floating in an undescribed void because I was so eager to get to their dialogue. So I've taken pains to pay attention to description, and I'll show some of my examples from *The Price of Thorns* in more depth in the example section. For now, I'll talk about the guidelines I use in description.

The first thing I try to do is visualize the scene in my head. Sometimes you can find resources online that will be helpful. For example, for a scene set in Amsterdam in *The Revolution and the Fox*, the final book in the Calatians series, I found images online of Amsterdam in the 1820s. I don't always keep a clear picture of scenes and characters in my head, so having a photo (or a drawn reference) is very helpful.

If you can't find a photo reference or have one drawn (or draw one yourself), then you'll have to do your best to picture what you're trying to describe. The way I usually start with this is to figure out what details are the most important to convey to the reader. What's going to be important to this scene? Next you want to filter those through what details the character will notice. Your character will, because of their background and history, be predisposed to notice people and settings in a certain way. What are your main character's interests and what are the key details they will pick up on the first time they enter a setting, or encounter a character. When coming back to a setting or seeing a character again, what's changed about them? What details were familiar that your character revisits?

Beyond what's important to the reader and the character, there are the details that are important to you. It may not matter that your main character's house is painted royal blue, to the plot or to the character, but in your mind that's one of the main things you know about it, and you want the reader to know it too. If your character wears a particular style of shirt because that's how you envision them, let the reader know that. These details help you build the picture in your own head and even though they might not seem important from a plot perspective, they help the reader share that picture. You might not know why it's important that your character wears that shirt, but it's part of them. Just as importantly, it helps you keep the character in your head consistently throughout the story.

In The Details

In mysteries, details of description are especially important, because they are often clues. Agatha Christie is a master in giving you just enough details that you will read the clue but not necessarily flag it, because the rest of the scene is so well described. One of her tricks is the specificity of detail.

There are any number of ways to describe the same object. As I mentioned above, different peoples' backgrounds shape how they see the world. You might see a pen as a tool, a weapon, a status symbol, or a clue that someone had visited a real estate office, for example. But just as importantly is how specific you get with the descriptive detail. Consider the different kinds of pens your character might have and how the following different statements communicate something about them:

They took out a pen and held it, ready to write.

They took out a cheap Bic pen, pulled the well-chewed blue cap off the end, and held it, ready to write.

They took out a gold-trimmed Monte Carlo fountain pen, carefully unscrewed the cap, and held it, ready to write.

They took out a pastel pencil, lavender, and held it, ready to write.

Okay, the last one is a pencil, but you get the idea. The first statement is generic; it tells you what's happening, but it doesn't give you any more information. The more detail you give, the more opportunity you have to communicate more information to the reader. Getting specific also helps the reader build an image in their mind. What image did you have of the pen when you read the first sentence? Some generic pen, maybe the last one you used? With the subsequent statements, you get a much clearer picture of the pen.

It might be that you don't have an idea what kind of pen

your character has. That's okay! Getting extremely specific with every single detail would result in prose that would feel exhausting to both writer and reader. But the more you know specifics in your head, the more you should include them, and the more specific you can get—especially about personal items like a pen or shirt, or about important details of your world— the better a picture you paint for the reader, and the more you show them.

And this is a good time to talk about…

Overloading

This is a term in software engineering referring to a single function or operation that can perform multiple different tasks. I use it in writing to talk about the ability to accomplish multiple goals with the same phrase or sentence. Elizabeth Bear taught in a lecture that a sentence can do four possible things in a story: establish character, advance plot, describe setting, and illuminate theme. Ideally, you'd like your sentences to do two or more of these things at once.

I talked about describing character and setting through interaction. That's what this is. Now, not every sentence has to do all four, or even aspire to do all four. Sometimes you get an opportunity that works out that way, but in general if you're always looking for ways to do one of those four things, you'll be able to craft sentences that can do many at once.

Why is this a good thing? The elements of a story should be working together in harmony: character, plot, setting, and theme. When you address multiple elements in a single sentence, it reinforces that cohesion that will make your book feel stronger. Your plot takes place because this particular character exists in this particular setting, and you've chosen these elements to illustrate your theme.

This also forces you to show more than you tell. You want to show your character taking some sort of action to advance the plot, and that is the surface level of the sentence, but the way your character thinks about that action reveals their character, and the way that action makes sense within the world tells the reader about your world building. If you put in those character, world building, or theme moments as context to other parts of the story, they grow in the reader's mind until they understand your character or world without you having to tell them explicitly anything about it. And coming to that understanding themselves makes it feel more real to them.

Sensory Experience

One good piece of writing advice when thinking about description is to incorporate all five senses. It's easy to describe what a setting looks like, and sound is a natural extension of that. But there's smell, taste, and touch as well. Maybe your character isn't tasting a room when they walk into it, but there are definitely smells and touches to experience, and taste can be useful to tell the reader if they've just eaten, just been drinking.

But there are other senses too. Interoception is the body's awareness of itself—are you cold, warm, hungry, full, dizzy, nauseated, sluggish, tired, alert? Is your heart racing? How's your breathing? You don't need to run through all of these when starting a scene, but it's worth going through a checklist with your character—do any of these apply? And proprioception is the body's awareness of motion and balance. If your character is moving, especially coming into a new setting, spatial awareness is important.

Describing your character's state helps the reader feel their experience. Moving on from what the character is experiencing to how they interact with the environment and other characters draws the reader along with them. Giving the reader a sympathetic party to experience the scene with helps a lot in making your descriptions effective.

Summary Points

• Describe the details in a scene that are important to situate the reader, that would be important or stand out to the characters in the scene, or that are important to you for any reason.

• Be as specific as you can about important details. Specificity makes your work feel more grounded and real.

• As with character, description through interaction is more engaging to the reader. The more purposes a sentence can serve (establish character, advance plot, describe setting, and/or illuminate theme), the more connected and powerful your narrative will feel.

• Think about the range of sensory experiences when writing description: not just sight and sound, but smell and feel, the body's awareness of itself, and the body's awareness of motion and balance.

Example: Description

Here's another very early bit from *The Price of Thorns*.

> Heat boiled out of the cave entrance. Nivvy stared at the dead bat stretched out on the wooden pole while Bella gathered her cloak around her and stepped into the cave.
>
> The bat had been there for some time. Spiderwebs clung to its fur, and its eyes had been ripped away, probably by birds, to judge from the claw holes in the wings. But it didn't smell, and the skin of the wings had an odd iridescent sheen to it. Nivvy's nose twitched. He looked back down the path to where their small boat rocked gently. "Say," he called into the cave. "What say we give this up for a bad job and go back to Spire to come up with another plan? I could use another round of those griddle cakes."
>
> Bella emerged from the cave, her black hair glistening with sweat around flushed skin. "Don't be ridiculous," she snapped. "We're here and we're going to go in."
>
> "Only I'm pretty sure this is nasty magic sign, here." Nivvy pointed to the bat. "Happy people with friendly magic don't kill bats and stretch 'em out to greet their guests with."

This is a first draft, so it's as much an example of "you don't have to get everything down in the first pass" as an example of description. For this, I thought it would be useful to show you the final text of this moment, after multiple revisions:

> [...] a blast of hot air assailed him and the light around him dimmed. Nivvy opened his eyes to see a small tunnel in the rock, lit with a

foreboding red glow, and a dead bat stretched out on a wooden pole right in front of him.

He yelled and stumbled back, and stared at the bat from there. Spiderwebs clung to its fur, and its eyes had been ripped away, probably by birds, to judge from the claw holes in the wings. But it didn't smell, and the skin of the wings had an odd iridescent sheen to it in the dim, hellish red light. What was more, from the bat's claws hung a loop of shimmering silver, big enough to be a necklace for one of the giants in Zein's story, and fastened to the thread at regular intervals were teeth. They looked to be human teeth, at least from as close as Nivvy was willing to get to them.

This was Bella's friend's home? This was how she greeted guests? The bad feelings he'd had over Bella trying to kill Zein resurfaced, stronger than before. He'd been able to explain that away to himself as the reflex of someone unsettled in an unfamiliar world, someone who with his guidance could find a better path. But Bella's best friend was someone who spent magic to make this grotesque tableau the first thing visitors would see? Some of those teeth looked not as old as the bat. If this was the company Bella kept…

Not that he hadn't done jobs for unsavory people in his time, but usually the unsavoriness hovered around the level of cheating customers, maybe some bullying, occasionally some truly reprehensible hygiene. One couldn't always be picky about one's clients. But he'd never knowingly worked for a murderer, magical or not, and he was starting to feel like he'd been hired by the latter to steal from the former, which was a worrying situation. Murderers tended to have an easier time murdering than other folks did, just as sailors were better at sailing and so on, and when you crossed one, it was harder to talk your way out of the situation.

Nivvy's nose twitched. "Say," he called to Bella, who had walked on past the bat without a second glance. "What say we give this up for a bad job and go back to Spire to come up with another plan? I could use another round of those griddle cakes."

Bella turned, her black hair glistening with sweat around flushed skin. Her lips looked even redder in the light; her eyes looked almost black. "Don't be ridiculous," she snapped, seizing his wrist and pulling him forward. "We're here and we're going to go in. Are you having second thoughts about your ability?"

"Only I'm pretty sure this is nasty magic sign, here." Nivvy pointed to the bat, ignoring the jab. "Happy fairies with friendly magic don't kill bats and stretch 'em out to greet their guests with."

It's useful here to look at the basics I got down in the first draft: Nivvy is first confronted with a blast of heat, the first thing he feels, then an impression of a rock cave or tunnel. But the thing that grabs his attention to the exclusion of everything else is a dead bat, preserved somehow. Spiderwebs and gouged-out eyes make it creepier. It doesn't have a smell, and there's no sound here, but we get heat, and in the revision I added a red glow and called it "hellish" to make it feel creepier. In the revision I also added a trophy necklace of teeth, elegantly presented on a silver loop. All this is building up the character of Scarlet, the fairy we haven't met yet, as well as showing us the obstacles facing Nivvy in the present moment, and we get a little bit of world building in that Nivvy interprets this (correctly) to be evil magic.

Most of the changes in the revision come in Nivvy's

internality, where he interprets the things that he sees and pulls in experiences from earlier in the book. In the revision, I knew more about his relationship with Bella and they had started to be closer on this journey—until this point. He has also met Zein, and called back to one of their stories.

It's also useful to see that while Nivvy didn't have reservations about working for Bella and breaking some rules earlier, this sign of evil magic makes him seriously consider abandoning her (in fact, he will not largely because he sees some vulnerability in her).

And lastly, the line about "murderers tended to have an easier time murdering" also reveals some of Nivvy's character and adds to the character of the narration, which, being tight third person, is intended to mirror Nivvy's thoughts and personality.

Also note in the revision that Bella's red lips and black eyes have been described to go with her black hair and flushed skin. Lots of black and red, good evil colors.

Exercise: Description

There are description exercises all around us. When we describe a meal or a person or a scene to a remote friend, we're doing the same thing as describing something to a reader. But there are a few exercises I've used to work on my descriptions in the past, so I'll share those.

The basic one is easy: keep a notebook with you (or your phone, anything you use to take notes, voice memo can work too) and walk into a room, an office, a building, a store.

First: Write down the first impressions that come to your mind from the following checklist. Don't worry about the wording yet, just write it down the first way you think of it.

• What does this space remind you of? (This can be other spaces that look the same, or a person whom you associate with the space, or any other memory.)

• What are the first five things you see? (Close your eyes a few seconds after walking in and list them off in your head.)

• What do you hear?

- What do you smell?
- What do you feel? (Carpet/flooring under your feet? Warm air, cool air, breeze?)
- What else are you feeling? Tired, excited, hungry, nervous? How do those feelings manifest physically?

Second: When you've written your impressions down, go back through the list and look at the wording you chose. How might you make your impressions more precise? Think of a few alternative ways to describe the things you've written.

Third: Now imagine that you're trying to describe this to a specific person. That could be a friend of yours or one of the characters in your story. Knowing their specific interests, how would that change what you prioritize in the description? What would that change about the wording you use?

Fourth: Put yourself in the mindset of one of your characters. What would they notice first? How would they describe the scene? What's important to them, what words would they use?

This is an exercise you can do with a group, too. Have everyone do the exercise separately and then compare notes with each other. This is a good way to discover new ways of looking at a scene and new words you can use to describe it. You can also do this exercise with people, either people you know or people you see out in public (but try not to stare, that's rude).

Chapter Seventeen

Voice

Finding Your Voice

One of the most pressing questions I had as a beginning writer, and one of the questions I see often from other beginning writers, is about "finding your voice." Voice is one of those qualities people talk about in writing but find hard to pin down, sort of an "I know it when I see it." It is generally the impression of the personality that comes through as the person telling the story. In some stories, the reader will understand that there is a fictional character telling them the story, and the narrative will be in that character's voice (for example, in first person stories). In cases where that isn't clear (most third-person POV narratives), people will assume that the voice in the narrative is the author's voice. In the first case, you will definitely want to think about how that character would tell the story to the reader. In the second case, you may just tell the story the way you talk (or the way you tell stories). Even if you don't think about crafting your voice, your personality will still show up in your prose in your word choice, the idioms you use, sentence cadence, the cultural background you draw from, the tone with which you approach stories, and other quirks of your writing. Voice is what people mean when they say that a story "sounds like your work."

Crafting Voice

If you want to craft your voice, my best advice is to imagine narration as a character telling the story to the reader. In first person stories, obviously the narration is also in the voice of the POV character, and you will have developed that character's background so you understand how they will be telling their story.

The narration can also match the character's tone even in a tight third person narration. In my own (non-first-person) books, I tend to go for a light touch with narrative voice and have it resemble my own voice as much as possible, but it also changes depending on the book. The tone of **Price of Thorns**, for example, is slightly different from the tone in the Calatians series. In neither case did I have a character in mind to do the narration, but I do think the narration takes its tone from the main character (as I noted above). Kip and Nivvy are both serious, but Nivvy is more prone to joking, and the narration in *The Price of Thorns* reflects that tone. I adopted those voices to make the narration feel consistent with the main character.

If you're writing in a distant third person POV (omniscient), you can invent a mythical character who's telling the story to the reader. Think about that character as you would any other character in your story. Maybe in a fantasy they are one of the gods of the world; in science fiction they might be someone recording the events or looking back on them through some advanced technology. You don't have to end your story with this narrator stepping forward from the shadows to introduce themself to the reader; this can simply be a vehicle for you to pin down how you want to tell the story.

Lastly, you can write as though you yourself are telling the story. In this case your voice is simply the way you tell the story to your readers. This isn't necessarily a bad thing. While there are readers who appreciate a strong narrative voice, there are also readers who find it annoying. They don't want personality in narration; they just want to know what happened. I know that having too much personality in narration always makes me think about who exactly is narrating the story and whether I need to consider them part of the story or not.

Using Your Voice

You can also craft voice to specific effect in your fiction. In the Dangerous Spirits series, each book has three separate stories, each of which I tried to imbue with its own voice. One was first person, one was present day, and the third was a historical era. In these, I tried to make the historical era voice give a feel for that era: 1900-ish Paris is (in my book) artistic and colorful; late 1800s Russia is cold and sharp and focused on political and physical power; early 1900s New Orleans is warm and agricultural and restless with class struggles. That series was inspired by David Mitchell's *Cloud Atlas*, which was introduced to me as a masterful example of playing with voice. *Cloud Atlas* is six nested narratives, taking place from the 1880s to some unspecified future date, and each narrative has its own very strong voice. It's voice that sets the characters of the narrative in a context that serves the function of world building.

Voice can be a powerful tool in your narrative. I've set this section here as you're starting your novel so you can think about voice as you write the draft. Like everything else, there's a good chance that your voice will evolve over the course of writing the draft, so you may want to come back to this section when you start your revision.

Summary Points

• Voice refers to the perception of a personality behind the narrative prose, made up of word choice, idioms, sentence cadence, tone, and other individual quirks of writing. It can refer to a specific character perceived to be narrating the story, or to the voice of the author if there isn't a narrator.

• To play with voice, imagine the character who is telling the story and what they think of it.

• Voice can be another tool in your toolbox to build your character and setting.

Example: Voice

In *The Price of Thorns*, the narrative voice hews closely to Nivvy's. He isn't telling the story in first person, but I imagined him being the narrator of his own story, as if he were telling it about himself in the third person. This gave it a somewhat irreverent, casual tone that worked well and as a bonus thematically resonated with the idea that what Nivvy wanted most of all was to be someone that stories were told about.

Here's an example passage from the second act, as Nivvy is exploring an underwater kingdom:

> Nivvy could hardly make out any details, not with these eyes and not underwater, but spots in the stretch beyond the castle shone reddish and white, and it wasn't hard for his imagination to once again turn that into the roofs of a sprawling city, perhaps a center of trade between the north and the west. A river must have run down out of the mountains here, and perhaps at one time had continued all the way to the sea.
>
> And now all that was left was this prince and the crown. Too bad, but that's what happened. There were ships at the bottom of the Copper Port harbor, long since picked clean of valuables, and farther out, some older wrecks from battles Nivvy had heard stories about. More experienced divers went out to them and brought back strange coins, or knives with unfamiliar beautiful designs on the handles. "Who made these?" he'd asked when a friend showed him a knife her father had salvaged. "Someone dead," she'd said matter-of-factly.

The first paragraph is light on voice—"it wasn't hard for his imagination to once again turn that into the roofs of a sprawling city" has some definite word choice elements there—and is mostly about describing the setting. Nivvy imagining what it might have looked like isn't really about voice; it's about his experience as a character.

In the second paragraph, though, the narrative voice is much stronger. "Too bad, but that's what happened" might as well be a spoken line of Nivvy's dialogue. And then the descriptions in the next sentence: "strange coins" and "unfamiliar beautiful designs" are all intended to invoke the wonder of stories—and that is set against the real-world practicality of the people living in this world, in the last sentence of the paragraph.

The voice in *The Price of Thorns*, reflecting and amplifying Nivvy's character, includes all of his wonders and insecurities. Mostly muted, because there are times when the narration just has to get you from one place to another or describe what you're looking at or experiencing, but visible enough that it's interesting to read and adds to the story as a whole.

Exercise: Voice

Take a few paragraphs from your early draft, mostly narration (ideally some action as well as description). Now imagine the description and action in those paragraphs being relayed by different characters, or different people you know. How would the word choice and tone change for each different narrator? Try doing one with a first-person feel to it ("I don't know what Jack was thinking when he tried to leap from one rooftop to another..."); try doing some where the narrator is hostile to the environment or characters; try some where the narrator is more awed or excited. Play around with voice.

Most of these will likely be too "voicey" for your narrative, but in doing them, you'll feel how the personality behind the narration can affect it. You can pick up this exercise at any point in your draft if you've written some paragraphs that feel a little off.

Part 3: The Soggy Middle

Here we are at Act 2! In your novel, this will be the point after which the protagonist has been introduced to the story and has decided to jump in.

There's a reason Act 2s are infamous for causing writers problems. When you're starting a book, often the bright, shiny ideas in your head are the satisfying ending and the exciting beginning. Few people start a novel excited to write the journey where the problem gets worse, or where the protagonist thinks they've solved it but they haven't. Maybe you're anticipating the moment when the villain reveals themself, or when a character dramatically switches sides, but in general, we are excited to start our stories and end them, and we figure we'll worry about the middle when we get there.

Guess what? We're there.

I hope that all the prep we did before starting has helped you build a road map for the second act, so you're not wandering into the wilderness where so many before you have gotten lost, stuck, or dispirited. I always have a moment in the middle of Act 2 when I feel like I've been writing the book forever and it's not going anywhere and I'm bored and feel like nobody's going to be interested in it. Having the outline to refer to reminds me that there's a plan, that the book *is* going somewhere, and that I'll get there.

So the big thing I'm going to talk about in this section is plotting, because that's the heart of any Act 2. You need to get your readers from the exciting beginning to the thrilling conclusion. I'll also cover character development—near and dear to my heart—because your characters need to grow and change as they race along the journey. I'll talk about villains and antagonists, because here is where they really get to shine, and I'll talk about midpoints, a good way to break up Act 2s in a couple different ways. Lastly, I'll cover some more general manuscript-wide topics like tone and theme/imagery, because if you haven't been thinking about them yet, this is the place to start, and if you have, this is a place to check in.

It's also a place to check in on your writing process. How's it going? Are you frustrated with your progress or scrambling to make time for your writing? Make adjustments if you need to. Keep track of what's working, and build on that.

Whether you've just started Act 2 or are close to finishing it, well done! You're working through the story, and you're not alone. Let's keep going!

Chapter Eighteen

Plotting

The Plot...Thicks?

I've talked a little about plotting already up when we were writing our outline. To summarize: plot is constructed of character decisions acting on the world and other characters, which then provoke answering reactions. When you were putting together your outline, you hopefully found a good sequence of events that all made sense, at least at a high level.

But maybe you didn't, and you felt your way through the first part of the book. Or you did, but now you're in the second act, and your outline isn't helping anymore. In my experience, one of two things happens here: either you get stuck—you don't know where to go next—or you get bored—the story seems pointless to you. I'll start with stuck, because a lot of the advice is the same and I think this is the easier problem to solve.

Feeling Stuck?

What happens when I get stuck in the second act is one of two things. Most often, I discover new character paths as I'm writing and I get to know the characters better, so by the time I get to the second act and I see what I'd planned, I say, "Oh, but that character wouldn't do it that way," or "that opportunity doesn't exist anymore." The other thing that can mess things up is that I've reached the point in the story with the setup and characters intact, but the sequence doesn't feel organic anymore. This can be because I've discovered new details that don't quite work with the plan or because I didn't think it through enough when I was making the outline. When I get to this point, here's what I do:

First, I remember that plot is constructed of character decisions, and character decisions are based on what the characters want. At this point in the story, if it doesn't make sense for the protagonist(s) to take the path I'd plotted ahead of time, what does make sense? What do they want right now, and what would they do to get closer to it in this situation? Then I look at how that action fits into the larger goal of the story. What do I want the characters to learn and achieve? Is this moving them toward that goal? And lastly, is this exciting for the reader? Does it have stakes for the characters and tension for the reader, or is it (just as a random example) multiple chapters of camping?

There will be times when what the protagonist wants to do —and should do at this point—feels right for them but not for the story. Does the Fellowship of the Ring want to go over the mountains or through the dangerous mines of Moria? Over the mountains, clearly. So Tolkien made that impossible for them with spies and storms, forcing them into the more dangerous path where they would lose a critical party member, beginning the dissolution of the Fellowship. When there's an easy path you don't want your character to take, put obstacles in their way. Either it makes sense for someone in the story to cut off that easy path (the antagonist would also know about this easy path and be invested in stopping the protagonist), or you as the author can put an obstacle in the way (more on that later).

Sometimes that works, and the logical thing for them to do will move the plot forward in the right way. Problem solved. But often the solution isn't that easy, so we have to move down the list.

If the protagonist action isn't going to work, then who else might take action to advance the plot? The next character on my list is the antagonist. What do they want? How are they trying to mess with our protagonist? We will talk about villains more in a later section, but the short version is: Your villain should have their own wants and needs and be acting to fulfill them. Their actions should affect our protagonist because their goals are aligned or conflicting, not (usually) just for the sake of being a jerk. In Ira Levin's classic novel *Rosemary's Baby*, the antagonist(s) are acting throughout the book, making Rosemary's life more difficult and strange, but their goal is to bring her pregnancy to term so she can deliver the child who will become the Antichrist. The more she tries to escape their influence—she wants a healthy child too, but her idea of a healthy pregnancy does not align with theirs—the more they act to stop her, first in subtle ways, then in more overt ways. However, they never ever take action unless it is with that goal in mind: to keep her and her child healthy (the way they want to) and nearby.

If it's not the right time for your villain to act either, then we move on to side characters. Discovering a new ally or a new enemy makes for a good plot complication. Farther along, a reversal (ally reveals themselves to be an enemy, or vice versa) is another good one.

The last rule for when I'm stuck, but maybe the most fun and important one, is: what would be the worst thing that could happen to them now? Within the continuity of the story, of course, but in those bounds…is there a secret they don't want revealed (there should always be a secret)? Who would be the worst person to hear it, and at what time? Who would be the worst person to discover what they're up to? What would be the worst time for something critical to break down or fail?

People want to see characters getting out of trouble, the worse the better. The plot of a book is in some ways the problem the protagonist is trying to solve (literally, in the case of plot-driven stories like mysteries and heists), and the trickier the problem, the more impressive the solution. But it's also a character device, because what we are trying to do over the course of a novel is to push the character to consider a new way of looking at the world. Change is difficult, and people are not inclined to it. To get them over this inertia, they have to have a lot of pressure put on them, and the worse the situation they're in, the more that's at stake, the more they are motivated to consider anything that will get them out of it (we'll revisit this more in the character arc section).

So if you're stuck, go back to your characters. What do they want, and what makes the most sense for them to do right now? What unexpected arrival or reversal of an ally or enemy can you throw in? What's the worst thing that could happen?

The Terrible Tedium

These are good solutions if you're stuck, but what if you're bored? The outline makes sense, the characters are doing what you wanted them to, but it doesn't feel compelling. You're on step 2 of a 15-step plan, and the exciting part feels so far away that you're having trouble motivating yourself.

Some of the above solutions will work here. A new character or a reversal will give your story something to react to; a new obstacle will give them a more immediate goal. Introducing plot complications like new obstacles or "side quest" subplots can be helpful, but they should always make sense in the context of the characters. Certain stories—I'm sure you can think of examples—can devolve into a series of "fetch quests," where the characters have to go to a place to get a thing, then go to another place to get another thing, and so on. The appeal of fetch quests is that having the characters chase a more immediately achievable goal (go get a thing) feels more exciting than the larger goal of the story, being a 2-step plan rather than a 15-step one. But if this happens without any character movement, where all the quests leave the characters in the same place on their character arc (another thing we'll explore later in this section), then it can feel static to the reader. Side quests are most effective when a character learns a lesson from them, when they affect the main plot, or when they present a different view of the problem facing the main character.

In *Watership Down*, for example, the rabbits find Cowslip's warren and General Woundwort's warren before finding the Down where they will make their home. Both of these adventures present dangers and tension of their own, but they also teach the rabbits important things about what their new home should look like. They know that they don't want to make bargains with men or live violently like men; at the same time they do take inspiration from parts of Cowslip's warren to build the Honeycomb in their own, and Woundwort's warren will prove to be the test that shows them their strength. But each of those warrens is an adventure unto itself, even though they're only a step on the larger journey. Hazel learns something about leadership in each location; the other rabbits all learn something about themselves too.

If you need something to happen but aren't sure how to make it work, there's a rule I follow: coincidences (used sparingly) are fine to get your characters *into* trouble, but not out of it. They should get out of trouble by their own agency and wits. This is why *deus ex machina* endings, in which the characters are rescued from a hopeless situation by some outside agency, feels unsatisfying. The ending is still a ways away here, though, and if you need your characters to stumble upon a new adventure, or be put in danger through a coincidence, go right ahead and do that.

Remember, too, that you're aiming for plots that are going to surprise the reader—but within a framework of things they expect. "What your characters do next" can and should be surprising, but make sense for that character. Hazel using the dog in *Watership Down* and Aslan's sacrifice in *The Lion, The Witch, and The Wardrobe* are startling acts that excite the reader, but they don't pull them out of the story. They are both deeply rooted in the character, and they work for that reason.

In general, you should be spending most of the second act getting your protagonist in worse and worse trouble. If you're stuck, ask yourself what your characters want and what they would naturally do next. If you're bored, ask yourself what would be exciting in your story. With these tools, you should be able to navigate your way through the soggy second act.

Summary Points

• Into the second act, your plot may be differing from the outline. Remember to focus on the decisions your character would make. Those may be different based on what you know about them now.

• The antagonist and side characters are also acting according to what they want and will affect the plot that way.

• If you're stuck, think about what would be the worst thing that could happen to your character(s) here. It's okay to get your character into trouble with a coincidence, but not out of trouble (they should get out by their own resources).

• Subplots or side quests should move the plot or character development forward; in other words, at the end of the subplot, the characters shouldn't be in the same place (plotwise or character development-wise) they were at the beginning.

Example: Plot

The first act of *The Price of Thorns* was pretty clear: Nivvy takes on Bella's job, they go to the fairy/djinn's lair, and Nivvy gets caught and turned into a weasel.

After that, my original plot outline was somewhat muddied. I'd written a scene where Nivvy convinces Bella to take him with her—which I quite liked—but then the next thing in the plot was "they find some old artifact of power." What was going to happen on that journey? They'd already been traveling together, their characters had reached some kind of understanding, and there didn't seem to be much further for that relationship to go.

What Bella wanted here was the artifact. What Nivvy wanted, now, was to prove that he was still a useful companion. I could have them travel together and throw more obstacles in their way. But Bella really wanted to go get the artifact, and more importantly, it would be much more interesting to watch Nivvy explore the abilities and limitations of his new body on his own. And as it turned out, the hinge points of the plot of the story all end up centering around one character choosing to rescue or abandon another. I didn't know that when I made the decision to have Bella abandon Nivvy, but that worked out well. It was purely a plot decision, establishing the character of Bella as someone who valued self over others, setting up a more exciting second act.

That was also fortuitous, because the only person Nivvy knew who could help him was Zein, the hawk they'd hired as their guide. And I liked Zein and welcomed the chance to make them a larger part of the story.

I had honestly very little idea of how Nivvy would get back to Spire, let alone meet Bella at Lake Beatrice/Glædeligdal, but part of the fun in plotting that act was putting myself in Nivvy's place. With only his wits, plus teeth, claws, and quickness, how would he escape the temple and convince Zein to leave Spire? I had not really set up much in the world that would work in his favor, but there were a lot of obstacles arrayed against him: his size, his animal body, his isolation from any support network.

The result was not only a fun adventure as Nivvy uses

stories to his advantage, but also an exploration of his character. Cut off from the identity he'd previously had, he had to discover who he was at his essence. Could he still be a thief? Would he be a friend? That was the underlying exploration that made this plot branch even more satisfying.

I made that decision because it felt right for Bella's character and more interesting for Nivvy's, and it turned into a fun arc of the plot that worked well for the book. You don't always have to follow your outline if your instincts lead you in a different direction.

Exercise: Plot

Simple exercise here if you're stuck on your plot, basically a condensing of action items from the main section. This is also a good exercise to stop and do periodically to make sure you're not forgetting some character or another:

Make a list of all the major characters in your story. Next to each, write the goal they're trying to achieve at this point in the story, and then what action they would take to achieve it.

Now look down the list and see what goals are most interesting to you right now. Which ones conflict with other people's goals? Which ones open up the story more (e.g. which offer the most possibilities if they're completed, or if they fail); which ones align with where you want the story to go?

If that doesn't generate enough ideas for you, think about your setting. How have the characters' actions been affecting the world so far? What might be a consequence of one of those actions?

And then think about where the characters are and what could be the worst thing to happen to them right now. Is it time for a coincidence to get them into trouble?

If you still can't make progress here, then talk to a friend. Explain the plot so far and ask them to brainstorm ideas with you. Having another person look at your plot can be really helpful to generate ideas you haven't thought of—and sometimes those ideas are so obvious that you feel stupid for not having seen them. You're not! This has happened to me multiple times.

Above all, don't give up here.

Chapter Nineteen

Pacing

Pace Yourself

Plot is the engine that moves the story forward, but that doesn't mean the engine has to be going at full speed all the time. Readers need a break now and then, and the characters do too. Pacing can refer to this cycle of action and reaction, as well as to the higher-level distribution of action and reaction in the story in general.

The higher-level pacing should be worked out through planning structure, but it's worth going over again. Just from reading, you should have an instinctive sense for how the major scenes of the story should fall—i.e., not right next to each other. Part of the reason to use a defined structure, or a structure template, is to situate the major plot events at the correct points of the story. We wouldn't have the Pevensies discover Narnia and be plunged immediately into the battle against the Witch—

the story and stakes need time to develop (we will talk about stakes later).

But that's easier to visualize than the ebb and flow of action in the scenes of the story itself. There may be stretches of the story where what seems to flow from one action scene is the next and the next and the next, or you may have sent your characters on a journey in which nothing much happens except them talking to each other.

Action and Reaction

The concept of action and reaction is something I first remember hearing from Jim Butcher, author of the Dresden Files books. He said that whenever there's an action scene, it should be followed by a scene where the characters regroup and reflect on what's changed with that action. Again, this is not only for the characters' benefit but the readers'. Action scenes are fun and exciting, and reading one after the other after the other can be exhausting. An action scene is supposed to not only be exciting but to change something about the characters' goals or the world, and so it makes sense to take a beat after something has just changed to regroup and figure out where to go next. This doesn't have to be a long scene, but it's good to give everyone a breather before they jump right into the next action.

Pacing is hardest when writing a first draft, because you're experiencing the story in very very slow motion. It can take you a few days to write an action scene, and at the end of it you won't have the excited feeling your reader will have when they finish reading it; you'll be moving on to the next piece. It can make sense to go right to the next action piece, because you're not feeling the rhythms of the story as a reader here.

As a result, pacing is often something you can address later, when you're going through your first revision phase. When you read through your draft, you'll feel the pace of the action and reaction, and you can see where you need to slow down or speed up the action. It's also an area where beta readers can help you out, because they'll be feeling the story as a reader for the first time, not as close to it as you are.

While you're writing, if you have the chance to skim back through what you've written, you can approximate how it will feel to your readers. Some writers like to do that while they're drafting and others don't; it all depends on what works with your process. In the meantime, though, a general pattern of "action, then reaction" will serve you pretty well.

It's worth mentioning that there's no one correct way to pace your story. Action-Reaction is a good model to start from, but every author has their own feel for how a story should be paced. Some authors will give you a fast-paced adventure; others will have long meditative stretches. The more you write, the more you'll find the pacing that appeals to you. As you read through other people's work, pay attention to the pacing. Remember, too, that "reaction" scenes need to be engaging, but they're engaging not because of external events, but because of how the character relationships and goals are changing as a result of the previous scene.

Other Concepts of Pacing

Pacing can also cover other aspects of the story. How quickly do you dole out information about the story? How quickly does the character adapt and change? There aren't basic "action-reaction" rules for these kinds of pacing issues, but they are things to be aware of as you're going through the story.

Part of the way to engage your readers is with little mysteries throughout the story. Elizabeth Bear, in a lecture, likened it to a backpack, with each mystery giving the pack a bit of weight. You want the pack to have some weight, or else it feels insubstantial and it doesn't sit well, but you don't want to put too much weight in it or the reader will get tired and set it down. So add a little mystery and a little weight, then reveal a piece of information and take out a little weight. I like this analogy because when the pacing is off, I can feel the weight of all the questions I have that haven't been answered yet. I start to get impatient with the story because my context is slipping away. The characters are forging forward and maybe making story progress, but I don't feel like there's progress, because I'm still wondering when this character's obliquely referenced trauma is going to come up, and why did that other character do that mysterious thing, and what's with the constant references to the world event that haven't come in yet, and when will the confusing orders from their superiors be explained? As the author, it can be difficult to see these issues if you know the answers to all these questions. You need to see the story from your reader's point of view—and that's where beta readers become very valuable, even after you get a feel for it yourself.

One method that I've seen used is to make a note in a separate document (or in your writing software, if it allows) every time you bring up a question or mystery that will be answered later, and every time you answer one. The questions should be weighted toward the beginning, then evening out until about two-thirds of the way through the book, where you shouldn't be introducing big questions anymore. The answers should have a reverse pattern, with a few small ones in the beginning maybe and then building to the end. There shouldn't be a point where the number of questions that haven't been answered is too large (find your own number, because it depends on whether they're big plot-important questions, character background questions, or smaller world building questions, and how many of each type you have); if it seems like the questions are building up without being answered, see if you can move things around to give readers that satisfying moment of having a question answered a little earlier.

Final Notes on Pacing

As an example of non-traditional pacing: Steve Kluger's brilliant *Last Days of Summer* is an epistolary novel told in letters and newspaper clippings (and occasionally cheating by including transcripts of conversations with guidance counselors and notes passed between apartments). Because the story is told in letters, nearly every scene is reaction—the characters taking the time to process and communicate about something that's happened. So one of the ways he keeps the reader engaged is by introducing mysteries about the two main characters. We begin with the protagonist in a juvenile detention facility telling some obvious lies about how he got injured, but enough truth leaks out that we can start to see a larger picture; the other main character, a professional baseball player, is introduced first through public news clippings before the protagonist writes to him. The relationship between the two builds through the letters, and meanwhile we are learning more about the characters and, as they react to world events, the world around them. But we never get to see an event happen in a narrative, because the characters live the events and then write about them afterwards. And this book still works, and works extremely well.

There are lots of ways to be aware of pacing in your story, and I know as we are going through all of this that it seems like a lot to be holding in your head in addition to all the stuff that is, you know, part of the actual *story* you're trying to write. The good news is, as I said above, most of these pacing issues become most noticeable in revision, when the story has already taken shape and you can worry about other things. So in your first draft, go by feel, but don't stress too much about it. You'll get to it later.

Summary Points

• The pacing of a story is hard to manage in a first draft, but a good start is to have a reaction scene after each action scene, time for the characters and reader to process what's just happened.

• The pacing of how you dole out information about the world and characters is also important. Leaving mysteries for the readers to try to figure out—but not too many at a time—is a way to make them feel more interested in the story.

Example: Pacing

Rather than pull an example of text from *The Price of Thorns*, I'm going to talk about pacing and how I structured the two halves of the second act. The act starts and ends in Scarlet's volcano, but a lot changes in between.

Nivvy has just heard Bella tell the story of drowning a kingdom, and during his theft he's been caught and turned into a weasel. This was an action-heavy scene, so I followed it with some processing. Nivvy realizes that now he has to justify his usefulness to Bella, and when a conversation fails to do that, he decides to act. He ventures into the dining hall, where we have another action scene.

That's followed by reflection when he gets caught and imprisoned, and finally we come back to action when he works to convince a visitor to the temple to break him out of his cage. He reflects on the next stage of his journey when he arrives in Spire and has to convince Zein to come with him, and then their journey north is time for further reflection. It ends dramatically, with more action, and Nivvy goes on to the lake by himself after processing that action. His adventure in the lake takes us to the midpoint, a very dramatic turn of events that will require a lot of processing.

After that, there's some minor action—Nivvy has to rescue Zein—but the rest of the second act is largely processing and buildup. I wanted to talk about that from a pacing standpoint because I've already mentioned that the "uneventful storytelling journey" didn't fit in the first half of the second act as well as it fits in the second half, so I wanted to talk about why that is (from my perspective).

The action of the midpoint shakes up the story so much that I thought it could bear a few chapters of reflection. And what's more, this was a good place to dive into the theme of storytelling a bit more. By this point in the story, Nivvy has now heard three more versions of how the kingdom was drowned—four total—and no two of them agree. What's more, he is traveling with Scarlet, who has very clear opinions about stories. As a result, much of the three chapters between Zein's rescue and the volcano reprise are taken up with stories and discussions of stories. This was (to me) a fun way to indulge in some reflection, because each story contains a little bit of action, even if there are no stakes to the characters.

What's more, over the course of these chapters, Scarlet is trying to convince Nivvy to challenge Bella. Her motivations for this aren't clear at first, but eventually are fully revealed over the course of the second act. This was one puzzle I used (a light one, admittedly) to keep the readers engaged.

Still, with all that, the chapters felt like they needed a little juice, mostly because Bella, the main antagonist, wasn't present. She'd left Nivvy with something like a threat that she expected him to rejoin her, but then she'd vanished from the story. So in order to reignite her threat and add a little excitement to the chapters, I added a scene in which she reaches out to Nivvy in a dream to remind him that she expects him to rejoin her. This brought her threat back to the forefront and also revealed to Nivvy that it would be harder to hide from her than he'd thought it would be.

Finally we arrive at the volcano and Nivvy has made his decision—but here, Bella attacks them, and there's another action scene, followed by a reflection that takes us into the third act.

I wanted to discuss this because the two halves of the second act are an example of how you can use the action-reflection model. The first half follows it very closely; the second half doesn't. For me, the second half was a time to synthesize a lot of what had been happening, because I was leading up to a big decision on Nivvy's part, and he had to process not only the change in his world (he had gotten his human body back, but the price of that was Bella demanding his service) but also his expanded knowledge about what went into stories. He'd now seen that events could be changed depending on the effect the storyteller wanted, and for someone whose ambition at the beginning of the book was to be in stories, that was also something he needed to think about. It doesn't come up much on the page, but hearing all of Scarlet's stories and talking to her and Zein about the state of world included some of that as well.

So the pacing I talked about in the previous section is a good rule of thumb, but there may be cases where you stray from that model. That's okay! If it feels right for the story, go ahead. Your beta readers will tell you if your story drags or needs rests. And as I said, you'll develop your own instincts as you write more.

Exercise: Pacing

Doing an exercise around pacing can be tricky, because it's a concept that covers long stretches of the book. I can't ask you to write a bunch of scenes to experiment with pacing. But what I can do is suggest that you take a high-level view of your story and see what you can glean from that.

You can do this either with scenes you've already written or with scenes from your outline. Jot down a quick sentence describing each scene in order. In this case, a scene is a segment of your story that has a beginning, middle, and end. It's up to you to delineate those. For example, you might have a section of your story in which your character sits down with three people for short conversations. If this is a job interview composed of three conversations, you might treat this all as one scene. But if it's three separate job interviews, you might treat it as three different scenes. It's up to you to figure out what's part of a scene and what isn't, and there's no wrong answer to it.

With each scene, add some note as to how long it is. It doesn't have to be exact word count, especially if you haven't written it yet, but some idea of how much time you'll be spending on that scene. Maybe "short, medium, long," or something like that.

Now go down the list and write down "action" or "reaction" next to each one. This should be pretty straightforward, but I'll talk a bit about what I mean by those terms. Action scenes are higher-energy; there is tension, events move quickly, and often there are larger implications for the story. A goal is achieved or an obstacle is overcome, and the path of the characters moving forward is altered, if only a bit. Reaction scenes are scenes where there is less tension, and the characters process what has changed as a result of the action scene.

(A side note: these definitions underscore another point that's worth lingering on. When you have a high-tension, active scene, like a fight or a sex scene or a chase, it should have some effect on the trajectory of the story. A big fight that doesn't change anything for the characters may feel exciting, but it ends up being rather dull for the readers. To take an example from movies, if *The Rise of Skywalker* felt ploddy to you despite having a lot of active scenes, it's because very few of those middle scenes had any lasting effect on the characters. Every step in the fetch quests just brings them one step closer to the end goal without affecting the story very much. Occasionally there will be events that seem to affect the story, major changes to characters, but— sorry for spoilers to a 5+ year old movie—those changes are rarely permanent and never require any of the other characters to process the changes or alter their course in any way. As a consequence, the less active scenes afterwards should be reaction scenes, but they end up just being map-reading to find the next destination because there's not really anything to process.)

Look at the alternation of action and reaction in your scenes. How well are they balanced? Do you have a lot of action scenes in a row? This might be a sign that they don't change things for the plot as much as they should. Do you have a string of reaction scenes? Maybe it's worth breaking them up.

This is a good exercise to return to when you've finished the story (because you will add and remove scenes) and after each revision. Your beta readers will tell you how they feel your pacing is, but if you can give them something with a firm foundation, it will be easier to fine tune, rather than asking them to do this kind of larger-scale work you can do yourself.

Chapter Twenty

Villains

The Bad Guys: Antagonists

We have talked a lot about the obstacles you need to put in front of your protagonist, about the action and reaction they have to go through, and about the pressure put on them to change their ways. So now it's time to spend a little bit of time giving those obstacles and pressure a name and a face. Let's talk about antagonists.

I prefer the term "antagonist" to "villain," just as I prefer "protagonist" to "hero," because not all protagonists are heroes, and not all antagonists are villains. In a romance, the "antagonist" can be the love interest who pushes the protagonist out of their comfort zone and to a space where they can accept love and a potential relationship (there can also be a more traditional villain antagonist in romances). The role in the story is the opposition to the protagonist, not evil or world domination.

Antagonist as Force

Of course, in fantasy stories (which are tilted toward morality plots of Good vs Evil), the antagonist is often evil. And there are some very good evil antagonists out there in the canon —Sauron, the White Witch (in the first Narnia book), Pennywise the Clown, Grendel—whose evil is never really interrogated or explained. They all want some kind of power that involves the death or subjugation of the hero. There is this effective kind of antagonist that I call a "force" rather than a character.

In many cases they can be embodied in a person, but in their most extreme examples they are literally a force of some kind. This is most common in horror stories (zombies) or disaster stories (a volcano): an antagonist that forces the hero to take actions they normally wouldn't, but not an antagonist that can be reasoned with. This type of antagonist has to present a unique challenge to the protagonist, something that: (1) they of all people are best equipped to deal with, but (2) they have to unlock that potential within themself.

You have some license with this kind of antagonist. You can make a zombie horde do whatever you want them to do, within the world building you've set up for them, to push the protagonist into the pressure you need them to feel in order for them to change. Sauron can mobilize any number of creatures, Pennywise can conjure any number of disturbing scenarios. But the endgame with this kind of antagonist is a personal, internal triumph of the protagonist. They dig deep and find something within themself; they overcome a personal trauma; they discover something new about life and the world they live in; etc.

These are all good and worthwhile stories! But it's important to know what kind of story you're trying to write as you develop your antagonist.

Antagonist as Foil

The second type of antagonist is the "foil." They're a character who has made different choices than the protagonist and highlights the choices available to the protagonist. In Lord of the Rings, Gollum fits this mold. As the foil to Frodo, he's the character who has succumbed to the spell of the Ring, which Frodo is trying to resist doing, and he serves as a vision of the future that awaits Frodo if he fails. General Woundwort of *Watership Down* is, like Hazel, a leader of a burrow that is under threat from humans. But his response to the threat is to try to become more like the humans, a betrayal of his own nature (as viewed in the context of the book). Hazel has a chance to follow that path, but elects to take the harder path of remaining true to his rabbit nature.

With this kind of antagonist, you have to think about them as a character. This category is where people want to see "believable villains," antagonists whose motivations are understandable. They are fully realized characters, or should be, and an interesting thought exercise is to look at your story from the villain's point of view. Does it make sense in that way?

(To take an aside about movies rather than books, this is part of the reason we find so many Marvel villains with the same powers as the heroes; it's a shortcut to show "this person had the same opportunities but took a different path.")

It's common in fantasy books to have both kinds of villains, because often fantasy books include an evil power that is the force behind the threat but rarely engages directly with the characters (until, perhaps, the very end), and then someone closer to the protagonist who is also trying to derail their quest. Often the closer villain is aligned with the greater power, but not always—Gollum and Sauron both want to stop Frodo's quest, but for different purposes of their own.

This is where I think there was a misstep in the Harry Potter books.[9] Voldemort worked very well as a force in the early

---

[9] If you have somehow managed not to be aware of this, the author of the Harry Potter books as of the time of this writing has for years been using her fame and fortune to promote anti-trans policies and beliefs, doing a great deal of harm to the trans community and their friends. I'm using this example because I am hoping you will already be familiar with the story, as many people are. If you aren't, please do not go out and buy the books or movies, or make any purchases that will benefit the author and her anti-trans crusade. Just move on to the next example.

books, with Draco as the foil, and then Rowling tried to convert Voldemort into a foil with a whole look into his backstory. The idea was: here's a kid who could've turned out like Harry, but he made different choices. This is also set up in the first book, to be fair, when the key to defeating Voldemort is Harry's mother's love, a thing Voldemort doesn't understand. But it's wielded as a barrier rather than something that strikes at his character.

A foil type of antagonist will often try to turn the hero to the wrong path. They are most likely to confront the hero and tempt them off their path, an interaction that isn't available from a force antagonist.

Where we see the biggest difference between a force and foil is in how the antagonist is defeated. A force is weathered or turned aside; you can't convince a volcano not to explode, but you can get out of its path. Similarly, you can't convince Sauron not to destroy Middle-Earth, but you can destroy his most powerful artifact to stop his plans from happening. With a foil, you defeat them by challenging the choices they made, or through proving that your choices were the correct ones. Frodo, at the last moment, suffers a moment of doubt, but because he kept his friend Sam by his side (Gollum, when he was Smeagol, murdered his friend, and has tried to drive Sam and Frodo apart), he can be rescued and redeemed. Gollum, giving in to the power of the ring, dies because of it.

Harry's defeat of Voldemort, by contrast, is something of a mess. If Voldemort is a foil, who spurned the idea of family while Harry has embraced it, you would expect that Harry's family would be instrumental in defeating Voldemort. If he's a force, you would expect Harry to find a weakness to exploit—something like the protection of his mother's love he had in the first book. While it's true that Harry's allies play a part in the victory (killing Voldemort's snake and final Horcrux) and that his self-sacrificing nature also contributes heavily, these incidents are spread out. The final battle is made possible by them, but it still comes down to Harry's strength and an odd quirk of wand magic. It's...not a very satisfying climax to their struggle, at least to me. Meanwhile, Draco, who had been Harry's foil, has a redemption arc in the last book but otherwise doesn't really play much of a part in it.

Defeat for an antagonist doesn't have to mean death or destruction, of course. "Defeat" in a romance can mean giving in to love. In a series, an antagonist can be defeated only to retreat and prepare for the next story. But whatever their defeat means, you should put some thought into what kind of antagonist they are, and make sure their defeat is meaningful to the protagonist and to the reader.

Summary Points

- An antagonist should be the perfect pressure to challenge your protagonist to change.
- An antagonist can be a force—something like zombies, an earthquake, a giant eyeball in a tower, that can't be reasoned with or reckoned with. In this case the protagonist succeeds by finding some strength within themself to overcome the peril the antagonist presents.
- An antagonist can be a foil, another character who tries to tempt the hero to the wrong path. In this case, the protagonist succeeds by proving the worth of the "right" path, often showing up the antagonist's mistakes.

Example: Villains

The main villain of *The Price of Thorns* is Bella. There are times when she operates as a force, but she is for the most part a foil to Nivvy. He starts out the story convinced that he is in the right and everyone else has wronged him, and the lesson he has to learn is to accept others into his life and value them. In the language of the world, he's focused on his own story but has to understand that he's part of everyone else's story too.

Bella, by contrast, is sure that she's the main character of everyone's story. She abandons Nivvy, even though she has been developing a friendship with him, because she worries he'll slow down her quest to regain her power. When she has her power back, she demands he follow her even though he expressly says he needs to rescue a friend. The way he "defeats" her in this case is to imply that she needs him, which causes her to recoil and leave. She can't conceive of needing anybody.

Throughout the book, though she is present only really in the first act and then briefly at the midpoint and climax, she is trying to force Nivvy to be part of her story, a fate he recognizes and tries hard to avoid. He starts out wanting to be the hero of the story as well, but putting his friends in danger during his adventure reminds him that he does need others in a way Bella can't.

There isn't really a moment where Nivvy realizes, "I don't want to be like Bella," at least not in the text, but the journey he goes on highlights the opportunities Bella lost or ignored. He finds a family, which is the thing she's been searching for, by taking a different path than she does, and ultimately, her insistence on being the hero of her story is her undoing.

Exercise: Villains

The first exercise to try when you're working with your villain is to decide if they're a force or a foil, a Sauron or a Gollum. How much do they interact with the main character outside of the obstacles they put in the way? Are they trying to convince them to change their ways, or just trying to stop them from getting to their goal?

If your villain is a force, look at the obstacles they're putting in the way and figure out how they enable your protagonist to grow. What is the protagonist's struggle, and how do these obstacles highlight those weaknesses and force the protagonist to address them? And then, how is this villain defeated? It should be, somehow, through the protagonist addressing their weaknesses.

If your villain is a foil, imagine the story if they were the main character. What actions would they take? How would they view your protagonist? How do they try to push your protagonist along a different path, the one that aligns with their views? And finally, how does their own weakness lead to their defeat?

If you're struggling with one or the other of these, try changing the way you view the villain. Would they work better as the other kind?

Chapter Twenty-One

Stakes

Stakes: What Is It Worth?

I've talked here and there about the stakes of the story, and it's worth giving that concept its own section. The stakes are the reason the character goes on the journey (the reason the character does the story, I like to say). There are many different kinds of stakes you can bring into your story: There are external stakes, the consequences that will affect the whole world if the protagonist doesn't succeed. There are internal stakes, the consequences that are personal to the protagonist. Both of those are distinct from the driving force of the character arc, the push for the character to change.

External Stakes

When people talk about the "stakes" of a story, they are

usually referring to the external stakes, whatever is at risk in the story. In fantasy especially, but also commonly in science fiction (and presently in that fusion of the two we call "superhero stories"), what's often at risk is the world, or humanity, or the universe, or all the universes. This is especially common in a series where the stakes might start small, but they have to get larger with each installment. Some people feel that fighting for the same level of stakes over and over again would be boring, and perhaps it would be, but inflation of stakes is also a problem.

Usually when the world is in danger, there needs to be some smaller personal goal for the protagonist. Not that saving the world isn't important (as The Tick once said, "That's where I keep all my stuff!"), but it's a very big and abstract goal. We can see in our everyday life how it is harder to motivate people to take action towards a large, abstract goal than a small, personal goal—for example, "stop the war" is a big, abstract goal unless you know someone fighting in it, and then "save my friend/family member" becomes an urgent personal goal.

Similarly, though the whole world would be in peril if Sauron regains the Ring, Frodo motivates himself by imagining the Shire being overrun. Early on, the hobbits want to put the Ring into other people's care to destroy and return to the Shire, where they hope they will be left alone because they no longer have anything Sauron wants. They come to understand, soon enough, that no place in Middle-Earth will be safe if Sauron gets the Ring back.

Having an external goal and an internal goal also gives you the chance to put the two into opposition. How many times have you seen the plot device that the protagonist must choose between the life of someone close to them or the entire world? The entire movie *Avengers: Infinity War* is just that choice repeated over and over. This kind of choice forces the character to make a difficult choice about what's important to them, which is an engaging, dramatic story beat.

You don't have to have the external stakes be as big as the universe, or even the world. Personally, I think that world-scale stakes are often used when authors aren't sure the reader will believe that smaller stakes are enough to spur the character on their adventure. It's an easy sell on the back cover blurb too: "The world is in danger!"

If universe-sized stakes are the way you want to go, more power to you! I like working in a subjective universe the best, the universe of one particular character (or two, or three). Remember, if you are going universe-sized, that you should think about what specific part of the universe your character most desperately does not want to be destroyed. Thinking about the world ending is a big, abstract concept, and most people—and characters—will need something smaller to hold onto.

One of the ways to do that is to remind the characters (and the reader) about the external stakes from time to time. In The Lord of the Rings, as the characters move through the land gathering allies, they have to remind them of what might be lost, and in each case find the small, personal part of the larger stakes that the potential ally cares most about (for example, Merry and Pippin cannot convince Treebeard to lead the Ents to fight until they learn how many trees Saruman has destroyed). Subplots can reveal another part of the danger to the world, heightening the stakes for the character, or they can form a bond that is now in danger. In Patricia McKillip's Riddle-Master series, Morgon travels around the land forming close friendships with the land-rulers, and when the whole world is threatened, he is motivated by those bonds (as are the land-rulers themselves).

Want: The Tangible Reward (Internal Stakes)

A good story will ideally have a protagonist with both a want and a need. The want is the external motivation—the stakes—that impels the character to jump into the adventure. The rabbits want a home that's safe from humans; Arthur Dent wants to go home; the Pevensies want to defeat the White Witch and rescue Narnia from winter. The want can be grand or it can be very simple, but it has to be important to the protagonist, so important that they will take all the risks you get to write about in order to achieve it.

In a comedy, the want is often out of proportion to the adventure taken to achieve it (the internal stakes are greater than the external)—in *Right Ho, Jeeves*, Bertie Wooster just wants to help his friend propose to the girl he has a crush on, a plan which keeps going wrong but in which he's so invested, because of his reputation as the problem-solver of his group, that he keeps coming up with wilder and wilder plans to make it work.

In a mystery, the internal and external stakes are balanced. The want is usually to solve the murder because of the detective's reputation, attachment to the victim, or affinity for puzzles; the external stakes are that a murder might go unpunished. There can be other stakes in a mystery; in Conan Doyle's *The Sign of Four*, Watson is invested in the mystery but also desperately in love with Mary Morstan, and he cannot act on that until the mystery is solved. Fantasy stories often have grand world-scale wants, but there is a subgenre (low fantasy) where more small, personal stories are told in a fantasy setting. And sometimes, as in Lloyd Alexander's *The Book of Three*, the story can start small (Taran wants to bring the oracular pig Hen Wen back to the farm where he works) and grow larger.

The two things critical to any want in a story are: One, it has to be important to the protagonist. Two, by the end of the story, the reader should know whether the protagonist got what they wanted. So a want like "the protagonist wants revenge" is not a good one, because it relies too much on a subjective interpretation of revenge. "The protagonist wants revenge by getting the antagonist fired from his job" is better, because we know for sure whether the antagonist got fired or not. Whether that ends up being sufficient revenge is part of the character journey, but setting out to get someone fired is a tangible thing someone can achieve.

Arthur Dent wanting to go home seems like an impossible want, because his home has been demolished. But that doesn't mean this is a bad choice for stakes for the story. It's a long-term goal, and it opens up the possibility of intermediate goals. For example, early on he decides that something that represents home for him is a really good cup of tea. His pursuit of this tea causes a lot of problems, but we sympathize because the tea is connected to home for him, so we understand that this is an important goal.

It's good practice to change the goal throughout the story.

Sometimes this means the original goal is abandoned, but sometimes it means that the characters are pursuing something else on the way to the larger goal. The reason we do this is to keep the reader engaged. Having the characters chase a far-off goal is important, but hard to keep interest in over the course of a novel. At the same time, you may not want your novel to devolve into a series of fetch quests, so it's important to make sure that each of the intermediate goals has stakes as well. They have to be significant to the character in some way more than just "we need a thing to get another thing."

It's also okay to end a story with the protagonist *not* getting what they want. Sometimes their journey shows them that what they thought they wanted isn't as important as they thought. Staying with Lloyd Alexander's Prydain series, in *The Black Cauldron*, Taran undertakes an adventure because he wants to be the hero who steals the terrible titular cauldron from the evil wizard who's using it to create deathless zombie warriors. But his companion is driven even harder by the lure of fame. In the end Taran does not get to be the hero, but he understands that it wasn't something he should want.

What he learns over the course of the story is that heroism is not always about the great grand flashy stories, but about sacrifice. That's the lesson he needed to learn—which is what I meant when I talked about a character's "need."

Need: The Personal Growth

We'll talk more about character journeys and how characters get pushed along them in another section, but I do want to talk about the need. It's not part of the tangible stakes, but the character's personal growth is important to the story. There are physical obstacles that keep the character from getting what they want, but what's really stopping them (from a story standpoint) is that they haven't learned this lesson yet. In some sense, the character can want something, but until they learn the lesson, they don't "deserve" it. It may be that getting what they want seems unrelated to learning that lesson—for example, the rabbits in *Watership Down* find their home after they've traveled enough, not because personal growth gives them an insight, but their growth is what enables them to keep that home in the face of the subsequent threats they face.

So when you're thinking about how to motivate your character in your story, make sure the goal is something important to them, but something that's out of their reach for reasons beyond the physical—they don't understand what it means, or don't appreciate it properly, or want it for the wrong reasons. If the character can't overcome these obstacles, not only will they not achieve their goal, but the world will lose something of value. That makes it much more satisfying when they finally achieve—or realize they don't need to achieve—their goal, benefiting themselves and the world.

Summary Points

• The stakes are the reason the character and the reader care about the outcome of the story. What will be lost if the character fails? It has to be important enough to motivate the character and keep the reader interested.

• When people talk about "the stakes," they usually mean the external stakes, the consequences to the world at large. In a series, there's often a perception that the stakes for the next installment have to be bigger than the last for the story to be as exciting.

• If the stakes are too large, it's helpful to have a smaller personal interest for the character. For example, our interest in a war on the other side of the world becomes much more focused if we know someone engaged in that conflict.

• There are also internal stakes, which is the "want" that motivated the character at the beginning of the story.

• Not really part of stakes, but paired with the "want," is the "need": what the character needs to learn in order to grow as a person.

Example: Stakes

In *The Price of Thorns*, when we meet Nivvy, his immediate goal is to get off the wheel he's been tied to. But even in the first chapter we get a sense of what's important to him: his reputation, proving himself to his community. He wants to get back to his Thieves Guild, or at least be part of a Thieves Guild again. And along with that, maybe even more important, is being someone stories are told about.

The importance of this is underscored because he's alone in this town, and being without his community has led him to this predicament he starts the story in. So we're shown why Nivvy wants these things as well as told through his thoughts.

But once he accepts Bella's job, that goal slips into the background as he tries to plan out how to get there. He takes her direction on going to steal the magic item they need—and then he's changed into a weasel, and the whole energy of the story changes. Bella abandons him, and now he has to figure out how to get back to her (his new goal) in order to be the kind of thief stories are told about. I've talked before about how changing this goal made the story more dynamic, but here you can see how the stakes have changed: initially he was getting along okay, but what he wanted was to be a celebrated thief. Now he's a former-human, and his prospects if he doesn't become famous are even dimmer (he knows from talking to Zein and from his old friend who was changed what life is life for former-humans). What's more, he suspects Bella is able to change him back, and nothing else in the world can (or will). In the first act, he could potentially abandon Bella at any time; he thinks he can trick her into signing a contract for him that will get him back into the Thieves Guild, so he holds on to that hope. But now he is choosing between an adventure and a life worse than one he's ever known. The stakes have gotten higher.

At the midpoint, the stakes change again. Nivvy now has charge of Zein and Scarlet, and once again he's at a point where he thinks he might be able to walk away from the adventure— he wants to walk away from the adventure, in fact. But Bella is pursuing him, and events convince him not only that he won't be able to evade her forever, but that she is an evil that needs to be fought. And Scarlet adds stakes to his decision; she tells him that Bella may well use up all the magic in the world. Now the stakes are not just for his life, but for the fate of the world— although Nivvy constantly tries to bring the stakes back to smaller, personal matters. If magic goes away, he wants to know, will his former-human friends survive? Scarlet thinks so, and that makes the matter less urgent for Nivvy. What finally adds to the stakes is that Scarlet may not survive—and that Bella is undoubtedly killing people up north, deaths Nivvy doesn't feel a connection to but which nevertheless weigh on his conscience. Here is where the theme of stories comes into play: heroes in the stories go off and do the right thing, and once Nivvy identifies what that is, it's harder for him to justify stepping aside. It would mean not just giving up on being famous, but giving up on all the heroes he's identified with his whole life.

In the final act of the book, he is aware that he may be putting his own life in danger, but the alternative is living in a way that doesn't feel honest to him anymore—either running away or serving Bella. The stakes here are his integrity and his spirit, which can only be served by taking an active role in fighting Bella.

Exercise: Stakes

Thinking about the stakes of your story can feel redundant sometimes—"what's at stake is that Frodo has to destroy the Ring or Sauron will regain its power and rule the world, that's the whole plot of the story, duh"—but especially here in the middle of the second act, it's a topic that can be worth revisiting.

It can be easy to lose yourself in the immediacy of what the characters are going through, especially if that's not apparently connected to the main goal. Your story has also evolved, and now that you know more about your characters' journey, you can evaluate how well the stakes fit.

Thinking about the stakes of your story means asking what's important to your protagonist at this point and in the larger scheme. I talked about how stakes can progress in stories, and how larger stakes can be supplemented with smaller but more immediate stakes.

So your exercise is to make a list of what might go wrong if the character's mission fails—basically explicitly write out the stakes. As you do that, take some time to think about what else is important to the character. Has anything been revealed over the course of your writing? What else might go wrong in the world? Are the things you have written down the most important, or at least important enough to make this journey worthwhile? ("What else can go wrong?" is a question every storyteller should ask at least at one point in their story.)

Now, you don't always want to pile more and more dramatic stakes on the story. Every adventure can't be about saving the world or the universe, no matter what Marvel tells you. Of course, one of the most important things to your character would be "does existence continue on?" But you can go a step or two below that, and that involves knowing your character, which you should be fast becoming an expert in. What means the most to your character emotionally? Are they adventuring for their own sake, or to protect a loved one, or for a cause? What else is in their life that might matter more to them? Have they formed attachments over the course of the story that could add to the stakes? This is a good place to explore whether their character growth has led them to value something they might not have at the start of the story.

Your story's stakes might be easy, but it's always worth taking some time to evaluate and make sure that your character needs to pursue their goal. It's worth repeating: if your character could walk away from the adventure, then your reader is likely to as well.

Chapter Twenty-Two

Midpoint

Whoa! We're halfway there!

The midpoint of a story, halfway through the second act, isn't always a moment of significance as large as the ones that propel the protagonist into the story and resolve the final conflict, but especially given the length of the second act, I find it useful to put a significant story event at the midpoint (this is a point Barbara Webb and Kij Johnson stress in their Novel Architects workshop). We talked in the pacing section about the need to keep the reader engaged throughout the story, and changing things up at the midpoint is a way to do that. In five act structure, the midpoint is the climax (in *Romeo and Juliet*, it would be where Romeo kills Tybalt—this alters the stakes and goals of the story).

Especially in our modern era, I feel it's important to pace a story for shorter attention spans. Immense novels still succeed today—see George R.R. Martin—but often they include multiple points of view and storylines, punctuated with enough change-of-goal events to keep the reader's interest. In an average length novel (90,000 words or so), the second act is going to be a large part of the book—over half of it in some cases. It's a tough ask for a reader to get through half the book without anything major happening. It can be done, but if you can figure out a way to break up that second act, it will usually help. (You could also fill the second act with subplots/side quests if you want, but this section will still be helpful as you decide how to structure and order them.)

In terms of the character arc, a midpoint event is also a place to put more pressure on the character. The general movement of a character arc is that your protagonist confronts the problem or obstacle the way they always have, because that's worked for them so far in their life. Over the course of the story, they're going to learn that they have to change, because this problem can't be solved unless they do.

There are a lot of tools we as authors can use to show our characters the error of their ways, but one of them is a spectacular failure. The protagonist is chugging along, thinking that they're handling things well and it's almost there, and then bang! Everything collapses around them and there is no more denying that their initial strategy isn't working (well, there is a little denying, but more on that in the character arc section). In *Romeo and Juliet*, for example, Romeo's duel with Tybalt shows him that he can't love Juliet and still abide by the feud between their families.

Along with the inciting incident and the climactic battle mentioned above, the midpoint is one of three places in the story where the major goals of the protagonist can (and should) change. At the beginning of the story, the protagonist has a personal goal that's important to them; at the end of the first act, the protagonist becomes aware of the main conflict and their goal is to resolve it. After the final conflict, the protagonist's goal changes again for the third act because the conflict has been resolved.

Those two, the first and last, are pretty straightforward as story beats go. The protagonist gets into the story, they get out of the story. So what happens at the midpoint? How do you alter the goals of a story before it's over? There are a few common options to get you started thinking about that.

Midpoint Story Beats: Some Suggestions

• False Victory. Here the protagonist thinks they've resolved the conflict only to find that they haven't; the real conflict is bigger than they knew, or their supposed resolution ends up not working. I always think of Beowulf for the classic example of this, where Beowulf slays Grendel and thinks that's the end of it, but then Grendel's mother proves to be the real challenge. Beowulf the poem does not necessarily follow three-act structure, but that twist is a perfect example of a false victory. In terms of story pacing, the false victory often comes as a release of tension after building up to a confrontation of some kind, and the release of tension it provides is immediately undercut with the uneasiness of realizing that the job isn't done.

• Real Antagonist Revealed. Often the midpoint comes with some kind of larger revelation that the quest isn't what it appeared to be. The protagonist might not have known the shadowy figure behind the thing they're fighting, but here at the midpoint is a good place for that antagonist to reveal themself—or be revealed. A variant of this is to have the goal itself be revealed to be larger or more significant than was originally thought—this is related to back when we were talking about stakes and said that stakes can be added. The midpoint is a good place to do that. This kind of reveal is a mirror of the false victory in terms of pacing, as it often comes when there's little tension and the protagonist feels like everything is going along smoothly. A big reveal at the midpoint dramatically increases the tension, as the protagonist's plans are ruined.

• Protagonist Suffers Loss. The arc of the story can also be changed at the midpoint if the protagonist's circumstances change. The false victory is one aspect of this; another is for the protagonist to lose something important that reframes how they look at the journey and changes their goals. If you've read a story in which a beloved character dies halfway through, you know what I mean here.

• World Changes. The goal can also be reset by a large change in the world. It's best if the change in the world results from the protagonist's actions—such as the false victory. This change in the world means that what the protagonist thought they were trying to achieve has also changed.

If you try, you can certainly imagine a midpoint event that includes all of the above ideas. Some of them have overlap in their conception and effect. You can also use them at different points in the story, not just the midpoint, if you're looking for ways to punch up your story. But the false victory especially is very commonly used at the midpoint because it is a big, significant thing that comes late enough in the story to feel climactic, but early enough to give the protagonist time to re-evaluate their strategy before the story ends.

And from the reader's standpoint, it shakes things up enough to keep their interest in the story high. It can also help you, the author, keep your interest in the story up as you work through the famously difficult and tedious (at times) second act.

Summary Points

• The second act is the longest act (in three-act structure) and breaking it up is helpful. The midpoint of the story, halfway through the second act, is one of three places where there's an opportunity to make a major change to the protagonist's goal. Unlike the other two (the inciting incident, pulling the character into the story, and the climactic battle, resolving it), there's less structure around that change, so you have more freedom.

• Some ideas for changes—you can use any of these or more than one in combination—are: a false victory (that turns out to be a failure and makes things worse), a real antagonist revealed, a loss suffered by the protagonist, or a major change to the world.

Example: Midpoint

In *The Price of Thorns*, the midpoint is a really important hinge point for the story. It contains a false victory, antagonist reveal, and I might argue a change to the world, all of which will come into play in the second half of the second act. Nivvy has a chance to accomplish the quest he set out to do, to help Bella get the artifact that will restore her to her throne, and potentially make him human again—a longshot, as this has not happened in his known world for decades. We don't really know what to expect from the story after that. Presumably she will go off to retake her kingdom; Nivvy can go with her but has also left Zein in some danger. She might dangle the promise of returning his humanity until she's queen again.

But when he retrieves the artifact for her, she uses it to steal the power from a djinn, which allows her to make him human again. Now his situation has changed: he has more power and agency in the world. But he's also made Bella much more powerful, which as we will see quickly is not a good thing.

So he's faced with a choice here: continue to serve Bella, or follow his friendship with Zein. It's not always necessary to have a character choice at the midpoint, but it does strengthen the moment, even if in this case it's not much of a choice. Underlying it, though, is Nivvy's character journey. He wants to be a hero, someone stories are told about, and if he wants to follow that path, the best decision is to go with Bella. A newly-powerful queen, riding off on a dragon to conquer her ancestral kingdom, is the perfect companion for a thief who wants to be in stories. But this moment is also an inflection point in Nivvy's journey. There is some allure to going with Bella, but she's scary and pretty definitely evil, whereas Zein is Nivvy's friend and is in trouble because of him. So this is also a moment where Nivvy decides he would rather be the sort of person who goes back to help a friend than the kind who joins up with a powerful witch for his own glory.

There are two reasons I can think of that I built the midpoint this way. First off, as I've mentioned before, the relationship between Nivvy and Bella wasn't interesting to me anymore. Originally I had Nivvy accompany her to the kingdom, realize there that she's evil as she massacred the royal family, and then figure out how to get out of it. But the more I wrote, the more I realized that, well, I liked Zein better than Bella, and I wanted Nivvy to also. The idea of pairing him with Bella again didn't offer much to me in terms of character development because he was already making the turn away from her. But to have him pick another path ("maybe I can just live a good life with friends") and have that path also run into problems—namely, that he bought that peace at the price of giving Bella free rein to destroy a kingdom—felt like a much richer opportunity for character growth. The whole arc of Nivvy's journey (I will talk about this more in the next section) is learning what it means to be a hero, and this felt like the more interesting path.

The second reason is that I wanted to mess with reader expectations a little. The story had been set up as "Nivvy and Bella's Excellent Adventure," and the logical way for the story to go was for Bella to get the artifact and then for Nivvy to rejoin her on her way north to regain her kingdom. But I like to surprise readers when I can. The trick to surprising readers is that the surprise has to be something that still makes sense; you can derail the story from out of nowhere, but it's likely to leave readers unmoored. In this case, I think most readers expected Nivvy to stay with Bella once he'd retrieved the artifact (a couple beta readers even told me as much), so setting up a situation where he'd changed enough to make a different choice felt like the more interesting story path.

And Nivvy has changed. The first part of the second act he spends as a former-human, with little power or agency, giving him more sympathy for how the world treats some people. He sees Zein through a new lens; previously they were a useful guide, but now they are a fellow member of an underprivileged class, with the same problems he has, and so their general demeanor strikes Nivvy differently, their friendship deeper and more important as someone who didn't abandon him when he had nothing to offer them.

So at this midpoint of the story, Nivvy decides that maybe he doesn't need to be a hero after all. Or if he does, it's only for the people who really care about him. This sets the rest of the second act on a different track, but as we will see shortly, it's not the end of his journey.

Exercise: Midpoint

Most of the exercises in this section have been centered around the story you're working on, but for this one I'd like to take a step back. Pick a few books you've recently read, or movies you've recently seen, and see if you can identify the event at the midpoint. If it falls into one of the categories I covered, great; if it doesn't, come up with your own category.

What you should take from it is: how does it change the protagonist's goal? How does it change the story? What character development does it signal in the protagonist?

Looking at the ways in which different writers break up their second acts can give you more ideas for doing the same in your own manuscripts. The midpoint is a great place to pause and say, "What might go differently here?"

Think back to talking about pacing, too, and ask yourself how these midpoint events break up the pacing of the book. Does it come at a point of high tension in the story as a release of that tension (this is often what a false victory looks like)? Does it come as a surprise in what seemed to be a lull in the story (this is often how you get a surprise reveal)? Looking at the pacing of your second act will help you figure out what kind of midpoint change will fit best there.

Chapter Twenty-Three

Character Development

Change is Difficult: Character Development

Characters are the lifeblood of a story. We talked way back in "character introductions" about engaging a reader by introducing them to a character who wants something, and one of the main ways readers engage with a story is by being invested in the characters of the story. Even in a plot-heavy story like a murder mystery, the reader wants to know which of the characters is a murderer.

But in a character-focused story, the character's journey is what the reader will be engaged with. In *The Lion, The Witch, and The Wardrobe*, readers want to know whether the White Witch will be defeated, but also whether Edmund will redeem himself. In Anne McCaffrey's *Dragonsong*, one of the first fantasy books I ever read, I loved the fire lizards but more than anything I wanted to know whether Menolly would find joy again after a hand injury robbed her of the ability to play music. N.K. Jemisin's Broken Earth series is about the remaking of a world, but the remaking happens because of the experiences of the main characters, and the fate of the world ultimately comes down to what the characters have learned.

So you want your characters to have an interesting journey, to endure trials, overcome obstacles, and learn something that will be of value to them and critical to the story. What can they learn? That's the point of the journey and in some cases the point of the whole story.

A Message, Not a Lesson

One rarely writes a story so singularly focused as to communicate just one thing; often it's a combination of many things, such as "I had this neat idea for how the world might work" and "I think this situation is interesting to explore." But one of the things a story is often (in my case, almost always) about is "I have learned something about how to live my life and I want to pass that on to you." I know that makes it sound like every story is a Very Special Episode, but that's not what it means. What characterizes a Very Special Episode is that the whole story is transparently about a single issue or lesson. Most stories are about a main character (or characters) coping with an unusual situation. How do they get through the obstacles and difficulties? By learning, changing, and growing. Think about how many adventure stories contain the lesson "what it means to be a hero," sometimes explicitly stated. Most people in the current age want to follow a character who grows and changes over the course of the story. That's what the character journey is about: presenting that growth and making it feel real so that the reward feels earned.[10]

---

[10] One of the fantasy series I read as a teen had an ensemble cast, and one of them was a character the author clearly thought was a Cool Guy. He went through the story just Being Cool and kept getting more and more power and success and never learned anything or was seriously challenged to grow. I hated him so much it almost ruined the series for me.

By the time you get into the second act, your character should be well along their journey. The second act is where things get really frustrating for them, possibly also dangerous depending on your setting, and they begin to realize that they need to change something about themselves in order to move forward. This is a good place to stop and take stock about where your character started, where they are, and where you want them to end up.

As I have been going through books looking for examples, I know that especially in fantasy and science fiction, character journeys aren't always at the forefront. This changed somewhat in the sixties with the advent of writers like LeGuin and Delany, and has changed even more in the last decade or two (I think, anecdotally), but you can still find plenty of SFF that focuses on the world building, on the quest, on the exploration of space, on the advancement of science. It's fine if the character journey isn't the primary focus of your story, but that doesn't mean it shouldn't get *any* attention. As I have mentioned, world building is most effective when revealed through interaction with characters. In one of the first SF novels I ever read, Anne McCaffrey's *Dragonflight*, the front-and-center plot is about an imminent threat returning to the world of Pern and a diminished culture of dragonriders remaining to fight it, but there is a strong subplot of romance and of how the main character(s) define their worth in society. The resolution of the plot also brings with it a sense of purpose and belonging that had been lacking for the characters.

The Journey Is The Point

I've talked about character journeys before in connection with the structure, with stakes, with the plot. These are all ways you guide the character journey, sometimes more sharply than at other times depending on how much you want to torture your characters. In *The Adventures of Tom Sawyer*, Tom and a friend play a game with a bug on their desk whereby they try to keep the bug on their side of the desk by putting obstacles in its way to guide its movement, never touching the bug directly. I think about guiding a character journey as a similar process, except that as the author, you are also controlling the bug, deciding where to go next in response to the obstacle you have placed in front of yourself. But it helps to have a bit of distance from the character, so you're not thinking "this is what I would do in this situation," but rather, "this is what my character would do."

The character's journey through your story is the movement from what they choose at the beginning of the story to what they choose at the end. Usually this is a change for the better; the character learns something that makes them a better person at the end of the story than they were at the beginning. Occasionally you may have a character journey explain how they got worse, if you want to do a villain origin story, but by and large when we write character-based fiction, we are trying to communicate to the reader a lesson we ourselves have learned through the story of a fictional character learning that same lesson. I have over and over again written stories about characters discovering that they alone get to determine their identity because I keep discovering that lesson for myself, and I find that I'm much happier when I am being myself. I want to help other people understand that, and so I keep writing stories where my characters find out that being the person they secretly know they are is okay.

Change is difficult! One of my favorite movie quotes is from *A League of Their Own*, when Jimmy Dugan (the manager) tells Dottie Hinson (the player) that "If it was easy, everyone would do it." The reason we're writing these character journeys, telling readers about these life lessons we've learned, is because it was difficult to learn them and put them into effect. Many of these life lessons have to do with identity because our own personalities and decisions are tied into our identity. We think of ourselves as "a person who does X" and "a person who doesn't do Y," and even if someone tells us "behaving in this different way can be better," subconsciously (or consciously) that's scary, because…if we stop doing X, or start doing Y, then we're a different person.

So in order to get a character to change, you have to put pressure on them. You have to dangle something they really want in front of them, something for which they would risk their identity—or at least a small piece of it. So let's go back to the discussion from the section on Stakes about what they *want* and what they *need*.

Want and Need (again)

The want (as we've discussed) is a tangible thing that motivates the character to go on the adventure. It doesn't have to be critically important to anyone but the character, and it doesn't even have to be the main goal of the story. Throughout the Calatians series, what Kip wants is to become a sorcerer (or reach another level of sorcery), but the main goal of each book is something larger.

Here are some characteristics of a good "want":

- It must be tangible; that is, the reader must be able to definitively answer the question "did the character get it" at the end of the book. Kip's wanting to be a sorcerer, for example, is too nebulous on its own, so in each book there is a marker: will he be accepted by the Masters to study at the school, for example? The acceptance is a firm yes or no that will be answered by the end of the book.

- It should relate in some way to the character's need; that is, the character wants this tangible thing because of the lesson they have to learn throughout the book. For example, in Ishiguro's classic *The Remains of the Day*, Mr. Stevens is looking back on his life as a butler. What he wants is to convince Miss Kenton to return to service at Darlington Hall (tangible: we know at the end of the book whether Miss Kenton is working at Darlington Hall again), while what he needs is to understand the sacrifices he's made for his career, including a possible relationship with Miss Kenton. In the course of reflecting on his life and leading up to his conversation with Miss Kenton, he will come to understand what his career has meant and how he should live the rest of his life moving forward.

- We should understand why the character wants it so badly. Not necessarily right away; in both of the above examples, the want is shown early on and the importance of it is built up over the course of the story. But at some point the reader should feel how badly the character wants this thing, and should have some strong feeling about them getting it (usually we root for them, but sometimes we can see that it will be bad for them).

- It should be something the character can't get easily, otherwise there'd be no story.

- It should be something that makes the reader a little curious and engaged, not only to find out whether the protagonist gets what they want, but how they get it. Who is Miss Kenton and why is she important to Miss Stevens? How does Kip get from being a non-magical animal person to earning the title of sorcerer? How will Arthur Dent get back home after the Earth has been destroyed?

All of the above is important because the want and the character's pursuit of it are what will keep the reader engaged through at least the first part of the story. You'll introduce other mysteries to keep them engaged, larger stakes from time to time, but your main character's initial push into the story is that they want something.

This want is separate from the need that the character has. A "need" is the way we talk about a lesson they have to learn, or a change they have to make to their life. Usually this will be related to one of the motivations you have in writing the story —a way you've changed your life or a lesson you've learned, something you want to communicate to others.[11]

Obstacles and Pressure

As I said at the top there, change is hard. Once your character wants something badly enough, they're open to change. Your job is to put obstacles in front of them, increasing in difficulty until the only way forward is for them to acknowledge that they have to do something differently.

---

[11] As an aside, studies have found that people do relate to fictional characters and try to emulate them in many ways. So writing a novel about some message you want to send is an effective way to help some people hear that message. Change is hard; a novel can be the instrument of change in the right circumstances. I've had people tell me that my gay romance books gave them the courage to pursue romance in their own lives, which is immensely delightful to me.

So the character journey maps to the structure of the story in these approximate stages:

- Character wants something
  - A situation arises that shows an opportunity for the character to get it
  - The character takes the opportunity! (First choice: This should make it hard or impossible for them to back out)
- Character tries to get what they want
  - There can be several try/fail cycles.
  - They are trying to get what they want without changing, without learning the lesson of the story.
  - There are several failures, and the obstacles[12] increase in difficulty (either with new obstacles or by revealing hidden parts of existing ones).

This should be around where you are in the second act right now. The midpoint is a great place to reveal to the character that what they think has been working, um, isn't so much. The false victory gives the character a good bit of confidence that they can handle the problem only to take it away again. The reveals at the midpoint also show the character that they're in over their head —or at least in deeper than they'd previously thought.

Where To Go From Here

So you've brought your character to this point in the story. There's no backing out now, but they are realizing that their existing skillset isn't going to be enough to get through this adventure. They need something more.

And this is the point in the story when they start losing the support they had. The latter half of the second act is when you torture your character the most: they lose friends and allies, they

---

[12] An obstacle can be anything in the story that is set up to prevent the character from moving forward, such as a character taking direct action against them (the antagonist or an antagonist's ally), a physical obstacle (a wall, a long distance), a lack of something necessary (knowledge, a key, a spell), or anything else you can imagine that makes your character's life more difficult.

lose everything they've relied on, and they descend into the "Valley of Death," the bleak spiritual land where they realize what they have to do and finally are pushed to the point where they can make their change. For Mr. Stevens in *The Remains of the Day,* this comes when he has been reflecting on his lord's Nazi sympathies and how disastrous they were, has met Miss Kenton (now Mrs. Benn) and realized that she had feelings for him, and is processing that his inaction was costly in both cases. For Kip (in the first book), it comes after he's been accused of endangering other students and his chances of being chosen to continue his education seem gone. In my gay coming-of-age novel *Waterways*, this point comes after Kory backs out of going to the prom with his boyfriend. I got a lot of letters from readers who didn't understand why he backed out, and the answer is this: Kory needed to reach the point where he understood that he could lose his boyfriend if he didn't change his view of the world. His boyfriend had been very understanding about his need to come out at his own pace, but it's this moment when Kory realizes that he can't drag his feet forever. This understanding forces him to make a choice: either keep his boyfriend and risk the censure of his family and friends, or remain "safe" in his community and lose the relationship that means so much to him.

It's important that in this critical moment, the choice presented to your character feels real. In the context of the book, of course we know that Kory is going to choose love, because we've picked up a romance book and that's how they go. But he has already chosen fear in the past, so this last choice feels real. There is a trope of a character's final choice being "cake or death," in which the right choice is full of rewards and the wrong choice is clearly wrong, and these choices feel unsatisfactory. Kory's choice contains a very real cost: he is going to lose the support of some of his family by choosing his boyfriend. If I'd framed the choice as "Kory's whole family now accepts his boyfriend and there's no risk to choosing him, but he might still turn him down and be miserable," it wouldn't feel like as significant a choice in that moment.

The risk, the cost of the choice is what makes it worthwhile. The desperation that comes at this moment propels your character forward. Kory chooses his boyfriend and makes a heartfelt gesture to demonstrate his resolve. Mr. Stevens spends time thinking about what his life means and comes up with an answer that suits him, but one he would not have arrived at in the beginning of the book. Kip realizes he cannot succeed simply on his own merits in a world stacked against him, and finally offers the human sorcerers a reason to keep him that he'd been keeping secret, because the goal matters more to him than the secret. This will be the beginning of Kip's learning to play politics, which will grow in importance in future books.

By the time you reach the climactic battle (whether it's a literal battle or not), the work the character has done and what they've suffered to get to this point will make the reward feel well earned. The change they have made will feel worthwhile, and your reader should feel satisfied with the progress they've made through the book.

Summary Points

• The main character's journey of discovery in learning something new about themself or the world is one of the things that will engage readers the most.

• Your story doesn't have to be only about some message, but putting your experiences into the story and, through your characters, showing how they can change someone's life, gives your story depth and meaning. It can also give readers the benefit of your experiences.

• Change is difficult! For a character to change, there has to be a lot of pressure on them. Often they have to be backed into a corner.

• One aspect of that pressure is to introduce something they want badly enough to change for it, and then put obstacles in their way. A "want" in the story should be a tangible thing; at the end of the story the reader should be able to definitively say whether or not the character got what they wanted.

• The "need" is the lesson the character has to learn. This can be more nebulous and often the character isn't aware of it until pressure is put on them and they understand that their current way of living is holding them back.

• After the midpoint of the story is when you should increase the pressure on the character. But their choice to change should always feel like a real choice. They can continue to live the way they have been and lose what they want, or change and achieve it.

Example: Character Development

Nivvy is the main character in *The Price of Thorns*, and his journey is the main one throughout the book. He starts out as a thief in trouble, exiled from his guild and tied to a punishment wheel in a small town after being caught stealing jewels. While in this desperate state, he's approached by Bella, who wants him to help her steal a kingdom.

Nivvy's response to this tells us something about him. What he wants is to be the kind of thief that someone tells stories about. What he needs isn't presented up front as clearly as that, but it becomes clearer as he dreams of heading a Thieves' Guild of his own. He doesn't just want to be a thief of stories, he misses the guild and the camaraderie there. He left his family to join the Thieves Guild, which became a replacement until they kicked him out.

So at first he thinks Bella will become the key to his new family, or at least to join a new Thieves Guild. He's not quite doing things "the old way," because he's already been shut off from those, but he's following the rules of the world: if he gets a contract from Bella, he can get back into the Guild. Bella offers a riskier path: help her overthrow a kingdom, and that has appeal, but he doesn't trust that she's telling the truth yet, so for the first act his goal is to get the contract from her.

Then he gets turned into a weasel, and his whole world is upended. Bella was telling the truth about her history, he learns, making her more dangerous but also a bigger opportunity than he'd imagined. But his short term goal is to get his body back, and she's the only one he can think of who can do that. Now he doesn't care about the contract; he wants to be human again.

But in order to catch up to Bella, he needs to convince Zein the hawk to help him. And Zein is so guileless that Nivvy can't bring himself to trick them. With a little help from a woodland "priest," he eventually reaches a level of friendship with Zein that he hadn't expected, so much so that when presented with an offer from a powerful, dangerous Bella to join her after he's been restored to his human form, he declines to go find Zein again.

This is an important point in his journey: Nivvy chooses

companionship and friendship over the things he ostensibly wanted: legendary adventure and success. At this point, he decides he's had enough of adventure. He agrees to bring Scarlet back to her home, but then he talks about staying with Zein in Spire.

Here's where another part of Nivvy's need comes out: he's always addressed his problems by running away, first from his family and then from the Thieves Guild. Here he contemplates that strategy again, but is nagged by the knowledge that he's leaving people in danger. He and Zein and Scarlet have a conversation about stories and what they teach us, and Nivvy realizes that being the hero of a story isn't just about doing something glamorous that's worth writing a story about; it is about doing something that needs to be done even if it's scary.

When Nivvy loses someone close to him in Bella's attack, he understands that not even his chosen family are safe. As scary as it is to face Bella, it's something he has to do.

The story goes on from here, but this is more or less the culmination of the character journey. There comes a point later when Nivvy is turned into a weasel again and has a choice between running away or standing and fighting, and he chooses to fight (it is always good to illustrate character growth with a choice). But the rest of the story is about him discovering and accepting the new family he's found.

At the very end, Nivvy and Zein attend a retelling of their battle with Bella, and so Nivvy has finally gotten to be the kind of hero stories are told about. But he isn't named in the story, and even though he's present at the telling, he remains hidden in the background, waiting to see the people who are part of his family rather than basking in the adulation of strangers. He ends the story having gotten what he wanted, but in a different way than he expected, and a way that addressed what he needed in his life as well.

Exercise: Character Development

For your own story, write down what your character wants (this should be easy) and what they need (this will be harder).

The want should be something the reader is told about very early on; the need might be something you don't fully understand until you've finished a draft of the book. You will circle in on it as you write the story, and so if you're partway through the story, or most of the way through, it's worth sitting down and thinking about what your character needs in order to live a happier life.

Once you know the want and the need, you can think about what experiences would teach your character what they need to know. This goes back to the chapter on stakes: what is important enough that your character would change the way they live for it? If your character is used to telling lies to get what they want, then put them in a situation where only telling the truth will get them to their goal. But first they will go through the story telling lies as they're accustomed to, even when (at some point) they realize they shouldn't be.

When you figure out the need and the way to get there, that will help you shape the characters and obstacles and even the villain. In this case, the villain would want the protagonist to keep telling lies and would tempt them along that path. Depending on how far you want to go with it, you could weave lies and truth into the theme of the book (we'll talk about theme in a couple sections here). You will want to give your character a real choice to make at the end of their journey, and not a "cake or death" option; there has to be a cost to doing the right thing.

A journey is a long adventure full of successes and failures, and centering your character's learning also makes sure that you're giving them plenty of agency—it's their actions, mistakes and successes, that move the plot. If you find that there aren't opportunities for your character to learn, then maybe they need to have more direct effect on the events of your story.

Chapter Twenty-Four

Relationships

No One Is Alone: Relationships

Back when I wrote about the four levels of story, I mentioned Kazuo Ishiguro's Nobel Prize acceptance speech,[13] in which he talks (in the course of discussing the little moments that inspired the way he wrote) about the importance of relationships in stories. "The thought came to me [...] that all good stories, never mind how radical or traditional their mode of telling, had to contain relationships that are important to us; that move us, amuse us, anger us, surprise us."

We love to follow characters, but even more, we love relationships. Even outside the romance-specific genre, there is

---

[13] Again, for reference: https://www.nobelprize.org/prizes/literature/2017/ishiguro/lecture/

often a romance or friendship at the center of any story. Your relationship arc doesn't have to follow the beats of a romance (the book *Romancing the Beat* by Gwen Hayes has a great rundown of those), but a relationship should have some growth and change over the course of your book—ideally, multiple relationships will, depending on how many characters you're focusing on.

A relationship arc can be intertwined with the character arc; that is, often the lesson the character has to learn, or the change they have to make, has a positive effect on their relationship as well as on the events of the book. Existing relationships start with baggage and unresolved issues, and new relationships start with many secrets to discover and a lot of progress to make to improve the trust between the two characters by the end of the story.

As you think about the different relationships in your book —most likely 2-3 primary ones—think about the basic arc you want them to follow. Where are they at the beginning? Where do you want them to end up? What happens to make that change?

Let's go through some of the essential parts of understanding a relationship arc.

Ghost

I will talk more about a "ghost" in Part 4. This is a screenwriting term for an incident in the character's past that affects their worldview and the way they approach the events of the story. Relationships can also have a ghost! If your characters are not meeting for the first time in your story, then there is likely some incident in their history that both of them remember. You don't have to include this in the story, but you should know it. It can be as simple as how they met, or it could be a significant experience (positive or negative) that they went through together.

In any of those cases, this experience or experiences form the core of why their relationship is the way it is. Siblings share a childhood in the same household much of the time, share experiences with one or both parents much of the time. Other relatives share other family experiences. Friends have a story about how they met, or maybe that story has been lost to time and they remember other markers of their friendship, times one of them stood up for the other (or didn't!). Romantic partners have a "how we met" story and have all the experiences of dating and sex to share.

Usually when we talk about a "ghost," we focus on a single experience that shapes the way the character—or in this case, relationship—approaches the events of the story. Any established relationship will have lots of incidents in the past, but there will be one that stands out as most relevant to this story.

When you're writing a series, this is an easy box to tick on your relationship sheet, because you have a whole book or several's worth of prior events. Often, an event in one book will spur your idea for the next one. This is one reason, incidentally, that I like working with series: the relationships have a chance to grow and the reader gets to see them.

But if your characters are meeting for the first time, or if this is the first story you've written with them, you'll have to do a little more work to establish their relationship. Think about their past together and how you envision their relationship. What might they have gone through together that would lead to the state the relationship is in now? We'll talk below about secrets and status—these things evolve over time, but often are cemented by particular incidents.

Secrets and Lies

At the beginning of your story, in any of the relationships you're focusing on, it adds tension to the story if your characters are keeping a secret from one another and are lying to them about it. The secret can be anything: something one character did for the other or to the other; something they're ashamed of or protecting the other from; something they know about the other one or about a mutual friend or relative; something one character thinks about the other. If the two characters have just met, it's easy to come up with the secrets they're keeping, because nobody bares all of themself to someone else from the jump.

These secrets can be kept with the best of intentions, but keeping them is difficult and that puts a strain on any relationship. They can make the character do things they wouldn't ordinarily, and force the character to justify their actions without revealing the secret. This can be played for comedy or for drama, but either way if the reader knows there's a secret at stake, that adds tension and keeps them more engaged to find out when the secret will come out.

Because—unless it's a multi-book series and the secret comes out later—the secret will always come out. You can build tension very effectively by having the secret almost come out, or by drawing out the reveal. Because every reader knows that if they read the words "they can never find out" in the first chapter, whoever it is is gonna find out.

Just as importantly, the lies at the beginning of the story provide an opportunity for character growth by the end of the story. We want our characters to be fully honest with each other, and even though they may be lying for a good reason, it's an indication that they don't fully trust each other. Over the course of the story, we should see their relationship evolve to the point where they can speak the truth—or maybe the relationship won't survive the truth. More on this below.

Status

In every relationship, there's a status of the two characters relative to each other. The status might change in different situations; for example, in *The Lion, The Witch, And The Wardrobe*, Lucy as the youngest does not get to decide what the four children do—until they arrive in Narnia, where she has experience and the others don't, and then she directs them. When the older children have learned enough to take charge again, they do.

This change in status didn't change their relationship, except maybe in that the older children trust Lucy more (they had thought she was making up the story of Narnia). But changes in status between characters can be a great tool for changing a relationship. Think of how many times a previously subordinate character takes charge and the others look at them in a new light; conversely, Joseph Conrad's *Lord Jim* is about a man with authority who utterly fails to meet a critical moment, and that failure follows him for the rest of his life.

Status is something to keep in mind with any interaction between two characters. Characters will often either affirm or challenge status with another character. These can both be in subtle ways—"Oh, let me do that," or "You're so good at this"— or more overt challenges. As you get a feeling for the ways a relationship will shift over the course of a story, you can put those affirmations or challenges into their interactions at key points to underscore the way the relationship develops.

Grand Gesture

This is a term from romances denoting an action one character takes to reverse their previous stance of "love between us is impossible" and show the other character that they do indeed love them. You all know the kind of thing this is from any rom-com. The term can apply even to non-romances, although the gesture then might not be as dramatic. But think about what one character can do to demonstrate the depth of their relationship to the other, and how that changes the dynamics between the two of them going forward. In *The Lion, the Witch, and the Wardrobe*, for example, Edmund puts himself at grave risk to defeat the Witch and is badly wounded; this noble effort fully redeems him in the eyes of his siblings (it happens offscreen, which is not optimal, but it happens nonetheless). Lucy, afterwards, heals him and remarks that he looks better than he had in ages, "since his first term at that horrid school which was where he had begun to go wrong."

When the relationship isn't the focus of the book, the grand gesture doesn't have to be integral to the plot. It can be a small thing in the plot sense but have great significance to the characters. In Patricia McKillip's Riddle-Master trilogy, a story built around beautiful small moments, it's no surprise that the "grand gesture" between Morgon and one of the other characters comes down to Morgon understanding and saying aloud that another character has acted out of love. This small moment upends their relationship but sets it on a more healthy path, and it leads immediately to another moment that affects the plot directly.

There can be many small gestures throughout a story, but there will often be one that affects the relationship more than others. Sometimes this is accompanied by a speaking of truth to the relationship, which is deserving of its own section.

Truth

Revealing the secret is a good way to challenge—or affirm—the status of a relationship. Kij Johnson and Barbara Webb in their Novel Architects workshop talk about the Unspeakable Truths in a relationship, the things characters know are true about each other but wouldn't dare to say aloud. There should come a point in the story when those truths come out.

This moment is helpful for character growth, because often that point in the character journey where they have to decide to change is motivated by someone telling them this truth. Also by losing their allies, running out of other options, etc., but if someone they trust tells them an Unspeakable Truth, that's the kind of thing that can motivate a character to really change. "Is that how you really see me? Is that how I really am?" A lot of self-reflection can come out of a revelation like that, and then the change necessary for the character to move on to the final battle.

In Ishiguro's *The Remains of the Day*, for example, Miss Kenton—now Mrs. Benn—confesses to Mr. Stevens in an almost casual way that she has thought about a life she might have with him. This is something the reader has known for a long time (that she is in love with him) but it is the direct statement of it that finally gets through to him and breaks through his certainty about the way he's lived his life.

When the truth is revealed, the secrets told and the lies stripped away, the relationship can become more honest, deeper, and move toward the final state you imagined for it. In many cases, we want the characters to end closer than they were, but as with tragedies, sometimes the truth-telling can damage a relationship irreparably. In the above example, Mrs. Benn's confession doesn't draw the two of them closer, but it reveals to

Stevens a truth about his life that he needs to acknowledge.

When we get to the final battles, we'll talk about how a relationship can be at stake, and sometimes that adds more tension to the story than threats to the life of a character, especially if it's the kind of story where the reader is pretty sure the character will survive. Just because the character lives doesn't mean their relationship will, or that it will survive in its current form. This doesn't mean that the main character's best friend or love interest dies (or fake dies, as in what TV Tropes calls the "Disney Death"). It can just mean that the relationship won't be the same again.

But whatever happens, the truth has to come out between the two characters so they are revealed to each other, and that is what will push their relationship to the end of its arc.

Summary Points

- A relationship arc is an important piece of a novel. Stories are not just about characters but about the relationships those characters have with each other.
- Elements of a relationship arc are:
     - "Ghost": an event in the past that still hangs over the relationship
     - Secrets and Lies: what is each person keeping from the other/lying about? There's usually a good reason that will affect the relationship
     - Status: Does one person have a higher status/more power in some way than the other? How does that change over the course of the story?
     - Grand Gesture: Borrowed from romance tropes, this is an action one character takes to prove their commitment to the relationship.
     - Truth: Eventually the secrets are revealed and the lies exposed. How does the relationship fare when that happens?

Example: Relationships

In *The Price of Thorns*, there are two primary relationships: Nivvy-Bella and Nivvy-Zein. I think the relationships that Nivvy, Bella, and Zein have with Scarlet are also interesting, but they are confined to the second half of the book.

Both these relationships start within the story, so there's no past shared between any of them. When Nivvy meets Bella, they both tell some lies to each other: Bella claims that this kingdom was stolen from her (this is technically a lie but Bella probably believes the emotion behind it even if she realizes it is factually inaccurate); Nivvy steps around mentioning that he's not a member of a Thieves Guild anymore and tells Bella that he's already a thief worthy of story (the first thing he tries to tell her is a story of his own exploits). These lies are related to the truths they will have to hear later: Bella that nothing was actually stolen from her, and Nivvy that he is not yet worthy of being in a story.

Zein is an interesting case because the lie they tell is a soft one, which is that they're happy with their life. It's revealed to be a lie because multiple times, Zein talks about things they'd like to do but don't feel able to: adventure, have a real community (they talk about the former-humans support group with affection, but it's also clear that none of them are really Zein's friend). However, Zein is the kind of character my friend calls a "cinnamon roll," just a sweetheart of a character who doesn't really have any ulterior motive. They're a catalyst for Nivvy to change, exactly the sort of person its easy to form a friendship with because they'll give as much as he's willing to give in return.

Zein doesn't really have a character arc through the story, but their relationship with Nivvy does. Not only does Nivvy have to learn to treat them as a real friend, but Zein has to learn to trust him. They live a solitary life, and though they like people, they don't necessarily trust them. They don't mistrust people, but they have learned not to rely on them. Nivvy changes this dynamic with two gestures: first, getting help for a wounded Zein (acting out of guilt for having put them in position to be injured), and second, returning to rescue them from Frankh.

These gestures are, in turn, inspired by smaller gestures that Zein makes, such as moving to shelter Nivvy from the rain while he sleeps. And whatever else Nivvy is (ambitious, a little too confident in himself), he is loyal and repays friendship. I didn't think of it in these terms while writing it, but they are exactly what each other needs: Nivvy needs someone who will offer kindness without expecting anything back, and Zein needs someone who will see their kindness and return it. Because both of them are looking for community but neither wants to state that openly, their relationship has to progress slowly until both of them can see that they are the community for the other.

The exchange of truths is soft with this relationship because the job of truth-telling is taken over by a magic mirror (I'll talk about that in a later section). But they do tell each other truths about their relationship, tantamount to confessions of love if this were a romance. And Zein says something very important to Nivvy when he asks if they think he's a hero; they say, "I think you could be." This is important because it confirms to him that he isn't, yet, but that that goal is within reach for him (and this line will come back to him later). A friend trying to talk up another friend might say, "Of course you're a hero," but Zein trusts Nivvy enough to tell him the truth here.

Nivvy doesn't have many truths to tell Zein about themself because Zein's character growth is milder, but he does coax some truth out of them, getting them to admit that they'd been looking for a family. Zein does say they love him in a very matter-of-fact way that can't count as a truth-telling or gesture, but which I loved for their character. I wanted this relationship to have softer edges than the Nivvy-Bella one, because that one was so full of danger.

By the time Nivvy has the chance to choose between Zein and Bella, at the midpoint, Bella's status has changed. He bonded with her when they were equals, when she could threaten him and he could threaten her, but now she has a djinn's power. She's not a person who feels safe to him anymore. And he's had a journey with Zein, who is the kind of person who feels safe. So here he's choosing which relationship he wants to pursue.

He and Bella started off getting to know each other in the way that he and Zein did, only they weren't helping each other honestly. Bella was deceiving Nivvy about her history and held back the information that he'd be stealing from a djinn/fairy, and Nivvy was deceiving Bella by getting her to procure a contract he could use if he decided to abandon her. Nivvy thinks this is perfectly normal in his world, even if he's not entirely happy about it.

Then things get more serious; they bond on the way to Scarlet's mountain, and when Nivvy has bad feelings about the job, he keeps going because he feels like Bella needs him. However, this consideration isn't repaid immediately after, when Nivvy is a weasel and needs Bella. She takes his horse and abandons him.

To get her to turn him human again, Nivvy can only conceive of one plan: to prove to her that he's useful. This means accepting her framing of their relationship, which is of master and servant. There's little question that they are friends now, despite how close he felt at one time. Bella feels a closeness to him that she explains as wanting to keep a reliable servant near her—but Scarlet, who knows her, tells Nivvy later that Rose is —like him—desperate for someone who understands her.

This is why their relationship works early on. Both of them want a companion, and they start a relationship cautiously reaching out to find out if the other person could be that companion. But where Nivvy wants an equal, Bella wants a subservient companion.

This is the same thing that binds Nivvy to Zein. When I'm exploring a new relationship in a story, I ask what need each character has that is satisfied by the other. Often I write romance, so "romantic partner" is the answer, but in this case it was specifically not a romance (I once tried to imagine Nivvy getting romantic with Bella and it felt like that would be either too funny or too disastrous or both to put in the book). And what I mean by "what need" is not, y'know, just "friendship," because that is usually what it is. I mean what kind of friendship, what area of trust are they missing? Someone might have a satisfying romantic life but be desperate for a companion in another area of their life, someone who can play chess as well as they do or who also likes going on quests for magical artifacts or who also loves the emptiness of space.

Anyway, back to Nivvy and Bella: When Nivvy spurns Bella after regaining his humanity, that's not the end of it, though he wants it to be. Bella's desire for a worthy servant who understands her drives her first to search for Nivvy in dreams, and then to send servants all over the land to get him back. This is her attempt at a grand gesture, but it's not the kind that's going to win Nivvy over. It does, however, clue him in that he can't just walk away from this relationship.

Bella never really tells him a truth about himself—as I said earlier, I leave that to the magic mirror in this story—but she does tell him a truth about their relationship when she sends a dream to him. She starts the dream by saying she wants to reward him, give him the Thieves Guild he wants, and offers to send a dragon to come get him. When Nivvy keeps refusing, she says, "Don't think that I can't have you brought to me." This drops the pretense that they are companions and lays bare the truth of how she sees him: as a servant.

And in their final confrontation, Nivvy tells Bella the truth that (with the help of the mirror) will be her undoing. Posing as her sister, he goes through some of their history and points out to Bella that her sister always loved her, that Bella's imagined slights that were the basis for her cruelty were all in her own mind.

This truth will defeat Bella, but Nivvy is left to reckon with the fallout from their relationship. Having helped her gain power, he bears a responsibility for a lot of the damage she left behind, but rather than dwelling on his guilt, he finds fulfillment in fixing his mistakes. However, with Bella's defeat and exit from the story, that is effectively the end of their relationship arc.

Exercise: Relationships

Pick a story you're familiar with and make a list of the relationships in it. For each relationship, write down the following for the beginning of the story and the end of the story:

• What secret is each person keeping from the other/what lie is each person telling the other?

• Who has higher status? If it's context-dependent, write it out.

• What is the Unspeakable Truth each wants to say to the other? (Beginning) and do they say it? (End)

Then, looking at the list, try to pinpoint the places in the story where the relationship changes. What gestures does each person make that result in a change? Is the relationship in a better or worse place at the end? Does it feel more honest to you, either way?

Chapter Twenty-Five

Tone

Crafting a Tone

Tone is the feeling you want to evoke in the reader. A tone can be whimsical, serious, scary, tense, and many other things. A book doesn't have to have a consistent tone all the way through; many tense or scary stories have moments of comic relief to ease the tension in certain areas. But you want to make sure that the tone you're creating is deliberately chosen.

In writing, tone is created through word choice. I've encountered problems like a character "chuckling" when being told about a tragic event. This kind of discordance can work, but you have to build it into the scene and be aware of how it affects the tone; you can't just drop a laugh or a smile into a sad scene and leave it there, because the reader will notice and wonder why a character is reacting that way.

When I look through a manuscript with an eye to tone, I

look for instances where a more specific word could evoke a tone better. For example: funny words and even funny-sounding words contribute to a lighthearted, casual tone; words that make you think of darkness or of small spaces can make your tone scarier and tenser; words associated with decay and rot contribute to a tone of disgust. This seems obvious, but tone isn't always something that's top of mind when you're drafting a scene.

This can mean using the right words, but it can also mean using evocative metaphors. A spaceship can be a fish or a locomotive or a junker; not only do these words give you different ideas of how a spaceship moves and looks, but they evoke different tones—fish (in this context) can bring up the natural world, a spaceship in a comfortable and organic setting; "locomotive" brings up an Industrial Revolution type of setting, people getting used to big machines they haven't quite figured out how to control yet, a tone of potential and peril; "junker" feels like a post-Industrial Revolution society where some machines have already been discarded, a tone of individuals struggling to make their way.

A Study of Tone

These are isolated examples; tone is many pages of these types of examples working together. Frederick Forsyth, famous for his thrillers (*The Day of the Jackal*), begins his short story "There Are No Snakes In Ireland" with an Irishman hiring someone to a construction site:

> "It's a quick in-and-out job, ye know. No questions, pack drill. You'll be working on the lump. Do you know what that means?"
>
> "No, Mr. McQueen."
>
> "Well, it means you'll be paid well but you'll be paid in cash. No red tape. Geddit?"
>
> What he meant was there would be no income tax paid, no National Health

contributions deducted at source. He might also have added that there would be no National Insurance cover and that the Health and Safety standards would be completely ignored.

This is an excellent use of setting and voice, and you can glean a lot about the story just from these lines. The setting will be a blue-collar job, physical labor, probably dangerous. The interviewee is a stranger to this culture. But pay attention to the tone, especially in that last paragraph. The author could have described the job any number of ways; for example, he might have simply said, "What he meant there was that the governments of the city, county, and country would be unaware of the money changing hands." Or he might have written, "What he meant there was that the job and the money paid for it were a contract solely between the interviewee and Mr. McQueen, that no other parties need be interested in it." But the way he describes it is with a series of negatives: *no* income tax, *no* National Health contributions, *no* National Insurance cover, Health and Safety standards completely *ignored* (not to mention *no* questions and *no* red tape in the earlier lines). By emphasizing all the things that should be part of this job and aren't, he's creating a tone of tension. There is an absence here that is going to come into play. The three elements of Health and Insurance give us a foreboding that there will be bodily harm.

And in fact, the inciting incident of this story is the protagonist being asked to do something dangerous, refusing, and being bullied for his refusal. Then, in the absence of any authority who might have stood up for him, he takes revenge into his own hands.

Correcting and Improving Tone

It is often easy to go through a manuscript and see words or phrases that don't fit your tone. It can be harder to look at places where the tone is neutral and see how you could strengthen it. I included the above example because it's rather subtle—there are no strong metaphors, no big adjectives. It's just the way a description is written that adds to the tone and builds it up over the course of the story.

Tone can shift in a novel, and probably should; even horror novels that have an overall tone of dread can have lighthearted scenes of comic relief to break the tension. The shifts in tone should flow naturally with the story and not be jarring to the reader, which is often something you can't see when you're drafting. Only when you go back through and pay attention to how you feel during scenes of the book will you be able to tell whether you need to tweak the tone. Pay attention to the feeling you get as you're reading through your scenes, and if a scene doesn't feel quite right to you, it's worth taking some time to examine why that is.

I've left the discussion of tone until relatively late in the book mostly because it is most often focused on in revision rather than in drafts. As your first draft grows, it helps to be aware of tone and thinking about it as you craft your scenes. Even if you can't think of the right word in the flow of writing, you can leave a placeholder like [MORE CREEPY] to remind your future self to pay attention when you go back.

Summary Points

• Tone is the feeling you want to evoke in the reader. It's created primarily with word choice, and builds up over the course of a novel; many small word choices add up to a consistent tone.

• Tone can vary throughout a novel; comedy and drama and horror and tension all benefit from a break.

• I find tone to be something I pay most attention to in revision, when I can read the whole thing, but if you're aware of it as you craft your scenes, you can make choices as you write or leave notes for yourself if you don't want to work on the tone right at that moment.

Example: Tone

The tone I strove for in *The Price of Thorns* is one I think of as "cheeky adventure." Nivvy, whom we follow throughout the story, lives in a world in which a thief can make his own way and his own fortune, but Nivvy is aware that he is very much in the lower strata of society, even if he is higher than the people he came from. So he uses wry humor as a way to express some power over his own plight. But he's aware that the dangers to him are very real, and so the tone of the narrative has to walk that line between real peril and humor.

Here's a section of the first chapter:

> Since parting ways with the Thieves' Guild a year or so prior, Nivvy had been searching for that one job that would make his reputation anew, one that would let him either return to the Guild triumphant or (in his wild dreams, but such things had been told in stories) found his own. In the course of that search, he had listened to many proposed jobs for an independent thief and found that generally what distinguished them from Guild jobs was that they paid much less. In the few cases where the payment felt sufficient, said thing was guarded by the kinds of large groups of well-armed paid murderers that Nivvy generally preferred to meet in nightmares, because at least then a body could wake up with no more damage than sweaty nightclothes. So by and large, when people asked him to steal something for them, especially people who didn't look like they could pay for his quality of thieving, his response was a polite but firm "take a walk into a wave." However, exceptional circumstances allowed for a rewriting of rules, and besides, this woman had an air about her, something different than the usual unwashed

unscrupulous undesirables he'd spent most of his time with over the last year. "What's yer job, then?"

The woman lifted her pointed chin and spoke formally, as though reciting. "My name is Bella and I have need of a good thief. Failing that, I could use a merely competent thief, and —"

Pride overrode the complaints of his throat. "I'll have you know that I am an uncommonly talented thief."

She arched one eyebrow up, which drew his attention to its thickness. "What is uncommon about your talents?"

"No, it's an expression. It just means very talented." Her eyes widened and traveled up from his to the leather bindings that lashed his hands to the wheel. "All right, yes, but look, you know the Tarisch Empire, across the eastern ocean?"

A lot of that tone comes from Nivvy's personality, of course; the narrative is centered around him. But I worked to get some of that tone into the narrative as well as into his dialogue. Here, there are a lot of elements I used in that first paragraph to convey that feel. "…what distinguished them from Guild jobs was that they paid much less" is a slightly humorous way to phrase that sentiment, better than something like "but none of them paid enough to be worth doing," which conveys the same thing. "…large groups of well-armed paid murderers that Nivvy generally preferred to meet in nightmares" is also an amusing phrasing. And "unwashed unscrupulous undesirables" isn't funny on the face of it, but the alliterative quality of to it gives it a little bit of whimsy to go with the image of the ruffians an unguilded thief would be hanging out with.

I tend to write very character-centric stories, and so the tone of the story matches closely the personality of the main character. This makes it difficult to talk about the tone independently, but the best way I can think of to describe it is that the main character is telling this story to the reader, and therefore the tone they're trying to set is the world viewed through their own experiences. This is most obvious when the story is first person, but it also works for tight third person like *The Price of Thorns*.

The tone varies, of course, depending on the plight Nivvy finds himself in. When Bella has gained her powers and is trying to convince him to come with her, the narrative keeps a little of the amusing turns of phrase, but on the whole it's more serious:

> She stared straight at Nivvy. "Would you like a dragon as well?"
>
> "Ah, I, ah, do you," he stammered, and then closed his mouth and swallowed. "Do you mean to change Rahila? I don't believe she would like that."
>
> "She's your horse. If you desire it, what does it matter?"
>
> "Indeed." Even in the battle with the eel, his situation had not felt quite so perilous. "The thing of it is, you see, I rather like her the way she is."
>
> "As you like. I can arrange for the dragon to carry her in her talons, or on her back."
>
> "On her…"
>
> She frowned. "You don't expect a mere horse to match a dragon's speed? She is a capable mount, for a horse, but that seems beyond her powers."
>
> "No, I—" He looked at Rahila in the shadows of the trees. "I'm sorry, what's happening now?"
>
> "You're coming along with me. You've

proven yourself a capable assistant, and I know from experience how rare those are."

"Oh." He tried very hard not to look at the eel. "Y'see, not that I'm not terribly grateful for the invitation, and honored, you know, but I've got a friend in trouble, and I've promised to rescue—"

"When you are the Master Thief in service to the Queen, you may bring an army down here to rescue whomever you please." Bella stared down at him, but she leaned forward, and the dragon, sensing her impatience, sat back on its haunches and exhaled a large plume of smoke.

"Right. But y'see, time—that is, it's, ah—" Nivvy tried very hard not to look at the eel. A day ago, he'd have wanted nothing more than to accompany Bella to the northern kingdom, but the imaginary Bella was a considerably nicer and less dangerous companion than the woman who now had all the powers of a djinn and a short temper besides. If he told her about Zein, she would probably turn Frankh into a grass-rat or kill him outright, go charging into the clearing with the dragon, whatever she thought would work fastest, and as much as Nivvy didn't like what Frankh was doing to his friend, he didn't want to kill the fellow.

He'd hoped that Bella would change him back and he'd be happy to serve her, and they would rescue Zein together the way he wanted before going on to live a magnificent adventure. He'd expected there was a decent chance she wouldn't, and he'd be on his own as a weasel, which was not ideal but where he'd proven himself capable. He had not imagined that he would be human again *and* that his best chance of remaining so would be to stay as far from Bella as possible, but that was how he felt. Unfortunately, telling someone extremely powerful a thing they didn't want to hear was rarely the safest course of action, especially when they might consider it a personal betrayal.

At his "I'm sorry, what's happening now," the tone changes slightly. He's wary and aware of how dangerous the situation is, but still assumes he has some say in what's going to happen up to that point. Then Bella tells him that her intention is for him to come with her whether he wants that or not, and the narrative turns serious while still keeping some of Nivvy's phrasing ("telling someone extremely powerful a thing they didn't want to hear was rarely the safest course of action"). He already thinks of his situation as perilous, but in the second to last paragraph, to emphasize that point, he imagines Bella rampaging through Frankh's clearing. No jokes here, just a plain feeling of dread.

And in the third act, when Nivvy has resigned himself to his heroic role, understanding that he might not survive this fight, he has a less snarky voice and more peace, and the narrative reflects that as well.

So when I went through the manuscript thinking about tone, what I looked for was whether the narrative matched Nivvy's personality and how he's feeling at the present time. Because stories are a major theme of this book (more on that in the next section), the idea that the "narrator" is some future Nivvy telling his story helped me feel out the tone throughout the story.

Exercise: Tone

I'm going to propose an exercise in two parts: First, pick up some stories you know fairly well. Read through the first few scenes and identify what tone the author is aiming for. How do they evoke that tone? What word choices and metaphors do they use? Write down some of the key words or phrases that solidify that tone for you.

Second, pick a scene from your own story that you're working on. What tone do you want this scene to have? Read through carefully and in each paragraph, note any words or phrases that contribute to the tone. If there aren't any, that's okay! Those paragraphs are opportunities to reinforce the tone.

When you're done, go back through your scene and look for places where you can modify the language. Does that help strengthen the tone? Does it feel too heavy or ham-handed? You can go through and tweak words here and there; make the prose flow naturally but in a direction you're dictating.

The more you do this with intention, the more natural it will feel. You'll gravitate to the right vocabulary and images as you write, and then going through and revising with an eye to tone will be a matter of tweaking and touching up here and there.

Chapter Twenty-Six

Theme and Imagery

I talked a lot about theme back when I covered pitches, thinking about what the themes of your story were going to be. It's worth revisiting here as you find yourself partway—or most of the way—through your draft. When you were planning the novel, you might have spent some time thinking about what the themes were. Now that the story has some shape, you can look at it and see how those themes are borne out. I'll also take a look at imagery, a related subject that I didn't discuss early on.

<u>Theme</u>

To recap: by "theme," I mean a conceptual situation that is explored several times over the course of the story, often from different points of view. I use the word situation to distinguish it from things like setting and subject matter—a theme, the way I'm talking about it, explores a situation that affects how a character relates to the world. A theme of your story could be navigating relationships with family, or exploring one's own identity.[14]

Even if you had an idea of the themes you wanted to explore when you started writing, other themes might emerge in your work as you write it. Our subconscious will help shape the story roughly, but it's not always great at applying finish and fine detail work, so reviewing what the story has become is the way for our conscious mind to look at the shape and see what finish best suits it—or, possibly, to say that the shape isn't right and work to re-mold it.

For example, you might have set out to write a story about family dynamics, but find when you review it that the main character's struggle isn't so much with how to relate to the family, but how to determine their own identity separate from the identity their family expects of them. This is the point where you can ask yourself whether that is the story you want to tell. If it is, you will likely have to revise some of the beginning, where you were setting up family to be important; if it's not, there will be revision later in the book to shift the focus back to the family issues you wanted to write about.

How to figure out what the theme is? The way I do it is to look at the big moments in the story. Look at where the protagonist(s) make decisions and what those decisions are about. What is the climax you're building towards? Let me add, too, that there is rarely only one theme in a book. A story leading up to whether the protagonist puts his own interest ahead of his family's is engaging with themes of exploring identity and obligations to family at the very least.

When you know what themes are associated with your big moments, you can figure out how to echo that theme in smaller moments. Side characters and subplots are opportunities to

---

[14] A note: people will sometimes say that a theme of a story is a simple noun like "family" or "identity," but that is usually shorthand for some particular aspect of a person's interaction with family or identity (or community or whatever). If the theme of a story is just "family," what does that mean? That everyone in it has a family? What aspect of family is being explored in the story? Is it our duty to family? Is it family as culture? Is it family as a cage? As I've said many times, interaction is important in a story.

explore your theme. How does your protagonist's best friend relate to their family? How does the villain define their identity? I said above that a theme is "explored several times" over the course of a story. We don't want to simply ask a question ("Should you put obligation to your family ahead of your own interests?") and have the protagonist come to an answer; we want to ask that question and think about what might happen in a number of different cases (What if your family is hostile to you? What if your own interests threaten your family? What about more nuanced cases? What compromises could be reached?).

Themes are also ways to build out your character. What hobbies or interests they have will help reinforce the theme? If they like to exercise, for example, do they go to a gym and meticulously track their workouts? Do they run outdoors? Do they exercise with other people or alone? Not all the little details in your book have to relate back to the theme, but the ones most pertinent to the character are the ones closest to them and therefore the ones where a coherent theme can be most effective.

What's more, exploring a theme can help you show the reader how to look at things in a different way, or open them to possibilities they hadn't considered. For example: one of the themes that I see in The Lord of the Rings is home, and threats to the place where one feels safe. This is explored in a number of ways: the hobbits are forced out of their home by threats; Sauron's ultimate threat is that by taking over Middle-Earth, he will destroy everyone's home and render them unsafe (there is rarely a specific threat other than "the bad guy will be in charge of everything"); Aragorn has been homeless for decades and doesn't feel safe anywhere. But in the middle of these stories about external threats, Tolkien includes internal threats to one's home. The Fellowship is a temporary home of sorts where all nine travelers feel safe, and that trust is broken by Boromir's betrayal. Rohan is another place that has succumbed not to an external threat but to an internal one (although that puts it in jeopardy from the external threat as well). All through the series, Tolkien is asking, "What does 'home' mean to you? What could threaten that? What would you do to defend or regain it?" Thinking of "home" as the theme allows you to think about the similarities of a close group of friends (the Fellowship) to a home; reminds you that threats can come from the inside as well as the outside; examines how an experience that changes you can change your relationship to your home even if the home itself doesn't change (as it did with Bilbo at the beginning and Frodo at the end). There are many other examples you could pull out, but the point is: finding that link between them guides you along a path to think about your own home and the threats it might face.

And of course, the protagonist is thinking about this too, all through their journey. This will strengthen their decision at the end of the story, and also provide better context for the reader to understand the question being asked and the answer being arrived at.

Imagery

Imagery is a way to help communicate the theme. Including motifs that recur throughout the story allows you to build associations in your reader's mind so that certain images become symbols of parts of your theme. These can be visual images or conceptual ones—for example, when people talk about "Christian imagery" in C.S. Lewis's Narnia series, there are both visual examples (as when Aslan appears as a Lamb; Jesus is called "the Lamb of God") and conceptual examples (as when Aslan sacrifices himself for Edmund's sin in the way that Jesus sacrificed himself for humanity's).

Your imagery can reference sources outside your story in that way if you like. Being in dialogue with other works adds to the richness of readers' experiences in general, and there's a thrill a reader gets from recognizing when a story references another they've read. What's more, stories like this can enrich each other through their dialogue. In the comics genre, capes and costumes are an enduring image and have become part of the language of those stories. Some people (Garth Ennis's *The Boys*, Rick Veitch's *Brat Pack*, among many others) use that imagery to show the ideal that their characters aren't living up to; others use the absence of capes and costumes to signal their outsider status (Marvel's *The Runaways*, DC's *John Constantine*). None of these stories have to establish in their stories that "superheros wear costumes"; this is something we all know from reading other stories in the genre. Similarly, science fiction and fantasy have several tropes that will have meaning to their readers.

But you can also work to establish an image in your book that is a new association for your readers. In Stephen King's *The Shining*, the boiler in the basement of the hotel becomes an image of the pressure the hotel exerts on Jack Torrance's mind. "She creeps," the maintenance worker showing Jack around at the beginning of the book tells him, a wonderfully evocative phrase (think about the tone that phrase evokes). What he means is that the pressure in the boiler builds up gradually and Jack will have to come down each night and vent it. Over the course of the book, the reader feels the pressure of the hotel building up in Jack's mind, and though there's rarely a direct connection made between the two, the parallels build up until it's no surprise that when Jack's mind cracks under the pressure, he forgets to vent the boiler.[15]

As you look through the images in your story, think about how they might be used in different ways in different parts of the story. For example, objects often reflect the state of the protagonist at various points in the story. It's easier to think about visual symbols in movies: two common types of symbol are the protagonist's clothes and their vehicle. A protagonist in disarray often starts a story with ragged or dirty clothes, disheveled hair, etc. Their car or bike might be old and broken-down. As they become more confident over the course of the story, they will upgrade their appearance and their vehicle. Imagery can be used in contrast, too; what does it mean to you

---

[15] I also, in *The Shining*, like the more understated image of Jack chewing Excedrin. It's associated with his alcoholism early on in the book—he chews it in anticipation of a hangover—and it's a great visceral image. We all know how bad medicine tastes, and chewing the chalk-like tablets made that stick with me. Later in the book when he chews Excedrin, it evokes in the reader the memory of his alcoholism and, in a more general sense, his addictive behavior. Toward the end of the book, too, when he is chasing his family, he screams at them to "take your medicine," an extension of this image which seems to be him telling them to join him in his addiction.

to have a disheveled character in a limousine, or a well-dressed character riding a rusty bike? This is more striking in a visual medium, but you can do the same things in your story.

One of the things imagery does well is build a connection between your characters and the setting. Having the setting, or pieces of the setting, echo or contradict your character's state gives the story a connected feeling that is very satisfying to the reader. We've talked about having your characters interact with their environment; imagery is, in a way, how the environment interacts with your characters.

Summary Points

- By theme, I mean a situation central to the story, often explored from many different angles. Some common themes are questions of identity and family.
- A story can explore many different themes, but there will usually be one main one.
- To think about a theme, think about the big moments in the story and what they hinge on. What question is the character forced to confront over and over?
- Knowing the themes in your story is helpful when thinking about side characters and subplots; these are ways to explore your theme by answering the main questions differently.
- Imagery consists of recurring elements in the story that go together and are associated with particular meanings in the story. This allows you to remind the reader of certain emotions, past events, character status, and other elements via an image in the description (for example, the changes in a character's clothing as their status changes).
- Imagery builds a connection between your characters and the setting/world.

Example: Theme

The biggest theme in *The Price of Thorns* is stories: how they're created, why they're passed along, what they mean to the people telling and the people hearing them. There is also a theme of transformation and identity, as all the major characters (except for Zein) go through a physical transformation of some sort in the text. One of the sub-themes of the "stories" theme is fairy tales, stories specifically passed down as part of cultural tradition. They're not called that in the text, but I used elements that will be familiar to many Western readers from some of our most popular fairy tales, mostly Sleeping Beauty.

The theme of transformation had a lot of associated imagery, specifically animal transformation. Zein has been transformed before the start of the story, Nivvy is transformed within the story, and Scarlet takes an animal shape within the story as well. Fairy tales have a lot of animal transformation imagery (Beauty and the Beast the most famous), so this worked for the theme of fairy tales, but to add to that, I used roses throughout, especially toward the end. Bella's original name is later revealed to be Rose, which also works as the character focus of the story: she is beautiful but uses thorns to keep people at a distance.

For the theme of stories, I used two major examples throughout the text: Rose's story of her own life and the story of Glædeligdal's destruction. The latter is more obviously about stories, because we're given four separate versions of the story (five if you count the bystander's version hidden in "The Honest Merchant"). Rose tells Scarlet a version in which the destruction was something she had to do because her daughter was threatened; Oigal tells Nivvy and Zein a version where the destruction was brought about by the kingdom angering the gods; Frankh tells Nivvy and Zein that the kindgom was drowned by an evil spirit for no reason other than evil; and finally, the prince's ghost tells Nivvy and Scarlet that Rose destroyed the kingdom because they "gave succor to her sister." Each of these contains seeds of the truth but also tells you something more about the teller, and in the process of hearing all these different versions, the reader is (hopefully) led to ask:

who decides how stories are told? Who benefits from those stories?

Rose's story is parceled out in less distinct ways. The first we hear is the story of her and her sister ("The Tale of Primrose and Just-Rose"), told by her to Nivvy and the merchant. Nivvy (preparing the reader for thinking more deeply about stories) uses the story to learn some things about Rose, correctly identifying her as sympathetic to the "Just-Rose" of the story. Later, Scarlet tells Nivvy and Zein about Rose's childhood more directly.

Scarlet, by the way, serves an important purpose in the theme of stories. As a being of pure power, she has no need to influence people's minds; she sees any story other than an exact retelling of history as fanciful and wasteful. So she is a trustworthy chronicler of history: when she tells us about Rose's history, we trust that she is telling it as accurately as she remembers it (and she gets irritated when she has forgotten a detail, as when Zein asks her about the precise name of someone who lived a thousand years ago). But she also serves as a guide for the reader to interrogate the point of stories, because she argues against them and forces Nivvy and Zein to defend them. By the end of the book, with less power but more friends, she is beginning to understand the importance of stories.

Other aspects of the theme of stories: Magic items require you to know their story before you can use them. Stories are used as currency—travelers exchange them, the first thing Zein does to introduce themself is to tell the story of the founding of Spire, and when Scarlet and Bella see each other for the first time after a thousand years, Scarlet asks for the story of Glædeligdal. The theme of stories intersects with the theme of identity and transformation in that Nivvy (and others) are told often that your identity depends on the story you tell about yourself. Literally, when Nivvy meets Scarlet, he sees a fearsome djinn until Scarlet says aloud, "I am Scarlet, a kind fairy," and then her image changes.

The theme of identity and transformation, similarly, is given several examples so the reader can see how different people cope with it. Zein has accepted their new life and doesn't wish to go back; Nivvy, upon his first transformation, desperately wants to go back. Scarlet, having lost her powers and being confined first to a ring and then to an eagle's body, wants to die. They all struggle with questions of who they are now that their physical form is different—and Bella, too, struggles with feeling worthless without her kingdom and power. Watching all of these similar situations unfold differently is how I chose to explore this theme, presenting Nivvy's solution as the healthiest, but with several others to illustrate how they might process it.

(And Nivvy being a trans man, he's already undergone a transformation to better fit his identity. This doesn't figure strongly into the story but adds to the theme. This was a transformation he initiated because of his identity, and that experience may at least help him cope with a transformation he's been subjected to.)

Having stories and transformation be themes in this book allows me to link them. A few times in the book, people are told that they shape their image by telling a story about themself to others. This is a lesson Nivvy learns early, but it is reinforced through all of the talk about stories and how stories change depending on who's telling them. The idea I had with this was to give the reader the idea that they have an amount of control over how their identity is viewed by others, and that power comes from storytelling.

The imagery of transformation is the physical transformation into animals, although there are other transformations in the book (Bella and Scarlet made powerless, for example). Someone who has been changed into an animal is visually, undeniably, different physically from whom they used to be, and has had to reckon with that. Part of the reason the book doesn't end with Bella's defeat is that Nivvy's storyline wasn't quite complete. The first time he's transformed, he wants nothing more than to regain his human shape. Now he and others are stuck in animal shape and so he has to find a different way to cope with that. I felt that wrapping up that theme—and Nivvy's character arc—was an important part of the story, if not the main plot.

Similarly, the theme of stories comes back at the very end... but I'll talk about that in a little bit.

Exercise: Theme

As with most of these exercises, the most useful things to do are to (1) read other books, and (2) study your own. So:

Think about one or two books you're familiar with. What sort of situations or questions do the characters face throughout the story? Can you pick out what the theme is? Often, for me, this turns into a game of thinking about the key moments in a story and trying to identify what they have in common. You've read about my thinking in *The Price of Thorns*, and hopefully that will help you look for similar patterns in other books. They may not always be easy to spot, and not all books will have a coherent theme, but often they are there. Sometimes you will find themes that don't feel fully developed, and I know that when that's happened in my books, it's because I wasn't consciously thinking about the theme. Themes tend to creep in anyway, because you will unconsciously try to relate parts of your story to each other, so if you can't pick out a strong theme from a story, you might be able to pick out "what was on the author's mind."

Imagery works similarly. Our minds will associate certain sets of images with the story and gravitate to using them even if we're not consciously trying to establish a pattern in the story. For instance, in a space opera, an author might give different characters different kinds of spaceships depending on their character: old but reliable, new and sleek, big and imposing. This is a language of imagery but it may not go any deeper than that. Think about *Star Wars* (or *A New Hope*, as it's now sometimes called): the look of spaceships is definitely a language of that story, as established in the very first shot of the small rebel ship dwarfed by the Empire's. The rebel fleet look all different, old and junky; the Empire's ships are very clean and uniform. The big bad guy is in a ship so large it defies belief. The language also tracks Luke's character journey, and this for me makes it feel a little more like thematic imagery: Luke progresses from his landspeeder to the Millennium Falcon to getting his own X-wing as his character journey progresses.

So look for these kinds of things in the stories you're familiar with, and then:

Look through your own book and apply the same methods to see what themes and imagery jump out at you from your story. What scenes feel like they go together? Do any feel out of place? Where are you using a pattern or language of images in your story?

If you go through looking for themes and images, you'll find a few, and you'll also find places where maybe they can be strengthened. Does your image language follow the character from the beginning through the middle all the way to the end? Or are there gaps? Are there side quests that don't follow your theme, or places where you drift away from it (this happens in the course of writing! Theme and imagery often get strengthened in revision).

Looking at your novel in the way that you look at other novels is an important part of revision, and I'll talk about that more later.

Part 4: The End...And Back Again

Chapter Twenty-Seven

Character Arcs

More About Character Arcs

I talked a lot a few sections ago about challenging your character to change and applying pressure to them so they are forced to make a choice at or around the climax of the book. As you approach the close of your story, it's worth looking back on that journey to see it in its entirety, and also to look at character arcs that you can give to other characters. Side characters usually have shorter character arcs, or at least ones that take up less of a novel's focus, but they can have a ghost, a want, and a need, and they can learn and grow.

We start, as we said, with a character wanting something (this is the tangible goal) and also needing something (this is the need to change in order to attain their goal). Characters often have what screenwriters call a "ghost," not usually literally (*Hamlet* being a famous exception), but representing a past trauma that is making it difficult for them to move on and make the choices they need. The ghost is a useful device for a couple reasons. First, it's a commonly relatable feeling. We all have some kind of past trauma that shapes our behavior. Second, it provides resistance to the pressure you're applying to the character to change.

If we want a character to learn over the course of a story, for example, that they have to value their own identity in addition to their duty to the family (and the proper way to do that), then there has to be a reason they're inclined to put the family first. Maybe that behavior stems from an incident where another family member acted selfishly, and people suffered, and the character's family never forgot it. It could be just that "family first" is how the character was raised and they have come to view that as part of their identity. Otherwise, making the leap we want them to isn't all that difficult and we wouldn't need to write a story about it.

Real Life, But Cleaned Up A Little

In *Waterways*, one of the examples I used last time, Kory's father left his family before the start of the book, an event that makes Kory doubt his own worth and much more reluctant to go against his mother for any reason. He's seen up close what abandonment does to her and to the family. But in the end, he realizes that he can't be happy and make her happy at the same time, and he has to make the choice that moves him toward his true identity and happiness.

Laid out like this, it sounds almost clinical, right? A character has a trauma about one specific thing, and then a series of events happen to make them rethink the way they view themself about that same specific thing. People aren't neat packages centered around one experience or one situation. We're messy and complicated and often the same experience can mean lots of different things, even to the same person. For example: Kory's father leaving his family might have made Kory angry and built up hostility toward his father, other male authority figures, or other things he perceived as responsible for his father's abandonment. Kory's younger brother Nick doesn't seem affected in the same way, because he was too young to really process what it meant at the time.

That's fine. A lot of things we do in stories are not meant to represent real life exactly. If we wrote dialogue the way people talked, it would have a lot of unfinished sentences and "ummms" and would be generally unreadable. For the reader's benefit, we clean up dialogue when we write it.

And in character arcs, we clean up the messiness of people a little. Not too much; you want your character to be well-rounded, to have lots of interests and quirks. But for the purposes of this one story you're writing, we're focusing in on this one aspect of your character's life. Doing this helps the reader focus on that part of their own life as well.

But we do want to hide this mechanism as best we can so it's not evident to the reader. Nowhere in *Waterways* does Kory say, "Man, I just feel like I'm not worth anything since my dad left." It's mentioned enough times that readers can make the connection, but people don't casually talk about their past traumas, and certainly—unless they're a certain kind of people who's been going to therapy—rarely say, "this past trauma is making it difficult for me to move forward in this situation."

Show the Problem Right Away

So we make sure the reader knows the trauma among all the other things they learn about the character when we introduce them. We want the reader to think of our main character as a person who has these habits, this job, these interests. They have some people in their lives, and the first interactions should tell us why those people are in their lives (not as in "we've been friends since first grade," but as in seeing them share an activity or an affinity). We should also see in the introduction something that's missing from the character's life—again, not in an obviously pointed out way, but in the sense of a situation that doesn't seem ideal, but which the character accepts as the way things are.

At the beginning of *Waterways* (to stick with this example), Kory is swimming at a different pool than his usual one because a teacher put up a poem he wrote and his friends are teasing him about it. He's embarrassed at this expression of his inner self and is running away from acknowledging it. And it's while he's at the pool that he'll meet a boy who also saw the poem and loves him for it (though he won't know that until later). Being embarrassed because your friends saw something you didn't mean them to is a very ordinary high school experience, and it isn't given a lot of special significance in the text (the teasing is mostly over by the time the book starts), but…it is an experience of someone who isn't comfortable with his identity. And so in a subtle kind of way, it sets up Kory's struggle over the course of the story.

How Do You Show Progress?

As the story goes along, the character will be changing and learning lessons, and again this is rarely (if ever) marked by them saying, "Wow, now I understand what I was doing wrong." The way it shows up in the text is by presenting them with another situation where they will behave differently than they would have at the beginning of the story. This difference can be slight, and often their intentions race a bit ahead of their actions; that is, they understand that they should do something differently, but old habits kick in when they actually have to take action, or they revert to their old habits when the new behavior doesn't work instantly.

Over the course of a novel, this change is a journey, and we should be able to see the change at each step of the journey. They will be presented with similar situations to those they met earlier in the book, but they'll respond differently, and that's how the reader knows they've changed. Ideally, you can use all the writing elements we've discussed here to show change. Remember: character is revealed through interaction. How does your character's interaction with the world and the other characters reflect their change as the story goes along? How does their dialogue change? How do they perceive the world differently? The tone of your story may shift; certainly you can use the imagery you've established to show character change as well. Many of these will be subtle things that some readers won't notice, at least consciously, but they will add up to make the more prominent markers feel right.

Change doesn't have to be linear, as I mentioned above. Your character or characters can backslide; they can change in the wrong direction before correcting course. Stories where the character arc is smooth, a series of lessons learned well and applied immediately, are not as interesting as watching characters try the way people do and fail the way people do, learn lessons painfully the way people do.

Plot Drives Character, Character Drives Plot[16]

Ideally, you want the character arc to be intertwined with

---

[16] A note here about Chosen One narratives: there is a temptation to make the character central to the plot by making the plot revolve around them intrinsically rather than by their own actions. What I mean here is a Harry Potter or Percy Jackson or Morgon from the Riddle Master series, who are central to the plot because of their birth, as opposed to a Frodo Baggins, who chooses to take the Ring to Mordor and therefore becomes central to the plot by his own actions. With a Chosen One, the plot does revolve around the character, but it's important to give the character agency to shape the direction of the plot even if they can't escape it. It's also important to make the danger to the character real despite their "specialness." Being a "chosen one" gives a character immediate investment in a plot and does bind them to it, but the story will be far more interesting if there is tension between the character and their destiny. This helps us relate to the character as a person.

There is currently some pushback against Chosen One stories because they are seen as elevating people because of the circumstances of their birth, rather than elevating people by their own actions. Western stories have long loved the birthright character as a reflection of their monarchic governments; they are ruled by someone chosen because of their birth, so birthright is important to them. Modern societies place more importance on the choices and actions people take, and elevate the individual regardless of their birth (in theory; in reality you can see many places in which the supposedly meritocratic countries still love royal families, literal or no).

Regardless of whether you make your character a Chosen One, your story's strength will rely on how strongly their *actions* drive the plot, and how well the plot forces them to change in response.

the plot of your story in such a way that the plot forces the character to change, and the character's change is what continues to drive the plot forward (this is what people talk about when they say characters should have *agency*, a word some of my early critique groups got very tired of hearing). I have seen many manuscripts from beginning writers (including my own) in which events just kind of happen to the character and they muddle their way through them. It's hard to build a plot that rests on a main character's actions (it doesn't sound hard, but trust me, as you're writing, it is), but it's important to do so because if they don't take action, and those actions don't have consequences, then none of the above works. They don't learn a lesson or change their way of thinking because they haven't experienced the consequences of a choice that didn't work out. And they will not, at the end, be faced with a choice that will show their evolution and precipitate the final battle. This all may, again, sound a little clinical, but with some practice, you'll be able to make it feel real to the reader.

A lot of this work will come in revision, as you notice sharp edges where the mechanism is more visible than you would prefer it to be, and you will have to sand it down, make the characters say less pointedly direct things to each other, tone down the weight of an incident here and there. In a first draft we tend to put things into the story more plainly than we want them to appear in the final (this is especially true in dialogue, where people rarely say exactly what they mean), and this is fine! It's expected that when you go back you'll have to conceal the gears of your story's clockwork. There will also be adjustments in the other direction, as you will imagine your character differently as the story goes along, and sometimes that change will not be as obvious on the page as you thought it was.

Summary Points

• A character's journey starts with a ghost (past trauma) that is part of the obstacle holding them back from getting a thing they want (tangible goal) and learning a lesson they need (personal growth).
  - Side characters can also have a character arc, though usually it takes less time on the page.
• In a story, it's okay to focus on the particular character journey you are interested in, which will be less complicated and messy than in real life.
• We want the reader to understand the character's problem relatively soon in the story so they can see where there's room to take a journey.
• Progress along the character's journey can be shown in the character making different decisions later in the story than they did in the beginning.
• The character arc ideally, as best you can manage it, should be intertwined with the plot: the character drives the plot forward, and the plot forces the character to change.
• Keep an eye on the character journey in revision, because in a first draft you may write your character's change too obviously or you may assume change without telling your reader enough about it.

Example: Character Arcs

Nivvy's arc in *The Price of Thorns* is a complicated one. I'll try to break it down in the way I thought about it.

His "ghost," first of all, is his expulsion from the Thieves' Guild for the crime of not doing enough to help a colleague, which resulted in that colleague's capture and execution. We don't get all of this at once—in fact, we don't get the full story until near the end of the second act, when Nivvy looks into a magic mirror and we replay the incident in his mind. But we know he feels he's been wrongly punished, and early in the second act when Zein gets injured because of Nivvy's actions, he is strongly motivated to act because of the memory of this other incident.

Apart from experiencing the consequences when he leaves someone (even in a case where he doesn't feel he should be blamed for it), this incident also spurred his community to turn against him. As a trans man, Nivvy already left one family so he could live as a man; now his chosen family is kicking him out because they feel he didn't act in accordance with their rules. So he has lost an entire family because of his actions, and as much as he thinks that they weren't that great a family if they kicked him out unjustly, he still very much misses the community that he was a part of.

These past traumas drive Nivvy's need, which is to have a community or family to belong to. As the story begins, he wants —well, his most immediate want is to get off the punishment wheel he's tied to, but his secondary want is to get back into the Thieves Guild somehow. He thinks this will take something extraordinary and he's also always dreamed of being the kind of thief that stories get told about. So when Bella shows up with an incredible story—and offers to release him from the wheel—the temptation is too great for him to resist.

His first instinct with Bella is to concoct a plan to make her sign a forged contract that will allow him to join a Thieves Guild in a new city—in effect, using her. But that goes awry when he's turned into a weasel. He has bonded with Bella a little, because she has also been cast out and is trying to find her place in her old community, and he leans on that bond to get her to keep him with her even though he's not human anymore. But she abandons him and he's left to rely on his own wits.

When he reunites with Zein and tries to convince them to take him to find Bella (his excuse is that she stole his precious horse, but of course the deeper reason is that he wants to prove to her that he's useful and should be kept around), his first instinct is to use them the same way he used Bella. But Zein's earnest assertions of their friendship and their care of him make him feel guilty about that. When an innocent remark of theirs makes Nivvy think they don't believe in him, it stings harder than he expected.

And then when Zein gets injured and Nivvy is responsible, at least somewhat, the guilt hits him hard. When he uses people for his own benefit, they get hurt: this is the lesson he learns. And in the same way that Zein showed care for him, he now finds it natural to show care for them as well. This is maybe the first true friendship Nivvy's had in a long time. We will see later what becomes of the other person he considered a friend.

Their friendship is enhanced with "medicated plants" that let them converse more openly with each other, and when Nivvy goes to find Bella on his own, he promises Zein he'll return for them.

Here we get to the midpoint of the story, and Nivvy's character has already changed, though he's not as far on his journey as he'll get by the end. Desperate to regain his human form, he gives Bella a powerful artifact and watches her steal the power of Scarlet (the djinn). This decision propels the plot of the rest of the book, and Nivvy will carry guilt for it all the way to the end.

Bella, now powerful, offers him the same deal as at the beginning of the story, only this time with more certainty. But this time he's wary of Bella's power and mercurial nature, and the promise of glory is offset by that fear and the promise he made Zein. He chooses friendship over glory in this situation.

Nivvy has a friend, but hasn't found a community yet. He doesn't have a way to get reinstated into the Guild, but he doesn't want to fight Bella, which Scarlet (the djinn he rescues) is pushing him to do. Zein lightly prods him to do the same, but stresses that it's his decision. Nivvy is taking Scarlet back to her lair out of kindness (he has also been guilted into it and somewhat threatened, but there is kindness at the heart of it), and this makes him a target of Bella's anger. So he learns that while there is a threat to him and his friends, he can't live a peaceful life. This is where he looks in the magic mirror, which recounts his past sins to him, and he decides he has to go atone for what he's done.

I admit that here, using a magic mirror to get him to confront his past is a bit of a gimmick, but I felt it was justified because the danger and loss he suffers makes him doubt himself in a way he never has before. That doubt is what leads him to look into the mirror, to see if he's really worthy of being the one to go fight Bella. So the doubt leads him to take action—he deliberately looks into a mirror he's been told not to—and that changes his view of himself (and as a bonus, tells the reader that the mirror works).

Now he decides to go back home and atone for the crime for which he feels he was unjustly punished. This is where Nivvy starts to understand that while friendship includes feeling responsibility and protectiveness toward your friends, being part of a community means the same thing for the members of that community. He wants to make amends to the Thieves Guild for what he did.

But he's betrayed because Bella has interfered again, putting a price on his head that leads his best friend from the Guild to betray him. Here again is a little fudging in the plot, because he makes the decision to fight Bella but then is taken to her as a prisoner. This felt a little off to me, I'll be honest, because his movement toward the final battle should be of his own volition, but I allowed it because he made the decision first, plus it restricted the ways in which he could prepare himself and forced him to rely on his friends to support him in the end.

And having made his decision to fight for his friends, he's presented with a last chance to serve Bella and become a part of the wrong kind of story. But he stalls until Zein and Scarlet arrive, and then in his final battle, has the chance to run away but chooses to stand and fight even though that's the most dangerous course for him.

In the end, he finds all that he wanted and needed, a

community of people who are common victims of a tragedy with him but who encourage the best in him. And in the last chapter, we see that he does indeed have a story told about him, although in keeping with the theme of community, it's told about the Order of the Knights of the Rose rather than Nivvy specifically. He also finds, when given a breathing charm by Scarlet that he'd used to fetch the powerful artifact for Rose, that while your past is a story that can't be erased, it is also a story that isn't over yet.

So while I talked in the last essay about the character arc feeling too clinical, Nivvy's holds together but is also a little messy. There are concessions to plot here and there, little tweaks I made that work for the story as a whole but which make isolating his character arc a little harder. But hopefully what stands out is that Nivvy's choices, by and large, shape the story. He takes Rose's job because he's desperate to get back to the Thieves' Guild; he brings her power because he's desperate to regain his human shape. He takes care of his friends until he understands that he has to take care of the world they live in, too, understands what it means to be a hero of stories, and then he sets off to battle the evil queen in her castle, and in the process he finds the community he hadn't realized he'd been searching for.

Exercise: Character Arcs

Pick a story you like with a character who goes through a journey and ends the story changed. Follow the character arc as closely as you can, noting where in the story the author shows you the character's initial want and need, what scenes mark changes in their goals or ways of thinking, and how the author shows you at the end that the character has changed.

Which scenes are more important to the character arc than others, and how are they distributed within the story? Are there places where the character backslides? Are there places where the character change isn't explained by the story? Does the progression of the character's journey feel smooth and relatable to you?

You can repeat this exercise as often as you like to get a feel for how different people handle character journeys. I do it with most stories I read or watch these days.

Chapter Twenty-Eight

Final Battles

At the End

So here we are at the end of your story, the final battle. This doesn't have to be a literal battle; in a romance novel, for instance, the "final battle" is the confrontation where love is declared finally. It's most often the place where the protagonist and antagonist meet for the last time and figure out once and for all who gets to achieve their goal.

The final battle has to do a whole lot of things. It has to wrap up the plot believably, and it has to provide a satisfying resolution (though not necessarily conclusion) to the protagonist's character arc as well as to the villain's story. It also should resonate thematically with the story and the plot. Oh, and it should be an exciting moment, thrillingly written. That's not too much to put on one scene or group of scenes, is it?

It's a lot for sure, but I find it immensely satisfying to write.

The more of the above I can wrap into the climactic scene, the more proud I am of it. For a lot of readers, this is the scene that will stick with them. Remember back when I was talking about the Final Scene idea in the Novel-Sized Idea section? That's a common thing because final battle scenes stick with readers and often become the feeling they want to reproduce in their own stories.

So here are my tips for writing yours:

Wrap up the plot believably

This should theoretically be an easy one. The plot is the engine moving the story toward a goal, often tied up in the character's want (though not always). So the scene of the final battle should tell you whether the hero (or villain) achieved their goal. The climactic battle in The Lord of the Rings ends with the destruction of the Ring; the climactic battle in Watership Down ends with the disappearance of the rabbit trying to take over the protagonists' warren, which assures them of peace for the relative future. After the final battle, there shouldn't be much movement left in the main plot. You can spend time wrapping things up, or if there are going to be more stories in the series, introduce those threads to be followed later, but the sense after the final battle should be one of stability. Things may not be perfect, but they should be okay for a while.

There's a sense of balance in the world at the beginning and end of stories that reminds me of a high school physics class where we learned about states of equilibrium. A marble balanced perfectly on top of a hill is at equilibrium, but a little nudge in any direction can upset that equilibrium and cause it to roll down. A marble in a valley is also at equilibrium, but a different kind: any nudge will move it in one direction and it will return to the bottom of the valley.

I think of the state of the protagonist and the world at the beginning of the book as being in the first kind of equilibrium. The world seems stable, but a nudge from somewhere can cause things to unravel. At the end of the story, by contrast, the world and protagonist are more in the valley—or should feel that way until the next one starts. If you're planning more stories, or if you just like ambiguous endings, you can leave the reader with a vague sense of unease. I'm thinking here of the end of *Watchmen*, the graphic novel, where Ozymandias's trick to solve the political turmoil of the world has worked, but Rohrschach has written down the facts that will expose the plan for the trick it was and has sent it to a right-wing journal. The story ends with a junior editor (or an intern perhaps) reaching for the pile of papers in which the journal lies, leaving the reader uncertain about whether the peace will hold, whether the plot will be exposed. I suspect that the reason Moore ends the story this way is to call into question the decision Ozymandias makes, the crimes he commits in the service of the larger good. Ozymandias claims that the crimes are justified because they result in this peace, and that's a question he grapples with at the end. By leaving the reader with this uncertain note, Moore reminds us that there is only so much in this world we can control. Even Ozymandias, the so-called "smartest man alive," cannot guarantee that his peace will last, if Rohrschach and an underpaid editor can destroy it.

All that said, even *Watchmen* wraps up the plot in its final battle. The peace does arrive in the end; the uncertainty is over whether it will last. We'll go into this more in the section on endings, but I don't want to leave you with the idea that you have to wrap up *everything*.

Resolve the protagonist's (and villain's) character arc

I've talked a whole bunch about character journeys and character arcs, and this final battle is where you can show the culmination of the journey. It doesn't have to necessarily be the resolution; sometimes the character journey resolution comes earlier and is what enables the character to reach the final battle. But the final battle is the proof that the character's choices were correct, and often they are pitted in that battle against an antagonist using the philosophy or choices they've just rejected.

You can see this contrast very plainly in movies (*Star Wars*) or in books aimed at younger readers. To the extent that anyone has a character arc in the Narnia books, it is mostly about whether they're going to be loyal to Aslan or not, but in *The*

Lion, The Witch, And The Wardrobe, Edmund's choice to choose the love of his family over the desire for power turns the tide of the final battle against a witch who is still fighting for power.

Because the final battle is intended to wrap up the plot, people often leave the character aspect out of it, but that's an important part of what makes the final battle feel satisfying to the reader. It's not just that the protagonist wins, but that they won the "right way." When the battle becomes the validation of the choices made over the journey, it feels right and earned in a way that a battle that doesn't take into account the character's arc won't. I mentioned *Star Wars* as an example above, in which Luke turns off his computer and trusts the Force to make the shot that destroys the Death Star. He succeeds where others have failed by his faith in the Force and his trust in his mentor.

When you think about books where the final battle didn't feel completely satisfying, a lot of the time that's because the character arc is muddled. For an example, I'm going to pick on *Harry Potter and the Deathly Hallows* here. Harry's character arc isn't really well defined in this book. He's mostly just reacting and solving puzzles throughout it. There's sort of an arc where he has to be willing to sacrifice himself for the good of his friends, which is the culmination of his character journey throughout the books (being a caring friend), and that resolution is an interesting, engaging scene. But it doesn't really affect the final battle itself (except in that Harry's available to fight it). Voldemort's embrace of power and a culture of pureblood wizards and fear also doesn't really affect the final battle. There's a small point where the Malfoys leave because Draco was shown mercy, but it isn't really clear that that affects the battle at all. The final battle, instead, comes down to... whether Voldemort is really the owner of the Elder Wand.

This final battle actually does more for Voldemort than for Harry, in terms of character arcs. Voldemort values power more than human connections, and so in his quest to become more powerful, rather than seeking allies, he looks for more powerful artifacts. He becomes obsessed with whether this powerful wand is his to control, kills someone he thought was an important ally to gain control of it, and in the end, this obsession with powerful artifacts is what leads to his undoing.

For this resolution to be effective, it's also important for the protagonist to win the final battle via their own agency (in Harry Potter's favor, he does choose to return to the world of the living and engage with Voldemort himself). In movies in the 90s, there was a short time when courtroom endings were in vogue, where the final "battle" between the protagonist and antagonist was decided in a courtroom, with a judge delivering the verdict, even though the story wasn't about a courtroom case. I get the appeal of a supreme authority reaching down to say, "this side is correct," but that removes the visceral impact of the choice being *proven* to be right. At the end of *The Stand*, a Stephen King book I otherwise quite enjoyed, there's an almost literal version of this, where the protagonists have fought the antagonists throughout the book, and at the end, the antagonist's hubris brings a nuclear weapon to the city and a mysterious hand cloaked in lightning reaches down and detonates it. "The hand of God!" one of the protagonists calls upon seeing it, in case that visual was too subtle for you. I should note that this isn't quite as bad as it sounds—there are multiple protagonists, and their character arc comes to a satisfying close, and this ending is the result of the antagonist's power to command loyalty to him (the nuclear weapon is brought by someone desperate to regain his favor), so it works on several levels. But the defeat of the antagonist is ultimately at the agency of a higher power, not the protagonists themselves.

Thematic resonance

The way the ending unfolds should, of course, match the themes you've presented in the rest of the story. If, for example, you were playing a video game with an adventuring style of gameplay, and then for some reason the final boss battle was a dogfight that you hadn't had any practice in, that would be jarring and you might not even finish *Starfox Adventures*. Similarly, if you've written a story about resisting authority and control over your social life and identity, and then you submit to the authority of a court to decide that you're right in the end (this was one of the courtroom-ending movies I mentioned above), that kind of breaks the message you're trying to send.

The Stand was always presented as a "God vs the Devil" story, and so the "Hand of God" ending, while unsatisfying on some levels, absolutely fits the theme. If you squint, you could see the Hand of God intervention as a sign that the protagonists have lived correctly and earned the favor of God and so he's stepping in to finish what they can't, being overmatched in a fight with someone who is, if not the literal Devil, at least one of his right-hand demons.

So when you're planning your ending, think about the themes you're exploring in the story, and try to make sure your ending is satisfying along those lines. Chances are you won't have to think very much about this—that should come to you as an idea that fits. But if you're feeling that there's something off about your ending, try looking at the theme and how you might strengthen it with your ending.

Make it exciting!

This feels like something we shouldn't need to say, right? That's what you're striving for. But I think it's worth exploring what makes something exciting.

Generally readers feel like a story is exciting if they feel tension and they want to know how something's going to resolve. Simply having a lot of action—a gunfight or swordfight or spaceship fight—isn't enough if the reader knows there's no way the hero is going to lose the fight. Here's where we call back to many of the topics we've covered. The reader must feel how important this battle is to be excited by it (stakes), and the prose should move the reader along at the right pace (pace). That doesn't mean that you need everything to be ACTION-ACTION-ACTION—you can pause to let the tension build up here and there—but you also don't want to interrupt your final battle with an extended backstory flashback, for example.

Think, as you write your final battle, about what the reader knows and expects. In a romance, for example, it's expected that the two leads will get together, and the tension comes from wondering what will be the grand gesture that gets them to the point where they get together. In a first-person story, the reader is pretty sure that the main character will survive, so put them in peril but don't make that the only source of tension. Disney's technique for introducing tension is to have a side character appear to die (this is so common that there is a TV Tropes section just called "Disney Death"). Since the side character's fate isn't as assured as the main character's, putting them in peril is a great way to introduce tension, as long as you don't overdo it.

Similarly, think about the other levels of story you're writing in. The individual level is resolved by this point: that's the character's internal journey. The plot is the part that the reader probably guesses the resolution to (although in many cases you can keep this open as well). That leaves the interpersonal story and the world story.

The protagonist's survival might be expected, but their relationships with the other characters need not be. Does your protagonist sacrifice a relationship to achieve a goal, or prioritize the relationship over the goal? The betrayal or abandonment of one of the main side characters (deuteragonists) who's built up a good relationship with the protagonist can be something the reader will feel deeply, especially if you've planted the seeds of this disagreement early on.

The world's story may not have any expectations attached to it. What upheaval is the world going through and how will this conflict affect it? The protagonist could survive only to live in a damaged world. All of these are part of the stakes of this final battle, and having multiple aspects of the story that the reader is invested in allows you a lot of room to keep them turning the page to find out what happens.

Another good twist to keep in mind is "the plan falls apart." Often the protagonist will go into the final battle with a plan to take down the enemy, only for some part of the plan to fail. Either the enemy knows about it or there's a betrayal or reversal, and now the protagonist has to improvise. Here, the tension doesn't come from "will the hero win," but from "how will the hero win," much as the tension in a romance isn't centered on the outcome but on how we get there. As a bonus, this allows the protagonist to show off, improvising in the moment and (hopefully) using the qualities the reader loves them for to rescue the moment.

Using the climactic scene to reveal a mystery you've been building up the whole book is also an excellent way to keep the reader engaged and excited. N.K. Jemisin's *The Fifth Season* begins with an orogene (broadly, a tectonic magician) unleashing an event that splits a continent in half. The book ends with the devastating events that led them to this desperate act. Throughout the book, we've been waiting to understand why this happened, and as the climax of the book unfolds, we ride along with the protagonist through some harrowing events and finally understand that this is why the continent was split. If you haven't teased the mystery earlier, this isn't the place for a sudden revelation that won't mean anything to the reader, but if your antagonist has a secret, this is a good place for them to reveal it.

To summarize the above (and allow you to think up your own variations): the reader knows some things and expects some things about how your final battle will play out between the protagonist and antagonist. Your job, to make the story exciting, is to give them what they expect but in a *way* they don't expect. Resolve the tension, whether it's from a mystery they're waiting to see solved or a situation they're waiting to see the outcome of. Think about the other stories in your novel: the interpersonal and the world. Try to surprise the reader—but surprise them in a way consistent with the story you've engaged them with up to now.

Summary Points

• A good climactic scene should wrap up the plot believably, provide a satisfying resolution (though not necessarily conclusion) to the protagonist's character arc as well as to the villain's story, resonate thematically with the story, and be exciting.

• Wrapping up the plot: does the protagonist get what they wanted? Does the antagonist?

• Resolving the character arc: has the protagonist demonstrated that they've learned what they needed to? Has the antagonist (if they are a character) been shown to be wrong in some way?

• Thematic resonance: does the climactic scene feel relevant to the rest of the story?

• Is it exciting: excitement arises from tension. The reader may not believe the main character will die, but other things can be threatened, such as side characters, relationships, or aspects of the world. Answers to questions and mysteries can be revealed here.

Example: Final Battle

The final battle in *The Price of Thorns* pits Nivvy against Rose in a final showdown. Heading into this battle, Nivvy has mostly completed his character journey; he has given up on the idea of being celebrated and famous and understands that he must confront Rose and try to defeat her even if it means losing his life. He is grateful for the friends and experiences he's had, having been able to compare Zein's true friendship to D'Alio's false one.

So this fight will represent the culmination of Nivvy's character arc. At first, he plays it cautious, trying to conceal that he is immune from Rose's coercive power, but she sees through that. When she turns him to a weasel again, there is a moment when he might escape the fight and run away, but instead, he uses the magic ring to take on the form of Rose's hated sister to confront her again. The choice to engage in the fight is a truly heroic one, which at the beginning of the book he would likely not have made.

Similarly, this fight closes Rose's character arc. Nivvy, posing as her long-dead sister, confronts her with the worst of Rose's crimes and attempts to convey the impact they had. Rose's motivation is that she believes the world has treated her unfairly, and so any action she takes is justified as a balancing of the scales. Nivvy presents to her the chance to see her victims as people and feel their hurt. But Rose rejects this chance to change her ways and ends the conversation, which brings about her defeat.

There's little to explore about how this wraps up the plot, except to note that it doesn't, not completely, and the story does go on for a few more chapters to allow Nivvy and his friends to find their footing in this new world free from the threat of Rose but forever altered by her. The events of the story center mostly around what Rose will do and whether she will conquer her kingdom; with her out of the picture, that takes care of that. The world story in *The Price of Thorns* is about how magic is declining in the world, and that story doesn't conclude in this volume, although the last few chapters do deal with the characters figuring out how to live in the aftermath of a magical catastrophe without any magic of their own.

Thematically, though, the final battle here works well with the rest of the book. Stories and the way they conceal and reveal truth is one of the main themes of the book, and here Nivvy confronts Rose with a true story that directly contradicts the stories she's been telling herself. It shakes her just enough for her to be vulnerable to the mirror whose magic is to do basically that same thing: it shows you the plain truth of the wrongs you've done in your life, removing the protections we all have of dressing them up in stories about how we needed to do it, we had no choice, or we were justified in it because we'd been wronged, because someone else did the same thing, because they deserved it. Faced with the undeniable horror of what she'd done in her life, Rose ends her own life magically, becoming a thorny rosebush (with, it will be later revealed, the power to make people very sad if they pick flowers from it).

So the theme of stories and what they tell us about ourselves is here, and the imagery of fairytales is carried through by the rosebush, by the magic mirror, and by the "evil queen being defeated with a terrible scream." I worked for a long time on this battle to get the elements to cohere in this way, but I feel it was worth all the work I put into it because it remains, on the whole, one of my favorite scenes I've written. It's emotional, resonant, satisfying (at least to me), and it's exciting.

I talked in the previous section about what makes a scene exciting, and I'll go through some of the things I think contribute to that in this final battle.

First, what does the reader know or expect? This story evokes fairy tales, and therefore the reader expects a "fairy tale ending." There's some uncertainty there because the book has been exploring the dynamics of stories, and so some readers may be thinking that ultimately the story could end in any way but will be retold as a traditional fairy tale. For the most part, though, I imagine most readers expect that the story will end with Rose defeated somehow, and that Nivvy will survive.

So the tension can come from a few places: *How* is Rose defeated? Will Nivvy get his human form back? What will happen to Zein and Scarlet? Most readers probably think Zein is safe because they're Nivvy's main relationship, and Western fairy tales rarely end with bittersweet notes (although in other cultures, like Russian fairy tales for example, "happy" endings are not a given). But Scarlet has (hopefully) engendered enough affection to be a character sacrifice at the end of the book. And her fate is somewhat uncertain over the course of the battle, as she distracts Rose and then pays a price.

Second, there are a lot of elements in play whose resolution is uncertain at the time of the battle. Nivvy has been told that he needs the magic mirror to defeat Rose, but he left it down south when he was kidnapped. He got to speak to Zein and Scarlet, but he doesn't know if they're on their way at all, much less when they might arrive. He doesn't know how long he'll be able to hide from Rose the fact that her coercive magic doesn't work on him. All of this uncertainty brings a lot of tension and excitement to the scene—and all of these questions are resolved in the course of the scene.

Third, the plan goes wrong. Scarlet and Zein arrive and Scarlet drops the mirror for Nivvy while attacking to distract Rose, but Rose has time to turn Nivvy into a weasel again, and the mirror falls to the ground and shatters. One of my beta readers told me that when they read that, they said aloud, "Oh, shit!" That's the reaction I was hoping for. Without the mirror, Nivvy is forced to improvise, and he returns to the familiar world of stories, hoping to use what he's learned about Rose to disarm her.

Fourth, there's a twist. When the mirror shatters, we think that's the end of it and we're invested in Nivvy's plan. But Zein picks up a piece of the mirror and arrives to back up Nivvy, so that when his new plan fails, they are there to hold the mirror up to Rose. It was tricky to conceal from the reader that Zein was holding a shard of mirror, but Nivvy was preoccupied and I think he would not have noticed it either at the time. As he's the main POV character, it doesn't feel like cheating to hide that for a few paragraphs.

And last, maybe less obvious but no less important, the characters all stay true to themselves and make consistent choices. Rose could have killed them all with a thought, yes, but she's shown previously that she prefers to leave her foes alive. Having learned that people can't turn back from animal forms without her, she favors that. So when faced with Nivvy's treachery, her split-second instinct is to turn him back into a weasel. Rather than kill Scarlet, she forces her to gouge out her own eyes and intends to feed Nivvy to her (though I am not sure she would have actually done that; she might have kept Nivvy as her prisoner). When faced with the ghost of her sister, she might dispel the illusion immediately, but the chance to gloat in front of her sister is too tempting to pass up. At the point where the conversation becomes too real for her, she does dispel it. Scarlet is motivated by her hatred of Rose to attack her; Zein is motivated by their love of Nivvy to help him. It is, I think, all as believable and consistent with the characters as I could make it, and that makes the scene more resonant than one of those where the villain just…refuses to use the power that might end the fight ("so the rest of the story can happen").

This scene was a lot of work to get right from all the angles, but I remain very pleased with how it came out. I often spend a lot of time figuring out these final battle scenes because they are critical to the story; they're one of the things that will stick with the reader if done right, and so it's worth all the time it takes to make as sure of that as you can.

Exercise: Final Battle

The best exercise for this part is "write your final battle until it feels right," but in the interest of giving you something to ~~procrastinate~~ help if you're stuck on your final battle, here's a critical reading exercise you can go through. You can do either of these as many times as needed to help get unstuck.

1. Pick a book whose final battle resonates with you. Read through it carefully and make notes on each of the aspects of final battles from this chapter: the character arcs, the excitement, the plot, and thematic resonance. Can you see how the author addresses each of these factors? Are there others that are important in making this battle resonate?

2. Pick a book whose final battle disappointed you. Read through it carefully and make a list of what it does well and what it does poorly. How would you rewrite it to improve it? Is there a simple solution or would it require changing earlier parts of the story?

Chapter Twenty-Nine

Endings

Here At The End Of All Things: Endings

The end of your book is the last impression your reader will be left with of your story and your work. I realized that last lines of books stayed with me more than first lines—or at least, a well-done last line sticks with me longer—and so when I set out to write, I spent more time crafting the ends of my stories than any other piece of text.

The end of a story—the very end, the last few pages—is much more about theme and character than it is about plot. At this point the plot should be mostly wrapped up. This is the space for settling into the new equilibrium of the world, for sitting a bit with the repercussions of the story we've gone through. It's a chance to show how the lessons your protagonist learned are serving them well now and a chance to revisit the theme one last time.

Call Back

It's not always possible, but if you can include some resonance with the beginning of your story, that gives your ending a bit of poetry. One of my favorite examples of this is *Watership Down*, which starts with the simple sentence: "The primroses were over." Primroses are a spring flower, and spring is a season of birth and renewal. What's more, many of the rabbits are named for flowers and plants (I don't think any are called Primrose, but it's been a while since I read it), so the beginning of the book foreshadows the destruction of the rabbits' warren that precipitates their adventure and journey to find a new home. The book ends with: "...together they slipped away, running easily down through the wood, where the first primroses were beginning to bloom." It's a small, subtle touch, but it shows that Hazel has guided the rabbits through the metaphorical summer and winter to a new springtime.

My book *Shadow of the Father* begins with the main character Yilon eating locusts, as there are a swarm of them moving through the kingdom, and animal-people have less hangups about eating insects than we humans do. They are crunchy and bitter, but they fly right into him, so he plucks them out of his fur and crunches on them for something to do. After a story in which he tries to escape or thwart the bitter (as he sees it) fate life has set out for him, and ultimately understands how to accept it and make it his own, he receives a gift of candied locusts and eats one at the end of the book, finding that of the sweet candy and bitter locust tastes, "it was the bitterness that faded first, leaving only its memory and the taste of sweetness on his tongue." I chose those words to leave the reader with the sense that things will be all right from here on out, but also to underscore that no matter how bitter you find your situation, it doesn't necessarily stay with you forever.

This Is Why I Wrote This

The ending is your way to tell the reader what was important to you about the story. This kinda means the same as "resonant with theme and character" but is a simpler way to say it. I think a lot about the end of Lord of the Rings, which concludes not with Frodo or Aragorn or Gandalf but with Sam coming back to the Shire after seeing Frodo off on the ships to the East. The story ends with Sam saying, "Well, I'm home." I talked earlier about "home" being a theme I saw in Lord of the Rings, and I'll admit that some of the reason I think that is working backwards from the ending. Tolkien chose that image, of Sam coming home, to be the one he left the reader with, and that gives it weight to me. Thinking about the story in the context of that ending provides a window into what was important for the author.

There's an element of poetry to a good ending, too, whether in the image you choose or in the words you use to describe it, or both. David Mitchell, who writes with an element of poetry in his prose anyway, does a fantastic job hitting the right note in the endings to his books. *Cloud Atlas*, a book about how people with power abuse those without it, ends with one of the characters vowing to fight for those without power. He imagines the scorn of his father-in-law upon learning of this decision, to which he makes his own, simple answer, and thus closes the book:

> "… He who would do battle with the many-headed hydra of human nature must pay a world of pain & his family must pay it along with him! & only as you gasp your dying breath shall you understand, your life amounted to no more than one drop in a limitless ocean!"
>
> Yet what is any ocean but a multitude of drops?

It's a beautiful image, and a call to action for the reader, and it's made more powerful by the journey we've taken with six characters into the future and back again (as this character is wondering whether this world must always be such). We have seen what he thinks the world will become, and whether it's in our power to change remains in doubt, but here he leaves us with the idea that the work to attempt that change is never wasted. And because this is the last line, this is the thought the reader takes with them as they close the book.

So as you approach the end of your book, think about all of these things. When you introduced your character, what image did you select? Can you return to that image, but in a way that shows how your character has grown, how their world has changed? What is your "closing argument" to the reader about the message of your book? How can you word it so that it will resonate and stay with them?

This can be a lot of work, especially as you've reached the end of your story and are likely very ready to be done with it. You've spent months, perhaps years, telling this story, and here you have wrapped up all four story elements, the world, the plot, the interpersonal and the interior storylines, your character is settled into this new world, and I am asking you to keep working on the last few words.

But I promise you, this work is rewarding. That ending to *Shadow of the Father*? I wrote it over fifteen years ago, but I typed it out from memory. I could probably recite for you the exact wording of the last sentence (or so) of half my books, and get a sense of most of the others. I don't know whether they are that meaningful to anyone but me, but I wanted them to be words I was proud of. I'll tell you in the next section about *The Price of Thorns* and that ending, but I could fill the rest of this section with another half dozen or more examples I'm proud of. I say this not to brag, but to encourage you to do the same: leave the reader with a sentence or a paragraph or a thought that you are proud of. Whether or not those words stick in their mind the way they do in mine, they are the last words of your story they will read. They're worth the time.

Summary Points

- Endings are more about theme, imagery, and character than about plot.
- The ending should leave the story in some state of equilibrium (if you are not writing a cliffhanger leading to the next book).
- If you can call back to the beginning of your book with the ending, it'll be an effective, elegant way to show how things have changed in the world and for your character.
- What do you want to leave the reader with? The ending is the last thing they'll read. If you have a "this is why I wrote this book" message, this is the place for it.

Example: Endings

Crafting an ending to *The Price of Thorns* was a tricky challenge. Because there were a few chapters after the final battle showing Nivvy trying to navigate the chaos Rose left behind, I wanted the last chapter to be set some time later, showing that at least some of the chaos had settled.

We get updates/closure on all four aspects of the story: in the world story, we learn that the kingdom of Heiterflus is thriving and that Heiters (the new name for former-human animals) can bear Heiter children, a huge step in normalizing their existence. The plot, which has been concluded with the defeat of Rose, gets an update in that we see how the story of her defeat is being told. Stories form such a large part of this book that I thought it important to hear how the events would be told going forward. What's more, we learn that the story has changed form at least once already. Our interpersonal story, between Nivvy and Zein, has resolved happily, and they get to renew their acquaintance with Scarlet, giving us a look at all our characters and how they're getting along. And Nivvy's character arc shows its resolution here in his contentment with his current life. Here he is, the hero in a story that's being told by a storyteller in Spire, and he's very happy not to be named or singled out for fame. In fact, his contentment will inform the last line of the chapter.

Before we get to that, he faces another leftover from his past: Scarlet gives him a magic item whose activating story is a reminder of how he helped Rose gain her power. He isn't pleased by this but accepts it as part of his past. And then Zein chimes in to remind him that that's only part of the story, that he made a mistake but he also fought to correct it. They suggest that he might add that to the spell, and Scarlet admits that she thinks that might make it part of the spell, in time. This was a section I put in to highlight again another way we craft stories to tell the message we want. The magic item itself is linked to Nivvy getting the powerful Crown for Rose, but that little scene isn't the entire story. Nivvy holds the item now, and he can change the story to be more complete.

So already thematically I've brought stories back into it and given the reader two examples just in this chapter about how stories can be changed. The fairytale theme comes back too, as the rosebush figures prominently in the ending of the story of Rose's defeat.

The book opens with Nivvy tied to a wheel, and I couldn't find a clear way to call back to that without being a little too obvious about it, but I do have Scarlet and Oigal talk about a society that believes that life is a giant wheel. The implication is that they are all "tied" to a wheel, in a sense. But for Nivvy specifically, where he had been bound and at the mercy of others, he is now the master of his own fate, talking about the travels he and Zein are taking.

As I came to the close of the story, I reworked the ending a few times to clarify the message. The traditional ending to a fairy tale is "and they lived happily ever after," which I altered a little here to be "happily thereafter," the title of the final chapter. But Nivvy had been so consumed at the beginning with living for a legacy and a story that he did not realize how unhappy some of the things in his life were making him. In my head, his years as a thief in Copper Port were good, but good in the way that happens when you're successfully working in a world you don't particularly like (my years working in tech were like this— I was good at it and they were good years but it wasn't what I really wanted to do). Over the course of the story, Nivvy has learned to live for the moment. He decided to rescue Zein rather than go with Bella at the midpoint of the book because Zein needed his help. He decided to fight Rose, not because that would put him at the center of a story, but because it needed to be done.

And so the last lines go to both Nivvy and Zein:

> Shantri touched Nivvy's arm on the embroidered rose and said, "So the Knights of the Order of the Rose did live happily thereafter."
>
> Nivvy peered up over her shoulder at Zein. "I dunno about 'thereafter,'" he said. "That's a long time."

"But we're living happily," Zein said.

"An' truthfully," Nivvy dropped his eyes to Shantri's smile, "who can ask for more than that?"

Exercise: Endings

Pick a couple books whose endings resonated with you, where you remember the final scenes clearly. Read through those final scenes and the final paragraph and sentence and try to feel why they are so effective.

Now pick a book you liked but whose ending did not resonate with you. Keeping in mind all that I've talked about with endings, try writing a concluding scene that you think would resolve the story better, or even simply a concluding paragraph that would stick with you more. It's okay, the author won't know you're doing this (do not tell them).

Part 5: Farther On

Chapter Thirty

Revision

Revision

So you've finished a first draft of your novel! Now comes the exciting part—which many writers hate, but I honestly love it—where you get to go back through everything you wrote and make it better.

There are lots of different thoughts on revision, so I'll walk you through what's worked for me and will include other practices I'm familiar with.

First, I celebrate the completion of a first draft. This can mean a nice dinner, a treat, a day off the next day, whatever. Finishing a novel draft is an accomplishment and you should allow yourself to feel good about it.

Then…I let the novel sit. Usually I leave it for at least a month, maybe longer depending on what other projects have priority during that time. It's important to me to have that time away from the manuscript to let myself forget about it somewhat, because if I go back and look at a first draft immediately after finishing it, everything still seems right to me. I need to get a little space so I can read it with at least a little objectivity.

Some people like to send their first drafts out for critique before they go back through it themselves. I generally don't like to do that because I know there will be continuity and grammar errors in the first draft that I can fix on a first revision, and I would rather my beta readers (I would call them "alpha readers" if they're reading a draft I haven't revised) focus on story problems that I *don't* catch. However, this is also a good way to make sure you don't look at your manuscript for a month or so while your readers go through it.

Basics of Revision

When I do come back to the book, the first thing I do is a quick read-through of the chapters. I try to write a one- or two-sentence summary of each chapter (or each scene maybe) that I keep in a separate document. Often I'll handwrite it on paper and then take that paper to a coffee shop to pore over it without computer for a couple hours, just focusing on the structure of the story, the character arcs and plot, making sure everything hangs together at a high level and nothing is missing. Having the short summaries of what happens makes it easier to look at the big picture without getting stuck in the weeds of prose—remember way back at the beginning when I talked about how big novels are? This is a way to manage that.

It's also helpful when looking at things like tone and theme. For my book *Azure City*, for example, I wanted to look at the main character's savior complex and his power to affect the world around him, how it ebbed and flowed over the course of the book. For each chapter, I noted a P with an up or down arrow, and where his savior complex came into play, I drew an S with a circle around it. Here's a picture of the first page so you can see the format I used and the way I made notes about what needed to change in the next revision.

(S) - Senior complex.
(P) - Athos's power

Azure City revision synopsis

1. Athos applying to jobs; Port City feels ghostlike. Gets a note from Allan. Takes Meg to meet him for a drink. Allan shows them the book. Meg doesn't like it; Athos intrigued. — Some tension over money - Meg buys the chunks

2. Athos and Meg meet Ferdy (muskrat), who cheerily takes them to boring houses. A financial advisor named Kendra (impala) tells them they can afford a house. Athos gets sick of Ferdy's good humor and blows up at him.

3. Athos visits Allan to try to figure out the book. Talks about his journalism job; Allan designs logos. They try different frequencies of light before Athos realizes it's sound. Writing appears and they copy it down.

4. Athos tells Meg about what they found, she's supportive. He translates the text and finds that it's the first line of the Bible. He reads more and then notices that he can see things written by Alex. He's excited but Meg won't look at the words. (Dinner)

5. First weird noises as Athos reads more of the book. He and Meg go to Craft Night where they and other friends work on craft hobbies and he hears a voice telling him to talk to a new person. He and Meg talk to her and she happens to know the publisher of his favorite book series. (Takeout Xaiqinese)

6. Athos hears whispers, definitely voices now, meets Preston Matheson. He demonstrates with Alex's letter that the book erases people from memory. Preston gives him a contract.

7. Athos meets with Allan, who has seen Alex's writing at the end of the book. They talk about their recovered memories of her. Athos tells Allan about the contract for Preston and Allan is vehemently against it.

8. Athos and Meg discuss whether he's going to continue with the book, fight with Allan. He looks back on his newly-recovered memories of Alex. They see a house they like and the voices like it too.

9. Athos talks to other people who knew Alex even if they don't remember her. He talks to voices for the first time. More discussion with Meg about the book and how far he can go.

10. Book appears in bed after an Athos dream! Voices won't let him give it to Meg to get rid of. He takes the book to Preston and conceives of a bargain, to give him to the book in exchange for letting him go.

11. Athos returns to Allan, who surprisingly isn't mad he tried to destroy the book (the voices betray him). He convinces Allan to look at Alex's Scentbook and then covertly looks at Allan's to see what he's hiding.

12. Athos chats with Allan's ex over SB, talks to Meg. Second craft night (Xaiqinese takeout), people don't remember Athos there. He uses the opportunity to be brutally honest with some of them. Trying to work with Meg on solving mystery of the book.

13. Athos dreams of the city and wakes up at Allan's condo. Allan, excited, shows him the book. The First appears and tells them to prepare for the journey; Athos is excited!

I find that this method really helps my mindset as I go into a revision pass. When I'm in the prose in the middle of chapter four, it's helpful to have this document on my desk to remind me of the higher-level aims as well as specific moments I noted should happen. As I'm in the middle of the prose, however, I'm experiencing what the reader is and I tend to trust my instincts in those cases as far as what works and what doesn't. It may be that something that sounded good at the high-level view doesn't work in the detailed view, or would require too much bending.

Revise with an open mind

One of the really important steps in the high-level view is imagination. With a first draft done, it's easy to fall into the trap of feeling that your story is set as it is, and all you have to do is make minor tweaks. This is a problem I struggle with all the time. I'd suggest as you go through making a practice of looking at various decision points and asking "what would happen if a different decision were made here?" (This, incidentally, is a thing your beta readers should be very helpful with, an argument to show your early drafts to them—more on this in the next section.) In many cases, you will find that your original decision works best for the story, maybe with minor tweaks. But here and there, you might find another avenue worth exploring. It's important to be open to them and to allow your mind to follow those paths.

When I have an idea of the changes I want to make, I will sometimes write a "revision plan" listing the things I want to change for quicker reference in a simpler format. I've also sometimes made chapter notes at the beginning of each chapter so I'll see them as I'm going through the document. You know best how you work; use whichever way seems most effective to remind yourself of the changes you want to make to your story.

As you're going through the document itself, put yourself in the place of the reader. Remember what information you've gotten from the text. Think about whether the actions make sense based on what you know of the characters. Sometimes—because I was thinking about the story a lot and trying out different options—I will find that a scene I thought was in the book ended up not being there, and that alters what we know of the characters. More often (because of the kind of writer I am), I will find that I put the same scene or situation into the book multiple times, and then I have to figure out where it makes the most sense to keep it.

On early revision passes, don't get too hung up on the language at a sentence level. If you see something, fix it, but you want to worry more about getting the story locked down. In later revisions, when you're getting near final text, that's the time to go through each sentence and make sure it's as clear as it can be. For the first or second, though, you want to make sure the story is as solid as you can make it.

The "if you noticed it" rule

There are times when I'm revising and I notice something doesn't quite flow well, or isn't quite right, but for whatever reason my first instinct is to say "it's probably fine" and leave it. I suspect that in my case this is fatigue from having spotted and fixed error after error and thought so much about ways the story could be changed. After a lot of these, if something comes up that is "fine, mostly fine, probably nobody will notice it," I can talk myself into thinking that it's not worth spending the energy to fix it. If you also have this instinct then it is useful to ask yourself, as I've made myself do, whether seeing this in your published book ten years from now will annoy you, and therefore if taking the five minutes to fix it now is worth it. Sometime the fix isn't that small, if for instance you're looking at a scene that will affect future scenes or which will require going back to previous scenes, but…this book is going to be set forever (barring future special editions) and I promise you there will be at least a few things that you and your proofreader don't catch, so take the few minutes and make it not just "fine," but good.

A common example of this for me is when I stuck something into the world building and didn't think about it too much. Does it work? Yeah, probably. Are there ramifications to the rest of the world that I didn't think through? Also probably. This is one of those cases where taking the time to think through all the possibilities will take a lot of energy, and the result may not feel worth it. You'll have to make that decision for yourself. If you're planning to write more stories in this world, it's worth taking the time, and even if you're not, it might be, depending on how you feel about readers coming along and asking you questions about your world.

Having patience with revisions is one of the hardest parts, and small, seemingly unimportant fixes are the most frequent casualty. Be aware of it so that when your mind suggests you just let something go, you have an answer ready and can make an informed choice about it.

Focused revision passes

One of the things I find helpful, especially if I'm worrying about a particular aspect of my story, is the focused revision pass. A focused revision just means going through your story from beginning to end looking only at one particular aspect of the story, to help you deal with how big the story is and how many elements of it you're trying to keep track of.

Elements I have done focused revision passes for include:

• Description—am I setting each new scene well enough? I tend to jump right into dialogue/action, so I know this is a problem.

• One character's arc or journey—thinking just about that, does it flow well and make sense?

• One character's dialogue—does it remain consistent?

• Tone—how does the tone feel at each stage of the story?

• Imagery—having thought about what set of images I want to use in the story, with an idea of what they mean, where do all these images occur? Are they all consistent? Is there room for more?

You get the idea. If there's an element of your story that you feel particularly worried about or invested in, maybe it's worth looking through it just at that element.

How do you know when it's done?

This is a question I get asked a lot. I typically will do a revision pass myself, send it out to one beta group, do a revision based on feedback, send it out to another group, then do a third revision based on that feedback. By the time I'm working on the third revision—plus any focused revision passes I might want to do—I should have a sense of how solid the story feels. Whenever a revision pass starts to feel like there aren't many changes happening this time through, it's time to wrap up the book.

There are conflicting impulses here. On the one hand, after a few revisions you might be anxious to be done with the story and/or worried that you are editing the life out of it. On the other, you will always find something to tweak every time you read through it. How to navigate between these two opposite feelings?

It gets easier the more you do it. As you write more novels, the process will become familiar. Until that experience comes along, though, my advice is to spend some time figuring out what you are comfortable releasing in a finished book. There will be typos here and there; there will be other mistakes, things the hundredth reader will find that the first 99 completely missed. That's just part of having an audience and there's nothing you can do about it. And maybe you're going to be working with an editor and publisher who will also go through the book, so you don't have to make it perfect before you send it off to them. But there, again, you'll have to work with them to figure out what level of problem they're able to help you with.

If you're doing this all yourself—or trying to get it ready before submission—and you're really worried, you can hire an editor or ask one of your trusted writer friends if they think it's ready to go. It does take a while to build up your confidence in yourself to the point that you can trust your judgment about a manuscript, so don't be shy about asking for outside help.

Last steps

For my last pass before sending to the publisher, I read the entire book aloud, which forces me to consider each word. That's how I catch a lot of repetition (Elizabeth Bear, at Clarion, told us, "Unintended repetition is the devil," and I've always remembered that), a lot of unclear phrasing, a lot of filler words that don't add anything to the text, a lot of dialogue that backtracks on itself, words or phrases I overuse, and other small problems that my eyes can skim over when reading in my head.

This is the most tedious part of every revision and I hate it every time, but I keep doing it because it catches so many little problems that every time I finish I know it was worth it. It has helped me to have someone to read the manuscript to—in my case, my boyfriend—and my fellow author Rukis reads hers out loud on a stream. One of my friends has a text-to-speech program that reads his novel aloud to him, but that wouldn't work for me because if I'm not the one talking, it's very easy to zone out. Still, it might work for you. Try a bunch of different things.

What you're listening for are things your eyes skim over but your ears will catch. Here's an example from *The Price of Thorns*:

> "Why should they have to?" Zein asked. "Why couldn't they ~~just~~ live their lives?"
>
> *You always live your lives at the mercy of a higher power~~,~~ ~~Just~~if not the ones you ~~usually~~ think you do. Someone turned you into a hawk and you live your life. Someone might decide to kill you, and if you're not stronger than them, they'll succeed.*

"Just" is one of the words I overused in this manuscript. Here it did not stand out to me until I was reading it aloud, and then I saw it used in consecutive sentences and asked myself, "what does it really add to either sentence?" I could've kept it in one, but I had already eliminated it multiple times, so I was trying to pare down its use as much as I could. And "usually" is a hedgy filler word in that sentence. Scarlet, who's speaking, is not worried about whether her opinion is 100% factually correct, and a word like "usually" goes with someone who is not as confident. "This is usually true," they will say, to allow for the possibility that in some cases it is not true. Scarlet, even without power, is full of confidence. I hadn't caught that because it's a common word and my eyes slide over it, but when I had to say it aloud, I caught it.

Here's another example, this time of clarifying dialogue:

> *[Y]ou worked against his god, if you believe in her, in a cause you believed in. You did not trust to a higher power; you acted. That is what I am ~~trying~~asking you to ~~tell~~do ~~you~~again.*

The original line was "That is what I am trying to tell you." It works tonally; it holds the exasperation I wanted. But it doesn't quite complete the call to action. When I read it aloud, I thought, "trying to tell him what?" In the original, the paragraph just points out that Nivvy acted and that Scarlet is trying to get him to understand that. But my intention here was subtly different. I wanted Scarlet not just to point out that he had acted to right a wrong, but to convince him to act again. So I changed the last line to be more precisely what I wanted Scarlet to be expressing. In addition, Scarlet's next line of dialogue also included, "I am trying to tell you," so I had to change one of them.

These are small changes, but each one is significant and makes the story better. That's the point of revision and why I enjoy it so much: I get to read a cool story and improve it. Revision can be tedious even if you enjoy it on that level, so find an incentive to do it. Maybe that's accountability to someone; maybe it's a reward after every chapter finished; maybe it's a state of mind you put yourself into. But embracing revision will give you the strongest result, whether you're handing the finished story to an editor, a publisher, or directly to your fans.

Summary Points

• Revision is your chance to improve your story! Try to view it as an opportunity rather than an obligation or a chore.

• I prefer to do one pass through a story myself before sending it off to others, but do what works best for you.

• I start with reading through the story and summarizing each scene, then putting the summaries together to get a high-level idea of what I've written. This lets me see high-level patterns.

• Keep an open mind when revising. It's easy to get locked into what you wrote in the first draft and feel like any changes hurt the story. At the same time, be confident in the story you want to tell so you can evaluate whether proposed changes will really benefit the story.

• If you notice something that bugs you, fix it. It might feel annoying when you've been revising for weeks, but it's better than leaving it to become a permanent part of your work.

• Try revision passes where you focus on a particular part of the story you're worried about: dialogue, tone, character, description, etc.

• It's done when you feel it's done. For me that's when the changes I'm making start to feel small and cosmetic.

• Your final pass should be to read the story aloud so you can catch little problems with word choice and flow that you might skim over when reading silently.

Chapter Thirty-One

Sharing and Critique

Sharing and Critique

In the last section, I talked about beta readers. If you aren't experienced with having peers review your manuscripts, I'll go through how to find beta readers, how to approach them, what to expect, and how to be a good beta reader yourself.

"Beta reader," in case you didn't know, comes from software lingo. In software development, the alpha version of the software is the first one (alpha is the first letter of the Greek alphabet) and is usually only tested internally. The beta version, or second version, is usually the first one distributed outside the company for end users to test. A "beta reader" of a story has therefore come to mean someone who reads a version of the work-in-progress sent out for critique prior to publication.

Finding the elusive beta reader

If you don't have a community of writers around you, the idea of finding beta readers might feel even more impossible than writing a book. But there are many places you might find beta readers.

At the beginning of the book, I talked about finding a writing group, and that's the best place to find your beta readers. The more you get to know someone and trust them, the easier it will be to exchange feedback on stories. As you work with someone else for years, they'll learn what sort of things you're trying to communicate with your stories and how you write; you'll learn the same about them. Your feedback will be much more constructive when it's built on this foundation.

If you don't have a writing group, you can still find places to exchange beta reads online; in fact, there are communities devoted to exactly that. When you find a community that offers beta reads, be sure to read their rules for members closely. Sometimes you might be asked to do a certain number of beta reads yourself before requesting one, or asked to contribute in some other way.

Lastly, there are affiliations of writers in online communities: writer groups like the Romance Writers Association, SFWA, etc., as well as other places where writers collect to chat. Here you will likely not be able to join and request a beta read right away, but join and spend some time there and you'll be able to pick up on the etiquette of exchanging beta reads with other writers.

This is a service most writers want, so it's not that hard to find if you go where other writers are gathering.

Care and feeding of beta readers

When you've found people willing to read through your novel draft and offer feedback, it's important to make sure you're both on the same page with regards to the time, the feedback content, and the feedback format. There are a lot of ways a beta reader can be helpful, and there are a lot of ways they can put in a great deal of work that isn't helpful or isn't what you need at this stage of the manuscript. For example, if you're going to rewrite or revise a few more times, it's probably not worth having your beta reader look for spelling and grammar errors. Make sure to be clear to them what level of feedback you're expecting: do you want their thoughts after each chapter? Just to answer some questions when they're done (see below)? A marked-up manuscript with a note every time they thought of a comment?

What you want your beta readers to provide is an outsider's point of view, someone who sees your story from a different angle and spots things you might have missed. It's very common to have so many pieces of story in your head that you don't remember which ones you've put on the page, or to have thought about a piece of the character journey or plot in a certain way and not realized that changing another part of the story makes that piece not work. Your beta readers, coming in without all your months of thoughts, feelings, and discarded ideas, will see the story on the page for what it is and can tell you where it's not working.

The areas in which I find this most helpful are:

• *Are there points where you feel bored/disengaged from the story?* — The biggest one, honestly. You're so involved in your novel that you know what every scene means, but your readers won't necessarily. They only know what they read. So identifying spots where the reader doesn't feel as engaged gives you a place where you have to fix something (identifying *why* they felt bored there is harder but you'll have to do that too if you can).

• *Does the plot make sense?* — Does each action follow on from the previous one understandably? Is there a shortcut that you missed (e.g. "Fly the Eagles to Mount Doom")? Is it clear why the plot is important to the characters?

• *Do the characters behave believably?* — Often people will wonder if their characters are relatable, but that is a more subjective question and I don't like to ask that one. If someone offers it, great, but not everyone is going to relate to your main character. That doesn't mean there's a problem. Behaving believably is also somewhat subjective but if you have a good beta reader, they'll be able to tell you whether the character's actions are internally consistent.

• *Do you get a good sense of the world and/or the setting?* — This is a question I ask a lot because description and setting is one of the places where I usually find my first drafts lacking. Whether it's a sense of the world in general or specific location in certain scenes, I always want to know if the story feels properly situated.

• *How is the pacing, both of action and of information?* — As we talked about in the Pacing section, this is something it can be hard to gauge on your own. Does the story have enough action punctuated with periods of reflection about what just happened? Does information feel like it's conveyed at a good rate, leaving some interesting mysteries for the reader throughout?

In addition to the above general questions, you will want to alert your beta readers to any areas you feel particularly worried about. "When did you pick up on this one thing?" "I'm worried that the villains might be coming across too sympathetic." "I got carried away with the historical research; is there too much detail in there?"

Now, having prepared all of your questions for them, make sure to ask them how they feel comfortable giving feedback. Some people may be comfortable emailing you their comments; others may want to talk you through them.

You'll also need to set a schedule. If you have a deadline, make sure to give them enough time for you to meet your deadline, and build some buffer into that time so it isn't a critical deadline. They're doing you a favor, usually unpaid, and life often gets in the way.

As for how much time is reasonable, tell them how long the story is and ask what timeframe feels comfortable to them, if you have that flexibility (I would never ask someone to read a novel in under a month, but sometimes people will offer shorter timeframes). Be sure to give them a firm date, so you both have expectations as to when it will be returned to you. If you have a deadline because of editor/publisher requirements, then explain up front that you need it by that deadline, and if they can't commit to that, thank them and keep them in mind for the next one.

And always, always remember: They are helping you make your story better. Maybe their feedback will be entirely useless to you, but make sure to thank them for the work they put in anyway. And if someone beta reads for you, you should offer to beta read for them as well.

What you'll get

What you will get from your beta readers—hopefully addressing the questions you posed to them—is one person's true experience of reading your story.

It's really important to keep that in mind. There will be points when your beta readers don't get the point, miss the clues, perceive a character's motivation differently, read a situation not the way you'd intended, etc. This doesn't mean they're wrong. It means that their read isn't what you'd intended. There are two things you can do about that.

One: you can ask yourself what led to this different read and make some changes. Maybe a character's motivation needs to be established earlier on; maybe some language needs to be added in or taken out. Often, I find that small changes can have a big effect if placed properly (in *The Price of Thorns*, I added a small bit in the first chapter about how Nivvy trusts himself to get out of any situation to establish that as his way of thinking when the situations get more perilous later). In rare cases, you might find that your beta reader's read is interesting enough to incorporate it into the book—what if this character really was going to double-cross the group? That seems to be set up, so how would you pay it off?

Two: you can say, "not everyone is going to get this," and leave your story as is. This is valid! Adding in small changes to account for every beta reader's views would be too much for the story to incorporate and can lead to a watered-down feeling in the story.

The decision between one and two is easier if you have several beta reads (getting critique from a writing group allows the beta readers to discuss their views, too). If one person has a read that nobody else has, you probably don't have to worry too much about changing it, unless you want to and it feels right for the story. If a lot of your beta readers all read the same thing, then it's worth making a change if you don't want people to have that experience of it.

Again: every beta reader's feedback is their true experience of your story. It might not be what you intended, but it's not wrong. They are doing this to be helpful, so thank them. It's okay to ask for clarification on some of their points ("why did you feel this way about my main character?") but don't argue with them or point out why their read wasn't what you intended. You can explain what you did intend, and ask them what might have helped them see it that way, and often that can be helpful feedback as well. Many beta readers won't offer that unsolicited, worrying about trying to rewrite someone else's story for them.

Lastly, it's always nice to include an Acknowledgments section at the end of your book where you thank your beta readers for their contribution to the final book. I did not always do this when I started out, and I wish I had.

How to be a good beta reader yourself

Be honest about your experience of the story, keeping in mind that the purpose of your beta read is to help the author make the story the best it can be at expressing what they wanted. Your feedback should be constructive rather than critical, meaning that as you find things you perceive as problems—plot holes, characters behaving inconsistently, inadequate description—you should try to phrase your feedback in a way that helps the author fix the problems if they want to. And don't forget to include positive feedback, too, if something works really well.

For example: A plot event doesn't seem connected to the event that just happened. Rather than saying "this didn't make sense," try to figure out why it didn't make sense to you. Maybe there's a linking scene missing ("how did the car even get ON the roof?"), maybe it's because it hasn't been explained ("the characters say the widget is important but I didn't pick up on why"), or maybe there's a character motivation that isn't properly supported ("Dix says it's important to do this but I don't know why they're so into wine-making"). If you can pinpoint why a part of the story is giving you the feeling it is, that will help the author understand how you're reading and how to address the issue—if they want to. Maybe they wanted it to be a mystery and feel disconnected.

It's all right to give your emotional reactions to the story, but don't give emotional reactions to the writing. The author wants to know how you're feeling throughout the story. But if, for example, you have a negative reaction to the use of the word "suddenly" in narrative (n.b. It is almost always better to describe the event happening suddenly than to say, "suddenly"; it's a "show, don't tell" thing), don't circle it on the manuscript and write "YUCK" next to it. Instead, suggest perhaps a way the author could make the event feel more sudden organically in the description.

However, when the author kills off a side character you like, by all means write, "OH NO NOT BETTY HOW COULD YOU." Our stories are intended to evoke emotions, and letting the author know that the death of this character affected you deeply is very helpful to them. I cherish the times my beta readers have called me a monster for my character deaths because I know then that they were as affecting as I wanted them to be.

As you're writing your comments, imagine that you are the author receiving them, and write the kind of feedback you would want to see. In general, unless the author has asked specifically, refrain from offering rewrites except in very small doses to address a specific concern. As you build up a level of trust, you may know that a certain author is receptive to potential rewrites, but if that trust isn't there, often a suggested rewrite can come across as "you should change the story to be this." A way we were taught at Clarion to avoid this is to tell the author, "if this were my story, I might…" This gives them access to your idea without making it feel like something you're telling them they have to do. And don't feel slighted if they don't take it! It's not your story, after all, and your idea might be great for a story you want to write but not quite right for what they want. I also like to use the word "opportunity," as in, "you have an opportunity here to show the character making a bad decision."

This lets the author see something that might happen, but leaves the choice about whether to include it entirely up to them.

In sum: communicate your honest experience of reading the story, making sure to write your feedback constructively. Keep in mind that this is just your experience of the story, a data point for the author to use in deciding how to approach the next revision. Note the positive as well as things that could use attention in the next revision, answer any questions the author sent you, and then leave the decisions up to the author.

That last point is important. Just as you may not take every bit of advice you get in critique, the author you're providing feedback for also will not. That doesn't mean your advice was bad, just that it didn't fit what they wanted to do with the story. Or maybe they found another way to solve the problem you brought up. Maybe they didn't view it as a problem, but the way they wanted the story to read. Whatever the case, I'd advise you to give your critique and then let it go. Don't get personally invested in whether they follow it.

Summary Points

• Beta readers are extremely useful in helping you find and fix problems with your story that you're too close to it to see.

• Find beta readers in your writing group or in online communities. Many communities have rules around membership and beta reading; learn and respect these rules.

• Be clear in what level of critique you're expecting from your beta reader and the timeframe you're expecting it in. No matter what they give you, they spent time reading your book and writing their feedback, so thank them for their work.

• Every beta reader's critique is valid! It is their authentic experience of reading your story. It's up to you to decide how much you want to alter your story to address that experience.

• As a beta reader yourself, try to understand what the author is aiming for and how you can help them craft the story to reach that goal. Ask them questions if you're not clear on how to give them a helpful critique. Limit the amount you rewrite their story for them unless they ask for that. And include positive feedback! Tell them what worked well for you, what evoked strong emotions in you.

• An author may or may not take your critique suggestions. This doesn't mean your advice was bad. It was still valuable as your experience of the story.

Chapter Thirty-Two

Publishing

Some Thoughts On Publishing

Publishing is mostly beyond the scope of this book, and the landscape of publishing is constantly changing in a way that novel-writing is not, or at least at a much greater speed, so I'll keep this section to an overview of the options that exist now as I know them.

Get an agent

A lot of publishing opportunities are open only to agented submissions, as these publishers don't have the time or resources to read thousands of submissions. Agents are a vetting layer between the author and publisher, someone they trust to read your manuscript and judge it worth publishing. Additionally, agents build relationships with editors, so they can often anticipate where a manuscript might find a home, and they keep an eye on the market so they can advise authors on the best strategies for their books.

There are a number of resources on the Internet for how to compose an agent query, and the best advice I have for you is to read a bunch of those and then write your query. Don't obsess over it—the book should be the strongest selling point, and if your book is something the agent wants, they will not pass on it just because you didn't word your pitch exactly right.

Oh, and if they ask for a synopsis, a good starting point (if you took my advice in the revision section) is the document where you wrote a sentence or two about all your scenes. Writing a synopsis sucks because you're going to lose a lot of what makes your story special, but that's why most agents also request a sample of the manuscript.

Submit to a small press

Some small presses do not require agented submissions. If you don't want an agent, or your story is too niche for an agent to be interested in, there may be a small press interested in it. Look for small presses that publish the kind of thing you're writing, and then *read all of their submission information carefully*.

Having worked for a small press, I can't emphasize that last point enough.[17] If a press says they are not open to submissions, don't send them your novel anyway (you can contact them to ask when they might be open again, though). If they only accept

---

[17] At one point, our submission information said that we were looking for short stories for specific 'zines only, and novels (over 50K words), to be sent to a specific email address in Word or text format only. The reason for this is that we had a process for submissions, and if things came in outside of that process, it was easy for them to get lost.

At a convention, a person we knew approached us and "submitted" their work by handing me a USB stick on which were stored a few novellas in WordPerfect format. I explained that that wasn't how we took submissions, and they huffily said that we had the stories now and just to let them know.

We never did, for (I think) obvious reasons.

Word or plain text, don't send them a PDF. Following their rules helps them guide your submission properly, but it also tells them that you're someone they can work with, someone who will listen to what they ask. That's as important as the quality of the book you're sending them.

A small press won't have the resources of a larger publisher, but you will usually be able to build a good relationship with them. They are in the business because they love books, and it's validating to have someone who cares about books love yours and be proud to include it in their catalog. Plus, if they're a niche small press, they will have a good idea of how to market to the exact people who will like your book. If you find the right small press, you can have a productive, fun relationship that lasts years over many books.

Self-publish

Once viewed as the "last resort" of publishing, self-publishing is not quite that anymore, at least not in everyone's view. It allows the author to have more control over every aspect of their book, from the layout to the cover design to the release date and marketing. The downside is that, well, you the author are responsible for the layout, cover design, release date, marketing, and everything else.

There are people you can hire to do good editing, layout, cover design, and even marketing for your book, and there are even more people who will tell you how you can do it yourself. My recommendation is that if there's something you're good enough at that you would charge other people to do it for them, go ahead and do it yourself. I trust my own editing, and other people have hired me to do editing for them, so I feel comfortable editing my own books (with beta reader help, of course). Same with layout, if need be. But while I have a decent eye for a good book cover, I would not trust myself to create one, so I always contract that out to an artist and/or designer.

Doing your own marketing is something you will likely have to do even if you're not self-publishing. Definitely you will need to do some of your own marketing for a small press publication, and even with some large press publications. There are a lot of places where you can find advice about growing your audience, but the only thing I've seen work consistently is to produce work, get your work and free samples out in front of people (there are websites that will allow you to serialize work, but your community may have more targeted places where they go for free work), and be pleasant to interact with. That's not going to lead to overnight success, but it's the most reliable way to grow an audience.

Being an author requires a certain degree of stubbornness, and even more so if you're a self-published author posting updates about your book to an audience of three. But keep going with it, keep doing the work, and the audience will grow.

Chapter Thirty-Three

Book 2

Not Done Yet: Writing the second book in a series

If you're writing a series, good for you! Writing a series requires you to think about the arc of the series and how each book fits into that, with respect to the characters, the world, and the plot. There are benefits to writing a series; I found that the more familiar I was with the world, the easier the writing became. But it also requires more work to think about the place of each book in the series as a whole.

There are broadly three kinds of series:

• Related books in the same world but with different protagonists each time (like Narnia or my own Dangerous Spirits series)

• Books with the same protagonists but in which each book is self-contained, though there may be an overarching plot (like the Percy Jackson books)

• A series that is one large story told over several books (the

Lord of the Rings series)

Same World, Different Characters

In my Dangerous Spirits series, each book has a different protagonist confronting a different problem, and the series does not really move toward a larger overall conclusion (except, possibly, in that the end of the third one semi-explained how the others had happened). For this kind of series—related books with different protagonists and plots—book 2 should be relatively easy. Readers who enjoyed your first book will want to see something similar in the second one, but not so similar that it feels like a retread. Find a different aspect of the world to explore, a new character to explore it through, and a plot that is related to the first book's plot without being identical to it.

Dangerous Spirits was a tricky series because the first book had a specific form challenge to include three POV characters: the main one, a narrative written in a book, and a sequence of dreams experienced through the third POV. I wanted the second book to also include three POV characters, but without resorting to the same methods of introducing them. So I included a first-person narrative that wasn't in a book—until the end, we don't know how we are hearing the narrative—and a narrative through letters written to the main character. In the third book, I went back to dreams for one of the secondary narratives, and the other took place in a comic the main character was drawing. Those were "the same, but different," enough so that I think each book feels fresh and different (and each of the three books has been mentioned as a favorite by fans, which I think is a good measure of how different they are).

Same World, Same Folks

If you're writing a series with the same main character(s) in the same world, then here's how I'd go about it. You need to consider three aspects:

1. Character. Your main character has already gone through a journey in book 1. So now you have to imagine not only a new journey for them to go on in book 2, but also an overall

series arc. Because once you start planning a series, you have to plan for the end of it, and final books in a series are a pain to get right. The more you plan in advance, the easier they'll be.[18]

When you were writing your character's journey in book one, there were stages along the way. Now take a step back and think of book one as the first stage in a larger journey. What's the next stage? That would be book two. If you know there are going to be more books, you should be thinking ahead at this point to at least the next two.

It's also possible that your main character is not the one with the arc in your second book. They can be a catalyst for change in another character if you want to make that the focus of your story. In Susan Cooper's *The Dark Is Rising* series, the second book (*The Dark Is Rising*) follows Will Stanton's growth from an eleven-year-old boy into an Old One who understands the weight of his birthright. In the fourth book (*The Grey King*), Will is again the protagonist, but Bran is the boy undergoing the character arc, with Will's help.

2. World. You're going to want to expand the world in each of the books of the series, either by widening the scope of the books or by moving to a different part of the world. In my Calatians books, each one grows the world the characters explore. Book 1 stays entirely in the town of New Cambridge. In book 2, Kip goes to London. Book 3 takes them all over the American colonies as well as London, and book 4 expands to cover the entire world. Rukis's series, specifically the Off the

---

[18]You may be planning a series in which each of the stories is a standalone episode, like a "monster of the week" TV show, featuring your characters in a similar plot in each installment of the series. If this is your plan, you might be saying that you don't need to think about an overall arc of the series, and maybe you're right—now. But even episodic series end up with world changes or plot changes that span several books, because writing the same thing over and over again will eventually bore most readers. James Bond, a very episodic book series, even had him marry and had the fallout from that marriage follow him into the next book; Fleming also played with different forms and plots (*The Spy Who Loved Me* is very different from the movie adaptation). The point is that these are good things to think about even if you think you don't need them right at this moment.

Beaten Path trilogy and the Kindred duology, do an excellent job of starting with a small personal story and expanding it to cover not just a larger area of the world, but larger plot problems in the world. In the Narnia books, or the Thomas Covenant books, the world in successive books is separated by time rather than geography, but expands nonetheless.

3. Plot. This is maybe the first one you'll think about. How do the events of the plot of book 1 affect the world and the characters? What complications might arise from that in the future? In David Mitchell's *The Thousand Autumns of Jacob de Zoet*, the titular character's actions in that book result in a plot point for one of his descendants in *Utopia Avenue*, which takes place hundreds of years later. Here, too, you may want to look at a progressive arc. What changes to the world are being driven by the plot, and what's their endpoint? In my *Out of Position* series, each book details challenges to the main characters' relationship, but the series overall has an arc of them coming to terms with their place in the world.

One Big Story

If you're writing one big story over several books, then your concern will be less about what goes into book 2 and more about where to break the story between books 1 and 2. Here I'd say to follow your heart. You could end the book on a cliffhanger to motivate people to pick up the next one. You could end it at one of the points in the story where a significant event has happened and the characters' goals have changed, leaving the reader excited for what's coming next without making them anxious about it (Tolkien ended *The Fellowship of the Ring* at the dissolving of the Fellowship, with Sam and Frodo going their own way and Aragorn, Legolas, and Gimli going off to rescue the kidnapped Merry and Pippin). You could end it at a place of closure within the story, with the knowledge that there's a larger problem remaining to solve. I've seen all of these work, so gather opinions from your beta readers and do what feels right to you.

Summary Points

• A series can be: books in the same world with different protagonists, a series of books with the same protagonists that each stand alone but may be part of a larger plot, or a single long story spread out over multiple books. Each of these presents different opportunities and challenges.

• Different protagonists: find a new character and a new aspect of the world to explore.

• Same protagonists, different story: where are the opportunities for character growth and movement now? What events from the first book will impact the world in the second?

• One long story: the challenge is more where to break the story between books 1 and 2.

Chapter Thirty-Four

Final Words and Other Resources

I said at the beginning that I expect most writers have several books on craft on their shelves, and I hope this one has proven valuable enough to be one of them. If you are interested in others, here are a few that are on my shelf and have proven valuable to me in the past, along with some that others have highly recommended:

- *On Writing*, by Stephen King
- *Wonderbook*, by Jeff Vandermeer
- *The Modern Library Writer's Workshop*, by Stephen Koch
- *Craft in the Real World*, by Matthew Salesses
- *Artful Sentences: Syntax as Style*, by Virgina Tufte
- *Romancing the Beat*, by Gwen Hayes
- "My Twentieth Century Evening—and Other Small Breakthroughs," by Kazuo Ishiguro

I have mentioned various writing workshops, and you can find more information online about all of them, but the ones I have attended and worked with and can personally recommend are:

Clarion and Clarion West: Six-week residential writing workshops with a different instructor each week. A great learning experience and a chance to bond with other writers over the six weeks.

http://clarion.uscd.edu and http://www.clarionwest.org

Novel Architects: A two-week residential workshop focused on novel writing, taught by Kij Johnson and Barbara J. Webb. Kij and Barb are among the smartest people I've met about writing, and this workshop was fantastic.

http://kijjohnson.com/teacher

RAWR: A one-week residential workshop aimed at furry writers. I've taught there several times and we have had some excellent classes come through.

http://rawr.community

In closing, I want to leave you with a repeat of one of the things I said at the beginning. Your book should be an expression of you. All the things I've said here, all the things the above writers say in their books, those are tools you can use to craft the best book you can. They explain things that many readers look for in books, shapes and techniques and aesthetics that it's useful to keep in mind because they are familiar and will resonate. They may help you understand why and how some of your favorite books succeed as well as they do. But ultimately, your book should represent what you want to say. If you write the best book you know how, and it is yours from beginning to end, with all your love and passion poured into it, then you will always have a book to be proud of. Even my very first book, which was not finished nor published and will never be either, still makes me proud for the writer who didn't know if he could write a novel but built the story in his head and tried to write it anyway. If I'd had a book like this, maybe I would've made the step from that first tentative story to a published novel more quickly.

That's what I want for you, because your voice, your passion, and your imagination are unique and valuable. We write because we want to communicate a feeling to someone else, and you picked up this book because you felt that need in you. A novel is a long journey to make, and it will be difficult and frustrating at times, but also exciting and exhilarating. Forty-plus books into my career, I still get a thrill when someone finishes one of my books and tells me how it reached them, every time. And somewhere out there is a person waiting for your story too, longing for something but not knowing what it is.

We all deserve a chance to tell our story. I hope that with this book, you find it easier to tell yours.

Acknowledgments

I have cited various people whose instruction has been invaluable to me, but here is a more complete list of writing teachers who have influenced me, even if they are not named in the text: my Clarion 2011 instructors Nina Kiriki Hoffman, John Scalzi, Elizabeth Bear, David Anthony Durham, John Kessel, and Kij Johnson; Chelsea Johnson and Carl Yorke at Stanford, and Barbara Webb of the Novel Architects (with Kij Johnson there as well). And of course, my very first teacher who started me down this path in the first place: my mother, Beth Susman.

In the course of writing this book, I got help from many of my friends and colleagues. Before this book was even an idea, I often talked writing with a number of friends, including (but not limited to) Alisa Alering, Ryan Campbell, David Cowan, Malcolm Cross, Jeff Eddy, Kevin Frane, Watts Martin, Rukis, Dayna Smith, Brooke Wonders, and Becky Wright, and those conversations helped shape my writing philosophy. Alisa, Dayna, Brooke, and Becky read an early version of this text and gave me excellent feedback. Special thanks to Steven Garcia, both for their critical role in founding a furry writers' workshop where I got to teach for many years and for the many conversations about writing and story at those workshops and outside them. And extra special thanks to my partners Mark Brown and Jack DeVries, who have also talked writing and story with me for years, in addition to being the best family a li'l writer fox could hope for.

Thanks to Watts also for their assistance with layout, and to Yena for assembling a bibliography; thanks to Mark Harrison and Grant Belles for their dedication to bringing cool new books to the world; thanks to the furry community for being generally awesome for a majority of my life, and to the furry writing community for the passion and energy they have. This book took shape as I was making notes for a panel I was going to deliver at a furry convention, so it's not hyperbole to say that without the furry community, this book likely would not exist.

Bibliography

A list of works cited and their writers, with URLs to works found online:

The Hitchhiker's Guide to the Galaxy	Douglas Adams
Watership Down	Richard Adams
Smothermoss	Alisa Alering
The Book of Three	Lloyd Alexander
The Black Cauldron	Lloyd Alexander
The Architect of Sleep	Steven R. Boyett
The Sword of Shannara	Terry Brooks
The Dresden Files (Series)	Jim Butcher
The Hero with a Thousand Faces	Joseph Campbell
The Heroine's Journey	Gail Carriger
Lord Jim	Joseph Conrad
The Dark Is Rising (Series)	Susan Cooper
The Dark Is Rising	Susan Cooper
The Grey King	Susan Cooper
John Constantine, Hellblazer	DC Comics
The Dragon and the George	Gordon R. Dickson
The Chronicles of Thomas Covenant (Series)	Stephen R. Donaldson
"The Final Problem"	Sir Arthur Conan Doyle

The Hound of the Baskervilles	Sir Arthur Conan Doyle
The Sign of Four	Sir Arthur Conan Doyle
The Tick	Ben Edlund
The Boys	Garth Ennis
The Spy Who Loved Me	Ian Fleming
The Day of the Jackal	Frederick Forsyth
"There Are No Snakes in Ireland"	Frederick Forsyth
Azure City	Kyell Gold
Black Angel	Kyell Gold
Camouflage	Kyell Gold
Green Fairy	Kyell Gold
Out of Position (Series)	Kyell Gold
Red Devil	Kyell Gold
Shadow of the Father	Kyell Gold
Essay: "We Live in a Society"[19]	Kyell Gold
Waterways	Kyell Gold
The Scarlet Letter	Nathaniel Hawthorne
Romancing the Beat	Gwen Hayes
Dune	Frank Herbert
Parasite	Bong Joon Ho / Han Jin-won
Zootopia	Byron Howard / Rich Moore / Jared Bush
Les Misérables	Victor Hugo
Kazuo Ishiguro's Novel Lecture[20]	Kazuo Ishiguro
The Remains of the Day	Kazuo Ishiguro
Fifty Shades of Grey	E. L. James
Broken Earth (Series)	N.K. Jemisin
The Fifth Season	N.K. Jemisin
Rose Madder	Stephen King
The Shining	Stephen King
The Stand	Stephen King
Last Days of Summer	Steve Kluger

---

[19] http://open.substack.com/pub/kyellgold/p/essay-we-live-in-a-society

[20] https://www.nobelprize.org/prizes/literature/2017/ishiguro/lecture/

The Left Hand of Darkness	Ursula K. LeGuin
Rosemary's Baby	Ira Levin
The Stepford Wives	Ira Levin
The Chronicles of Narnia (Series)	C. S. Lewis
The Lion, the Witch, and the Wardrobe	C. S. Lewis
Star Wars: A New Hope	George Lucas
Avengers: Infinity War	Christopher Markus / Stephen McFeely / Stan Lee
Life of Pi	Yann Martel
Runaways	Marvel Comics
I Am Legend	Richard Matheson
Dragonriders of Pern (Series)	Anne McCaffrey
Dragonflight	Anne McCaffrey
Dragonsong	Anne McCaffrey
The Riddle-Master of Hed (Series)	Patricia A. McKillip
Moby Dick	Herman Melville
Twilight	Stephanie Meyer
Cloud Atlas	David Mitchell
The Thousand Autumns of Jacob de Zoet	David Mitchell
Utopia Avenue	David Mitchell
Watchmen	Alan Moore
The Heroine's Journey	Maureen Murdock
Harry Potter and the Deathly Hallows	J.K. Rowling
Kindred Duology	Rukis
Off the Beaten Path Trilogy	Rukis
Old Man's War	John Scalzi
Hamlet	William Shakespeare
Romeo and Juliet	William Shakespeare
Save the Cat	Blake Snyder
MAUS	Art Spiegelman
Snow Crash	Neal Stephenson
Dead Right	Tim Susman
The Calatians (Series)	Tim Susman
The Price of Thorns	Tim Susman
The Revolution and the Fox	Tim Susman
Slow Surrender	Cecilia Tan

The Rise of Skywalker	Chris Terrio / J.J. Abrams / Derek Connolly
Brooklyn	Colm Tóibín
The Lord of the Rings (Series)	J. R. R. Tolkien
The Fellowship of the Ring	J. R. R. Tolkien
Artful Sentences: Syntax as a Style	Virginia Tufte
The Adventures of Huckleberry Finn	Mark Twain
The Adventures of Tom Sawyer	Mark Twain
The Girl Who Circumnavigated Fairyland in a Ship of Her Own Making	Catherynne M. Valente
Brat Pack	Rick Veitch
The 90-Day Novel	Alan Watt
The Time Machine	H.G. Wells
Right Ho, Jeeves	P. G. Wodehouse
"Writing Advice from Matt Stone & Trey Parker @ NYU"[21]	Matt Stone / Trey Parker

---

[21] https://www.youtube.com/watch?v=vGUNqq3jVLg

Also By the Author

acceptance. *(mature readers)*

Divisions – As Dev's team fights to make the playoffs, Lee fights to keep his sense of self. *(mature readers)*

Uncovered – The playoffs are here, and Dev needs his focus more than ever. So when Lee becomes too distracting, something has to give. *(mature readers)*

Over Time – Dev and Lee try to plan their future while dealing with crises all around them. *(mature readers)*

Ty Game — Dev's teammate Ty navigates an arranged marriage while also falling in love. *(mature readers)*

Tales of the Firebirds — A collection of stories exploring the lives of some of the other characters from the Out of Position series. *(mature readers)*

Titles – In the two weeks leading up to Dev's third try at a championship, Dev and Lee face new challenges and changes in their lives. *(mature readers)*

Dangerous Spirits

Green Fairy – A gay high school senior struggling through his final year finds a strange old book that changes his dreams and his life.

Red Devil – A gay fox who fled his abusive family in Siberia seeks help from a ghost who demands he give up his gay lifestyle.

Black Angel – A young otter struggles to understand her sexuality as her friends prepare for post-high school life and dreams of women in other times plague her.

Azure City — A fox adrift in his thirties after losing his job finds a blank book that promises him escape, but also may be erasing him from everyone's memory. (Coming 2025)

Argaea

Volle – The story of how Volle came to Tephos, a spy masquerading as a noble, and the first adventure he had there. *(mature readers)*

The Prisoner's Release and Other Stories – The story of how Volle escaped from prison, and the story of what happened after, plus two other stories following characters from "Volle." *(mature readers)*

Pendant of Fortune – Volle returns to Tephos to defend his honor, but soon finds himself fighting for much more. *(mature readers)*

Shadow of the Father – Volle's son, Yilon, must travel to the far-off land he is meant to rule, but he will have to fight treachery to take the lordship. *(mature readers)*

Weasel Presents – Five short stories from the land of Argaea, including "Helfer's Busy Day" and "Yilon's Journal." *(mature readers)*

Return From Divalia — Years after a night of adventure ruined his life, a young wolf gets a chance at redemption. *(mature readers)*

Forester Universe

Waterways – The full story of Kory's journey to understand himself and what it means to be gay. *(mature readers)*

Bridges – Hayward seems content to set up pairs of his friends. But what does he really need for himself? *(mature readers)*

Science Friction – Vaxy never took sex seriously, until he found out the professor he was sleeping with was married… *(mature readers)*

Winter Games – Sierra Snowpaw was an unsure high school student when someone he thought was a friend changed his life. Now he's fifteen years older and still looking for answers. *(mature readers)*

The Mysterious Affair of Giles – A servant in a British manor house tries to solve a murder.

Dude, Where's My Fox? – Lonnie chases down a fox he hooked up with at a party as a way to get over his breakup. *(mature readers)*

Dude, Where's My Pack? — Lonnie tries to navigate relationships old and new. *(mature readers)*

Losing My Religion – On tour with his R.E.M. cover band, Jackson mentors the new guy in the band as his own life falls apart. *(mature readers)*

The Time He Desires — A Muslim immigrant struggles with the betrayal of his son and the dissolution of his marriage, as well as his own long-past trauma.

Camouflage — When Danilo is sent 500 years into the past, he must choose between safety in an unfamiliar world and his own sense of what is right. *(mature readers)*

Squeak Thief — While plotting a daring jewel heist, unexpected feelings turn a high-stakes caper into an even more risky game of hearts. *(mature readers)*

Other Books

The Silver Circle – Valerie thought the old hunter was crazy when he warned her about werewolves—until she met one.

In the Doghouse of Justice – Seven stories of superheroes and their not-so-super relationships. *(mature readers)*

Twelve Sides — Twelve short stories about side characters from the above books. *(mature readers)*

Do You Need Help? — Writing advice for furry (and non-furry) writers.

Writing as Tim Susman:

Breaking The Ice: Stories from New Tibet (editor) - On a hostile ice planet, survival is guaranteed to nobody.

Shadows in Snow (editor) - More stories from the unforgiving ice world of New Tibet.

Common and Precious - A kidnapped heiress comes to sympathize with her desperate captors, while her father discovers the limits of his power in trying to rescue her.

Patterns in Frost - Return to the world of New Tibet with six more stories.

The Calatians

Book 1: The Tower and the Fox - Kip and his friends encounter prejudice and mysteries in their first few months at Prince George's College of Sorcery.

Book 2: The Demon and the Fox - The forces of revolution grow in Massachusetts as Kip and his friends rush to solve the mystery of the attack on the College of Sorcery.

Book 3: The War and the Fox - Kip and his friends are drafted into the fight for independence from Britain, but there is more at stake.

Book 4: The Revolution and the Fox - Two years after the war, Kip and his friends face their greatest threat yet.

Wolftown

Unfinished Business — A detective uncovers a plot against him and must turn to his werewolf ex-boyfriend for help.

Dead Right — A detective rescues the ghost of a teenaged activist and must get her to safety while being hunted by a sinister government agency.

Other Books

The Price of Thorns - A down-on-his-luck thief meets the actual evil queen from many fairy tales when she offers him the job of a lifetime.

About the Author

Kyell Gold has won thirteen Ursa Major awards and a Cóyotl Award for his stories and novels, and his acclaimed novel "Out of Position" co-won the Rainbow Award for Best Gay Novel of 2009. He helped create RAWR, the first residential furry writing workshop, and has instructed at each of its sessions through 2022.

He lives in California, loves to travel and dine out with his partners (when possible), and can be seen at furry conventions around the world. More information about him and his books is available at http://www.kyellgold.com. You can follow him on Mastodon at @KyellGold@furries.club, on BlueSky at @KyellGold@kyellgold.com, and find his newsletter at http://kyellgold.substack.com.

www.ingramcontent.com/pod-product-compliance
Lightning Source LLC
Chambersburg PA
CBHW060239100426
42742CB00011B/1582